My Life Dancing With The Stars

MIRIAM NELSON

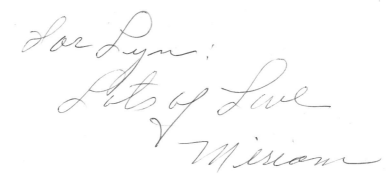

For Lyn;

Lots of Love
& Miriam

Published in the USA by:
BearManor Media
P O Box 71426
Albany, Georgia 31708
www.bearmanormedia.com

ISBN 1-59393-333-9

Printed in the United States of America.
Editing and Proofreading by Gary Clason.
Cover Design by Joe Yakovetic.
Book design by Brian Pearce.

TABLE OF CONTENTS

DEDICATION

To my wonderful son, Chris,
who's always been there for me,
(By the way…did I mention, as an editor, he's been
nominated for an Emmy? *Four* times?)
his wife, Jenna, my three grandsons, Christian, Josh and Matthew,
and my darling great granddaughter, Emma.
In addition, my mother and father who were always behind me.

I love you all very much.

PREFACE

A friend called, "Miriam, you have to read this book — you're in it!"

Here it was again, another book. When I had finished reading the book, I counted it to be the eleventh book that mentioned me. These books were written by or about: June Allyson, William Holden, the Lennon Sisters, Rusty Frank, Larry Billman, Jane Powell, Al Jolson, Joshua Logan, Betsy Blair and *two* Doris Day books. I toyed with the thought of writing my own book.

It wasn't until I was asked to do an hour-long show on a cruise ship (telling my stories about working with movie stars and showing film clips) that the process began. Diane Davisson, a tap teacher friend of mine, knew I was writing my show in longhand, so she said she'd put it on the computer for me. We spent days together. In fact, she was the first one to say, "You have so many interesting stories to tell, *you should write a book.*" The seed was planted. Thank you Diane. Before long, I was carrying a yellow pad and sharpened pencils. My idea was to write a chapter of each star I had worked with.

After I had written several chapters, Jane Napier, another tap teacher and good friend, came to my rescue. She had me bring all my scribblings over to her house, and she put them on her computer. It took weeks of work. While writing, we kept being interrupted by my getting jobs.

When I finished my manuscript, I sent it over to my friend, Larry Billman, a Disney alumni, dancer, choreographer, writer, and producer. We have worked on many shows together. His first comment was, "Miriam, people reading this will want to know how you got to do these things and who are you. You need to tell something about Miriam!" So back to the drawing board, I went, rewriting and adding *me*.

Then Joe Yakovetic, who also works a lot for Disney, creating Fine Art, illustrating numerous books and designing sets, costumes and attractions, read this new version and challenged me to write how I felt about things, advice I could offer and how situations affected me.

Once again, I picked up my pencils to rewrite and there was Boss (Greg Williams). We met through Diane Davisson's tap class. He had a good business going and he loved dancing. He was also a computer whiz (by now you must know I'm not). He picked up the mantle to type and did some research for me.

Along the way Rusty Frank went through this book three times and made notes.

I can't say enough about her. She is my sometime dancing partner and my some-time agent. She has been responsible for my teaching master classes in Sweden, Finland, Germany and New York. Greg Gast and Will Ryan, more talented friends, put their eagle eyes on this, too.

Finally, my newest friend, Nick Santa Maria, read it, picked up the phone and called a publisher he knew. Nick is a brilliant actor and the funniest person I know. He makes me laugh all the time.

So here I was, with a publisher and a book — I thought I was done. Then I found out that I needed pictures *and* editing.

Back to Larry, who edited this manuscript and made constructive suggestions like, "This chapter would work better if you put it here, instead of there." Of course, he was right. All his suggestions have helped make this book so much better. Along with Joe, they went over this book more times than we care to count, fine-tuning, adding everyone's notes, and making sure the names of people and titles were correct.

Then Joe went through hundreds of my photos and letters and scanned them — for days. I'm still looking for a good picture that I know I have of Lucy and me. After that, he organized the index and with input from Larry, Greg, and Rusty, designed the book cover.

Originally I wanted to call the book, "Ingrid Bergman didn't tap dance." My team put their minds together and came up with our current title, thus keeping the book about me, and the wonderful stars with whom I worked.

I'm extremely lucky to have so many smart and talented friends who took the time to encourage and lend their expertise in helping me tell my story as well as I could. I would also like to acknowledge the many assistants who have been such a major help to me through the years. Please forgive me if I forgot to include you. *Feel free to pen your name to the list.* Larry Billman, Leslie Bouchet, JoAnn Dean, Randy Doney, Rusty Frank, Ray Hesselink, Alexander Ivashrevich, Sandy Johnson, Sarah Kawahara, Toni Kaye, Amy Nelson, Dolores Nemiro, Charlene Painter, Mariana Pergora, Phil Phillips, Jack Regas, Bob Squire, Bob Street, Tad Tadlock and Eric Underwood.

Thank you, my friends, I am eternally grateful and dearly love you all.

Always,
Miriam

Miriam is a dear friend.
It is a pleasure to read her personal story,
which is told
with a keen overview of
Hollywood and
the way it works...

Blake Edwards
And
Julie Andrews Edwards

CHAPTER ONE

My Early Years

I didn't always work in Hollywood — it started in Chicago.

From early on I knew I wanted to be on the stage. Both parents supported me from the get-go. They would have supported me if I wanted to be a garbage collector. Once I started tap lessons, my strongest desire was to be a dancer like my idol, Eleanor Powell.

My mother, Miriam Elizabeth Bly, was very talented. She taught herself to sew and create beautiful oil paintings. To this day, I have many of her paintings on my walls. She was raised in Des Moines, Iowa. She was of Irish, English and Scotch descent. She had one brother who died as a child, and then, her mother died while she was still young. Her father remarried a woman who wasn't as loving or attentive as my grandmother. I remember, in particular, my mother telling me her new mother didn't dress her up or fuss over her hair, like her own mother had.

My mother toyed with the idea of going on the stage. She was working as a cashier in a café in Des Moines when a magician passing through town asked her to be in his act. About the same time, Daniel Frankel, the proverbial 'traveling sales-man,' came to the café. After a whirlwind courtship, Daniel made her a better offer. They were married and that was the end of her stage career.

Everyone called my father "Danny" which tells a lot right there. He loved every aspect of show business. He especially liked comedy. Many of his friends were come-dians. My father had a pretty good sense of humor, too. In fact, his sense of timing was so good he could have been a comedian himself. I have been told I have a pretty good sense of humor. I believe I either inherited it or absorbed it by being around my funny father during those formative years.

On the surface my parents marriage seemed to have major differences that many would have considered insurmountable. While my mother was from a small Protes-tant family my father was raised in a large Jewish family in St. Louis. In spite of this, they moved to an apartment in Chicago.

I made my debut at the Edgewater Hospital in Chicago on September 21, 1919. My mother liked her name "Miriam." It sounded like an actress. Being the second

Miriam, I was a Junior. It was confusing to have two Miriam Frankels in the house. When I got older, and jobs started coming my way, my mother changed her name to "Mildred."

I never really knew why, but my father had little to do with his family. I only saw his sister, my aunt Fanny Frankel, once and that was on the big screen. She was in a movie and it was a very big deal to us. I remember going to see it with my mother and father.

"That's your aunt Fanny!" my mother yelled out when she appeared on the screen. She was portraying a Florodora Girl, a member of the historic theatrical song-and-dance sextet who, coincidentally, performed the first synchronized tap number on Broadway in 1900 in the show "Florodora." I met some of my uncles a couple of times. I saw my mother's father twice in my life, but I never met Aunt Fanny.

It never seemed out of the ordinary to me to be half-Gentile and half-Jewish, either. In fact, I liked it. I went to Methodist Sunday school, which I liked a lot and celebrated all the Christian holidays. Then I got to be Jewish on the Jewish holidays. What this meant was that I got to be out of school more than the rest of the kids.

As I grew up my family moved from time to time. We always lived in rented apartments which never had more than one bedroom. I remember sleeping on a sofa in the living room or a rollaway bed that opened up. We never had much money, but I was happy. I guess most of us didn't have much money back then except for the occasional rich kid.

Christmas, in contrast, was another story. It was really magical. One Christmas I wanted a baby doll with eyes that opened and closed. It was our custom on Christmas Eve to open one gift. I picked the biggest package. To my delight, it was a doll about my size with curly hair and blinking eyes. I was so excited and loved her so much I wanted her to sleep with me. I woke up Christmas morning and to my horror I had somehow managed to poke out her eyes. My mother calmed me by telling me we would take her to the doll hospital. We did and she was good as new.

I was about five the first time I remember being on stage. I was cast in the leading role of a kiddies' recital and spent hours learning my lines. When we started rehearsing on stage my teacher kept yelling, "Miriam, speak louder." But try as I might, I couldn't. Finally, I was replaced. I didn't mind because I wound up in the chorus where I played a red poppy. My mother made me a costume of red satin. A year or so later my father took me to a local theater to see a comic friend. We watched him perform from the wings. When the comic finished his act he exited the stage, said "hi" to us, and returned to the stage to take a bow. He came off again, grabbed me by the hand and took me out on stage for his final bow. I thought I was in show business!

It's funny, but I have no recollection of my parents ever fighting or not getting along. In fact, I would describe our home as "happy." My father always seemed to be in a good humor. And my mother enjoyed his good-natured teasing. It always seemed so harmless. For example, after my mother changed her name to Mildred she let us know she didn't want to be called "Millie." So, of course, my father called her Millie.

But about the time I turned eight they separated. My father moved into his own apartment. And my mother had to get a job to make money to support us. On the

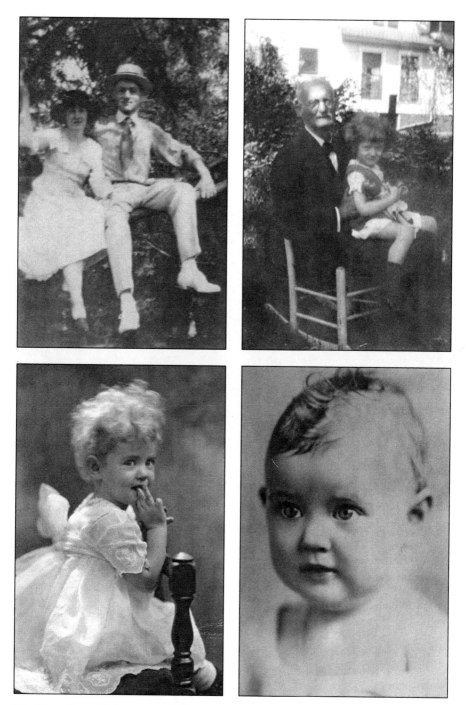

Top: My mother and father up a tree (left). On my grandfather's knee, my mother's father, Albert "A.B. Bly" (right). Bottom: You see, I was a blonde (left). Starting to get a curl in my hair (right).

In our Sunday clothes.

Top: Mother wrote on this photo, 'Waiting for Charlie Chaplin" (left). Always posing (right).
Bottom: The beginning of my love for horses (left). Miss America at summer camp (right).

Ah, youth! The photographer Maurice Seymour was actually two brothers, Maurice and Seymour.

side, she sewed lovely nightgowns and negligees. She took samples to the nurses at local hospitals. The nurses liked them so well they always bought the samples.

I know divorces have scarred many a child. But if I was scarred, I was never aware of it. I do know that I never felt in any way that the divorce had anything to do with me. And I know that both of my parents cared deeply for one another and they loved me.

I was, however, traumatized to learn I would be going away to school. My mother decided I would be better off at a Catholic boarding school. I would get a better education and the nuns would teach me to be a lady.

The school was called Our Lady of Bethlehem; it was in La Grange, Illinois. I didn't want to go and tried everything I could think of to get out of it. I begged. I pleaded. I cried crocodile tears, to no avail.

We boarded the train at the station in Chicago in February of 1928 and rode it to La Grange. It seemed as though we had gone hundreds of miles. As I was writing this book, I checked the distance out of curiosity. Imagine my surprise when I learned La Grange is only fourteen miles outside of Chicago!

My mother took me into the school where I was introduced to the nuns, and then she got in a waiting taxi and pulled away. She wasn't at the end of the drive when a wave of homesickness washed over me. And I learned why they call it a sickness. I felt such an ache right there in the pit of my stomach. That night, when I was lying in my bed, I could hear the train whistle blowing in the distance. How I wished I were sitting on it, going home! To this day, whenever I hear a train whistle, a little forlorn feeling comes over me.

The other girls were, indeed, ahead of me scholastically. When a nun would ask a question, they'd shoot their hands up. Not me, I always struggled. My spelling, in particular, wasn't very good. I never got over the feeling of being the dunce.

I participated in many of the extracurricular activities like the winter sleigh rides. It was so much fun to get bundled up and be pulled lickity-split over the hills of La Grange by a beautiful horse. When we got back to the school the sisters made us hot chocolate. But I didn't really spark until I heard they were putting together a show for parents.

One of the girls and I were teamed up to do a song and dance. We rehearsed in the gymnasium after school for weeks on end. We would enter, walk ten steps, face left and go into our number.

The big day of the show arrived, along with my mother. My partner and I were so excited. When our turn came, we entered the stage as we had rehearsed. As I walked the ten steps I realized something was different. The audience was not to our left, but straight ahead. So when we went into our song, I stayed looking at the audience and my partner turned left and faced the wall. No matter how I tried I couldn't get her to turn around. I can only imagine what our act must have looked like. After the show my mother told me I was quite the pro!

Prayer was a major part of the schooling and, even though I wasn't Catholic, I had to learn the catechism and abide by all the rules. When we awoke early in our dormitory, we'd throw our covers back, kneel at the foot of the bed and pray. Then we'd wash and dress, line up two-by-two, kneel and say another prayer.

We walked to the dining room for breakfast. A bowl of Holy water was beside the door. We dipped our finger in the water and blessed ourselves with it by making the sign of the cross. Then, before we ate, we said grace. Afterward, we went to school. Once situated at our desks, we would kneel and say another prayer. After school we would play, do our homework, and then go to church where we would, of course, pray.

Sundays we were required to go to Mass. Most of the girls would go to the altar to take communion. Once, one of the sisters asked me if I would like to take communion. I said, "No, thank you, sister." When I related the story to my mother she asked why I said no. I said, "Communion would make me Catholic and I don't want to be Catholic." (I was too naïve to realize there was more to being Catholic than eating a wafer and sipping a bit of sanctified wine.)

"Why don't you want to be Catholic?" my mother asked.

"They pray too much!"

I had been at the school for one semester when I got exciting news. My mother had made enough money selling negligees and she could support us by sewing at home. I would be able to live with her again.

Mother made only enough for us to eke by. If there was any extra money, it was the loose change she threw in the bottom of her Singer sewing machine. She could almost always scrounge up ten cents for me to go to the movies once a week and five cents for candy. Mother used thirteen cents for her pack of Lucky Strikes. I would steal a cigarette once in a while when she wasn't home. I stood in front of the mirror and watched myself smoke. I got pretty good at blowing smoke rings. I'm a bit ashamed to admit that smoking cigarettes became a habit that would stick with me for many years.

I went to the neighborhood movie house every Saturday. I stayed there all day watching and re-watching the shorts and the feature. After they showed the movies they would show them again. In those days they never cleared the house, so once you were in you could stay as long as you liked. I never wanted to leave. My mother would have to come get me. She'd walk down the aisle to the front row, her path illuminated by the flickering screen, where I could always be found.

"Just let me watch a few more minutes," I'd beg. It didn't matter that I'd seen the upcoming part at least four times already.

Saturday was prize day at the movie house. They drew tickets to see who would win items like dishes or movie passes. One Saturday, the manager, who knew me pretty well by now, asked if I would like to draw the winning ticket next Saturday. I was so excited! My mother, bless her soul, spent the next week making me a fancy dress and matching tam. When Saturday rolled around I was in the first row, as usual. I sat on the edge of my seat waiting through several shorts and serials and a feature before the drawing. Then the big moment arrived. The manager came out on stage and asked for a volunteer to draw the winning ticket from the fish bowl. My hand flew up and so did I. I didn't even wait for him to pick me.

Life seemed to go on like this for a good long while without incident until about the time I turned ten. I almost died. I was sitting in a big box on the roof of a garage. When I went to get out, the box tipped over and out I flew. I landed on the stairs of a fire escape and rolled the rest of the way down. I won't even dare tell you how many feet, since after the La Grange story I don't quite trust my childhood memory, but I do know I had severe pain in my mid-section. One of the children I was playing with said she would get my mother. I told my friend not to because my mother would be mad I was playing on the roof.

As luck would have it, my father was visiting at the time. He was playing cards with my mother when they heard the ruckus. He raced out and rushed me to the hospital. The doctors performed a rare surgery to repair my spleen. In those days, if you had a problem with your spleen, they removed it. The operation was so rare, they wrote it up in a medical magazine. While on the operating table I opened my eyes and saw my father lying on a gurney next to me. I remembered wondering what they were doing with him. I found out they were doing a direct blood transfusion from his arm to mine.

My doctor told me "Don't cough or sneeze. You could die." Talk about getting someone's attention! I did exactly as the doctor instructed and under the good care of my mother I slowly recuperated. Pretty soon I was able to go back to my Saturday movies.

I got to know most of the people who lived in our building. It was like one big, happy family. One of my good friends at the time was Margie Mandelbaum. She had a Jewish mother and a Gentile father, the exact opposite combination of mine. We used to joke that if you put us together you got one whole Gentile and one whole Jew.

And then, a new tenant moved into our building, down the hall. The sign by his door advertised: "Ted Arkin, Tap Dancing." I ran to my mom.

"I want to take tap lessons," I announced.

She told me we didn't have enough money. That didn't stop me from listening at Mr. Arkin's door. I heard the most wonderful tap sounds. Rhythms I never heard before. One day it was quiet and the door was open. I could see Mr. Arkin behind his desk. I don't know where I got the nerve, but I went in.

I don't remember much other than saying I wanted to be a tap dancer. When Mr. Arkin found out I had no money he told me he was sorry, but he had to make a living. He went back to work.

I made a habit of dropping in at least once a day. I think "hanging around" is probably more accurate. I guess I wore Mr. Arkin down because one day, without even getting off his chair, he surprised me by saying, "Brush forward, brush back." He demonstrated the movement. "Now put your foot down," he continued. I did exactly as instructed. "Put your weight on it. Now do it on the other foot."

Pupils started to arrive and it was time for me to leave, so I raced into our apartment and told my mother I now knew what I wanted to be when I grew up. I wanted to be a tap dancer!

At that time my father was producing nightclub shows. Sometimes he would take me to rehearsals. I was allowed to stand behind the dancers and would try to pick up the steps.

I continued my daily ritual of talking Mr. Arkin into teaching me another step. This went on for about a year. I never had to pay for a lesson. To repay him, I started teaching classes for him.

And then my mother got a job as head wardrobe lady for The Chez Paree, a newly opened supper club which quickly became the most famous club in all of Chicago. That was really big time show biz to an impressionable twelve-year old. Every major star of the period like Sophie Tucker, Jimmy Durante, Harry Richman, Ray Bolger, Helen Morgan, Texas Guinan, Veloz and Yolanda and the De Marcos appeared there. I got to go to the first show at 8:00 on Friday nights. Everyone loved my mother so I was treated royally. I'd go backstage and the dancers and showgirls, named The Chez Adorables, let me try on their costumes. They even showed me how to apply makeup. I was in heaven!

Sometimes my mother called me at home to say she was bringing some of the girls to our apartment between shows. That was fun. They would rush in, make a batch of fudge or fry donuts, then rush off to do the midnight show. I would go to bed, comforted by the lingering fragrance of their perfumes and the memory of their girlish bantering. By the way, one of those girls was June Taylor - who would later create The June Taylor Dancers who became a "Household Word" with their appearances on *The Jackie Gleason Show*.

As if life couldn't get any better, about that time my father got a job working for a professional photographer named Maurice Seymour. It was my father's job to get performers to have their pictures taken so I guess you could call it a sales job. I feel really lucky to have been surrounded by show people in many capacities all my life.

One summer, Miss Hutchinson, a secretary who worked for Mr. Seymour, suggested I might have a good time if I went to Michigan to stay with her parents. They had a farm in a small town called "Glenn" on the shores of Lake Michigan. Glenn was a kind of summer get-away for well-to-do people from Chicago.

I boarded the bus at the station in Chicago and rode along for a good part of an afternoon. We pulled into a town that was nothing more than a gas station and a grocery store which also served as the post office. I think they also had a church and that was about it. You could have missed it all if you blinked.

The Hutchinsons met me at the bus stop. I rode in the back seat of their truck out to their farm. It was a big, old working farmhouse in the middle of nowhere. I was shown to my room upstairs. It was a true country bedroom with antiques and a quilt on the bed. The basement was where they had the stove and did all the cooking. I went out to the barn where farmhands were milking cows and taking care of animals. I loved it immediately.

In the morning, just as the sun was rising, everyone gathered for breakfast. Mrs. Hutchinson (by now I called her "Grandma") scrambled eggs that came from the henhouse and served them with toast and preserves she had put up herself. I washed it all down with milk fresh from the cows. All of this was new to a city girl like me and a true education.

However, the most thrilling part of the entire farm were the eight horses that could be found stabled in the barn or running free. If you ever wanted to know where to find me, you just had to look for the horses. I fell in love with a white one I named "Silver." The man who cared for the horses, an old rodeo rider with a broken hip, taught me how to saddle and bridle a horse. Then he taught me how to ride. I was so crazy about riding I'd go out in the field before the sun was up with a flashlight, a halter and an ear of corn. Silver would come over for the corn and I'd throw the halter over his neck and lead him into barn where I'd saddle him and take off. I learned to ride like the wind.

There were several cozy cottages perched alongside the Lake. I got to know many of the occupants, most of them city people like me out for a relaxing summer. I remember as if it were yesterday trotting on Silver's back down the dirt road that ran behind those cottages. I'd slow up at the first house with a light on in the kitchen

In a borrowed costume from the Chez Paree.

A Merry Christmas
and a Happy New Year

Miriam Franklin

Top: My mom cooking and I listening to music in our New York apartment. Bottom: Christmas card. I was now Miriam Franklin.

and an opened window. I'd poke my horse's head through the window and call out "Good Morning." One cottage was home to a kid named Seymour Burns. At that time we had no way of knowing Seymour would grow up to be a director and that our paths would cross again many years later out in Hollywood.

I became friendly with a boy and girl about my age. Every once in a while they invited me over for dinner. Another fellow I thought of as "the rich kid," because he had nice clothes and his house was nicer than the rest, lived just a bit down the road toward town. He had a new horse and always wanted to race me. We'd line up beside each other. He'd yell "go!" And off we'd go galloping. That boy never could beat me. So he'd get another new horse. It seemed as though he had several new horses that summer, but try as he might he could never beat me and my Silver.

The farm rented out horses to a girls' school a couple of miles down the road. I would ride Silver and lead six horses on ropes to the school and ride with the girls. When I'd return with the horses I'd take off the saddles and bridles and curry them down and put out the feed.

The rodeo man taught me a few tricks. One was to take my right foot out of the stirrup and swing all the way around until I landed on Silver's neck in front of the saddle. And then back around into the saddle.

I used to ride down a narrow, steep road that led right into the Lake. Silver was the only horse I knew who was sure-footed enough to go down that hill. Once down, we would ride along in a couple of feet of water along the beach. We both loved that! My mother came to Glenn once and watched me do this stunt. She told me it "scared the daylights" out of her!

The boys in town had a baseball team. They played all the neighboring schools. Saturday nights someone from Glenn would project a movie onto the school wall. We'd all bring blankets to sit on and watched those magical flickering scenes with awe and laughter.

I stayed in Glenn most of the summer. As summer drew to a close I said a tearful good-bye to Silver and Grandma Hutchinson and returned to my life as a city girl, unaware that I was about to be on my way.

CHAPTER TWO

Broadway in the 1930s

The year was 1935. Tony Bruno, of "Bruno of Hollywood," a famous Los Angeles based photographer, offered my father a job at his new office in New York. My father jumped at the opportunity. Once my father was established, he wrote my mother asking her to consider getting back together. He also thought New York would afford me better opportunities. So you can see how he always supported my desire to be in show business. I was sixteen at the time.

I know the reconciliation of divorced parents after years of separation is like a story right out of the movies. And something about which many children of divorce dream. But my parents had always remained friends. There was never any anger or vitriol or "if only's," so it didn't really surprise me. But I was thrilled about the prospect of moving to New York. New York was definitely the "top of the ladder."

Before I knew it, my mother and I were selling everything we owned, packing up our old car and taking off for New York. We left Chicago in the dead of winter; it was cold and snowing. The car didn't have a heater so most of the trip I was wrapped in a down comforter. We stayed overnight in bed and boards. I wasn't old enough to drive, but I was the navigator and keeper of the maps. We ate at the diners where the truckers stopped, because they knew the best (and cheapest) places to eat.

The closer we got to New York the more excited we became. The night before we planned to arrive, we were too excited to stop and sleep. My mother decided to keep driving until we got there. We arrived about 4:00 in the morning. I didn't believe we were in the heart of New York because the lights on Broadway were turned off. Even when I read a sign for 42nd Street, I still couldn't believe it.

My father found an apartment in a terrific location, so close to Times Square I could walk there. And he had several photos taken of me. He hung them in drug stores around the city to advertise the photographer's services.

And now I must confess something that's never been easy to admit. After we moved to New York, I never enrolled in high school. I would have been in the tenth grade. Instead, I focused all my energy on my dancing career. Keep in mind it was

Top: *The best tap instructor in 'the City', Earnest Carlos. Bottom: My first Union card, Chorus division. Now it was official.*

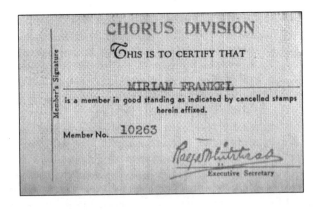

what I wanted to do and it was with my parents' full support. But for the duration of my life — especially when I was working with the sharpest minds in the entertainment world — I would harbor a deep-seated fear that I had never learned enough about the three "R's."

My father found me the best tap dance school in the City. It was owned by Ernest Carlos, a really terrific black tap dance teacher. Because I had learned everything Mr. Arkin knew, I thought I knew everything about tap dancing. I could do trenches, single wings and double wings with my arms flailing around like windmills. That style of tap dancing was called "Buck and Wing." It didn't take more than a second for a rude awakening. Mr. Carlos taught steps with millions of little taps and no flailing arms. Instead of being intimidated, I was enthralled. I was at the studio every day!

Mr. Carlos called each of us "professor" even though he was the *real* professor. He'd say, "Come on, professor." The piano player was called "Handsome." There were people of all ages in my class. Betty Bruce, a terrific dancer and actress who later appeared as "Tessie Tura" in the film version of *Gypsy*, also took classes with me.

One of the dances Ernest taught me was "Tea for Two." Tap dancing has such a glorious tradition. It is passed down from one generation to the next like story-telling. I recently was on a street corner in New York a few months ago when I bumped into Harvey Evans and the choreographer Alan Johnson, who both began their dance careers on Broadway in *West Side Story*. I showed them "Tea for Two." So here I was, back on a street corner in New York almost seventy years later, passing along a dance dear Ernest Carlos had taught me when I was his young and eager student.

My father brought the paper home every night and I would scan it for show auditions. The following morning I'd grab my tap shoes and off I'd go. I'd show them what I had. I was only sixteen at the time. It was against the law to hire anyone underage and when I was asked my age, I couldn't bring myself to lie. Every time I'd get the same response: "Come back when you grow up."

Then, one day when I was walking down Broadway I ran into Harry Rogue, a fellow from my tap class who was on his way to a rehearsal. He told me that Harry King, the father of Bobby Van, one of my dancer friends, was putting together an act for vaudeville. I didn't care that vaudeville was on its last legs. They were putting together an act for six guys and six girls and they needed one more girl. I think I beat Harry to the rehearsal hall.

I was hired on Harry's recommendation alone. I didn't even have to audition. I was about to make my debut as a professional dancer. Our act was called "The Aristocrats," no connection to the successful singing group of the same name.

We rehearsed the next three weeks and I was so excited I hardly slept. We were going to perform two numbers: a jitterbug and a tap dance. Off we traveled by bus to do a split week, meaning the show would spend half the week in one city and the other half in another. We were to be in Troy and Schenectady.

When we got to Troy, we girls waited in the bus station while the guys looked for a boarding house. They finally found a place we could afford. Three of us girls shared one room. To save money we cooked our own meals on a hotplate and ate together. Even at that, we barely made enough to pay the rent.

The theater ran movies four times a day and we performed our stage show between each showing. We opened on Thanksgiving Day and I had the worst menstrual cramps of my life. After every show the girls would put towels on the floor and a

Early headshot.

rolled up jacket under my head. I lay doubled up with aspirin and a hot water bottle until the next show. When I was on stage I didn't feel pain, just excitement, fear and exhilaration. As soon as I got off the stage I'd go back to the floor. What a way to break into show biz!

Our boss sent a telegram to his partner in New York. It read, "I got a turkey for Thanksgiving." I don't remember being bad. In fact, I thought we were quite good. Nonetheless, we played the rest of the week in Schenectady then I was back in New York, scanning the paper for audition notices again.

A friend of my mother's got me an audition at Radio City Music Hall. I thought being a Rockette would be neat. "Neat" was definitely the word I used at the time.

I arrived for my audition at Radio City. The backstage was a city in-and-of itself with a commissary, a small hospital and a huge wardrobe department. I rode a spacious elevator to a rehearsal hall. I was told to wait until someone came to see me. It was the largest rehearsal hall I'd ever seen and it was the same size as the real stage below.

I stretched at the *barre*. A young man came in at the other end of the room. He put his foot on the *barre* and began to stretch, too. He was so young I thought he was one of the dancers from the show. Suddenly, he walked to my end of the room and asked my name. I told him.

"All right, Miriam," he said. "Let's see what you can do."

What a shock! As it turned out, this young man was Russell Markert, dance director for the Rockettes. I immediately got a flush of anxiety. He wanted to see my high kicks. I kicked. He said they were fine. Then he wanted to see me tap. He was so nice I wasn't scared anymore. I did my tap dance and he seemed genuinely impressed. He told me the original Rockettes started in St. Louis, as "The Missouri Rockets." When they were to appear at the Roxy Theater in Manhattan, they became "The Roxyettes" and when they moved to Radio City Music Hall, in Rockefeller Center, they became "The Rockettes."

"To be a Rockette," he told me, "you have to have great stamina because they perform up to five shows a day and rehearse a new show in the early morning and sometimes between shows." I was really thin at this time and Russell thought I needed a "little more meat on my bones." He would arrange an appointment with the Rockettes' doctor to find a way to fatten me up. Then he asked how old I was.

"Almost seventeen," I said, thinking it sounded better than sixteen.

"Well, Miriam," he told me, "Be sure to come back when you grow up."

When I got home my mother said I had a phone call about a nightclub show I had auditioned for weeks ago. It was so long ago I had forgotten about it. The next day I found myself rehearsing with seven other girls for a show to be performed in Boston at The Mayfair Club. The star singer was Carol Bruce (who would go on to star in several Broadway musicals, including *Show Boat*) and the comic was Billy De Wolfe (who later co-starred in several Doris Day pictures I worked on at Warner Bros). I was still underage, but they didn't ask. And I didn't tell.

My parents weren't thrilled about me going to Boston, especially to perform in a nightclub. Nightclubs were thought of as a bit "seedy" in those days, especially for a young lady. They knew how badly I wanted to go. They talked it over and decided it was a good opportunity and they trusted me, so they let me go.

When we got off the bus in Boston we went to the nightclub to rehearse. We weren't there long when the much-dreaded question was directed right at me.

"How old are you, Miriam?" one of the nightclub owners asked.

"Here goes my job," I thought, but I told him anyway. "Almost seventeen," I said. He clapped his hands to get the men's attention.

"Miriam is off-limits!" he announced. After that the men nicknamed me "Jail Bait."

We gals doubled up in a rooming house, again taking turns cooking. My specialty was the fudge and donuts I learned to make from those wonderful times with my mother and her dancer friends.

After we opened, I received a couple of nice reviews. One read: "Line closed with an intriguing jungle routine, with Miriam Frankel soloing with a nifty tap." The show ran for six weeks then we returned to New York and it was time to get out to more auditions.

I went to one audition to find more than five hundred girls waiting at the stage door. They were lined up halfway around the block. We were ushered in twenty girls at a time and told to stand in a straight line. I heard someone humming loudly. I looked up and down to see who it was. I almost fainted when I realized the humming was coming from me. That's how nervous I was!

"Girl in the pants," a voice called out from the dark, "step forward." He meant *me* and wanted me to step forward from the rest of the line. "What's wrong with your legs?" he wanted to know. All the other girls wore shorts or bathing suits while I had on pants. "Nothing," I called out. The voice asked me to roll up my pant legs, which I did. After showing my legs I was instructed to sit in a section of the theater seats with a group of girls. I didn't know if I was in or out, but I took my seat.

It took the better part of the day for them to see the rest of the girls. I was to find out later that, at this phase of the audition they were selecting girls on looks alone. And fortunately, they liked my looks. Those of us sitting in the audience were asked to come back the following morning for a dance audition. They were seeking tap dancers to go to Cleveland, Ohio, and toe dancers for Texas.

Having lived in Chicago, Cleveland didn't sound as glamorous as Texas. I wanted to see Texas, but I had never even set foot inside toe shoes. Even so, I borrowed a pair of toes shoes and showed up at the audition. As I think back, I can't believe how naïve and stupid I was.

Robert "Bob" Alton was the choreographer. By this time he had already choreographed several Broadway shows. In fact, he was the best and most famous choreographer on Broadway and would later go to Hollywood and create many wonderful dance sequences in many of the best MGM musicals. He asked one girl at a time to step out and do an *arabesque, glissade* and a *tour jete*. He might as well have been speaking Greek. It was my turn to audition. Mr. Alton asked me to step forward, which I did. He asked me to do the combination.

"I can do this," I said, "and all the other steps. I just don't know their names." If the other dancers snickered, I didn't notice. "If someone could demonstrate the step," I suggested. Oddly, Mr. Alton did ask another dancer to perform the steps. I did my best to imitate her.

I would quickly discover that Mr. Alton was quite a tease. He asked me to do continuous *relives* on one point. That meant I was to go up on my toe, drop flat on my foot, up on my toe and flat on my foot. I struggled to comply. "*Ugh,*" he'd say every time I tried to go up on point.

When he announced the selected dancers I couldn't believe it. He chose me! He couldn't give us an official start date for rehearsals for at least a week and he said someone would call us.

The weeks ticked away and I slowly realized I wasn't going to get a call. I found out later that the tap dancers did go to Cleveland as planned, but they selected the toe dancers from Texas.

SING OUT THE NEWS

I had been dancing enough by now that I was in the dancers' grapevine. I heard about an audition for a new Broadway show called *Sing Out the News*. It was a revue, rather than a "book" show, produced by Max Gordon in association with George S. Kaufman and Moss Hart. Harold Rome was to direct. I grabbed my tap shoes and off I went.

After my audition, a man came up to me and said, "I'm sure you're in." He continued, "There's a little blonde we all like, too. But she doesn't have a routine to show us." He told me if she got a number together, he could arrange for her to be seen again. "Would you help her, Miriam?" he asked. I was so thrilled about the prospect of being in a Broadway show I would've done anything. So I took the "little blonde" off to a rehearsal hall to teach her something. I think it was a jazz routine. When she was ready they did see her again. She was chosen. It was her first Broadway show, too.

Her name was June Allyson.

One of my parts was as a Florodora Girl. Life is interesting the way everything seems to connect. It hadn't been long ago when I had seen my Aunt Fanny performing as a Florodora Girl on the big screen. And here I was, a Florodora Girl myself, about to sing and dance to their signature song, "Tell Me, Pretty Maiden," right there on Broadway.

It was during *Sing Out the News* that someone suggested "Frankel" wasn't an attractive name and wanted me to come up with something better. At first I thought a six-lettered name would be great on a marquee. Something like 'Pat Bly,' Bly being my mother's maiden name and Pat was 'tap' spelled backwards. Then I thought "Franklyn" was pretty close to my real name, so I selected it. When the show programs were printed, someone made a typo on my name. They spelled it with an "i." I kept "Miriam Franklin" as my stage name.

If there was any anti-Semitism in the suggestion of a name change, I wasn't aware of it. Shortly after, I did face anti-Semitism in another way — one that was far more painful. There was a singer named Pete in *Sing Out the News*. I had a big crush on him and we started seeing each other. We got so serious we even discussed marriage. Then Pete surprised me one evening. He hemmed and hawed for a few minutes then he came out with it.

"Miriam," he told me. "I can't marry you."

"Why not?" I wanted to know.

"Because you're Jewish." It was the first time in my life I realized being Jewish could have a negative affect.

Sing Out the News was politically oriented, as the title suggests. Truthfully, most of the time I didn't know what I was singing about, I was just thrilled to be in it. After we learned several song and dance numbers, the choreographer started staging

Sing Out the News – *June Allyson is on the far left and Pete King is with me on the far right.*

the opening. We were to walk across the stage in a straight-line singing *Sing Out the News*. I was chosen to lead the group across the stage. Being the first person on the stage in my first Broadway show was pretty special to me.

The show opened on September 24, 1938 (only three days after my nineteenth birthday) at The Music Box Theatre. I stood in the wings on opening night, waiting to go on. The orchestra began the overture. All of a sudden strange things started happening to me. First, my mind went blank. For the life of me, I couldn't think of my opening lines. And then my bladder began to swell. I thought, "Uh, oh, I'll never make it if I don't go to the bathroom." But before I could do anything about it I heard my cue. I walked out and all the words came out just right. And I forgot all about the bathroom. I later learned that what I experienced was pretty common.

BILLY ROSE'S CASA MANAÑA

When *Sing Out the News* began singing its last notes (which happened quickly as it closed on January 7, 1939), the big Texas nightclub show I had auditioned for was coming to New York. The show would be performed at Billy Rose's Casa Mañana on 753 Seventh Ave. Built originally in 1922 as the Earl Carroll Theatre, it had been converted into a nightclub in 1934 as the French Casino and in 1936, Mr. Rose leased-and-converted it to present the New York version of his spectacular Texas revue. Bob Alton was still the choreographer and they brought most of the Texas dancers to New York. Five girls were unable to come from Texas and had to be replaced. They held another audition and, of course, hundreds of girls showed up. They picked Rene (nicknamed by the dancers "I-can-get-it-for-you-wholesale") Russell, Grace Gilron, Vera-Ellen, Billy Rose's sister, Polly Rose and me. I don't know what happened to the toe dancing episode, but thankfully it was never mentioned.

The Texas girls were great. They went sightseeing every chance they got. One showgirl was six-feet tall. Her nickname was "Stuttering Sam." She had such a sense of humor that soon she became well-known in the city. One day, while stepping off a curb, Stuttering Sam got her foot run over by a cab. Miraculously, no bones were broken, but her foot was sore for awhile.

The rehearsals went along smoothly until one night when everyone was getting ready to go home. "I have to keep you all until John Murray gets here," Mr. Alton said. "He wants to see the couples' number with all the lifts." He was referring to John Murray Anderson, one of the producers of the show who was an acknowledged master with his use of innovative lighting and new scenic design and techniques. Well, we waited and waited. Finally, Bob told us to get dressed and then come back on the stage to get our call for the next day. It was the middle of winter, bitter cold, so we changed and put on our heavy coats, boots, hats, mufflers and gloves.

At that moment John Murray walked in. He was a nice-looking, white haired gentleman who exuded power. He wanted to see the number. We headed for the dressing room, moaning because we had to change back into rehearsal clothes.

"No, no, don't change," someone called down the hall. "Do it just as you are." We couldn't believe it. Some types of dancing would not be difficult fully clothed, but this included lifts. My partner in that number was Van Johnson. He had to put me on his shoulders, waltz around, then drop me into a "fish" (that's practically upside

Top: Billy Rose's The Big Show. *Bottom: My rehearsal pass signed by Billy Rose.*

down), while holding on to each others' hands. We did it, but I can't imagine what we must have looked like in our gloves and mittens. At the end of our number John Murray said, "That was fine. Go home."

Of course, we were so hot from dancing we had to undress and cool and down before going home. I guess Bob Alton got his devilish sense of humor from doing so many shows with John Murray Anderson.

The Casa Manaña was a precursor to the flashy Vegas nightclubs of the Fifties and Sixties. The shows were big, full of acts, lots of girls. The showgirls wore glitzy, revealing costumes (this was before dancers were allowed to perform in the nude) and big headdresses and had to walk down a long staircase. One of the costumes was a black net skirt with glitter on it. Billy Rose wanted us to wear G-strings under it. We all rebelled and finally were allowed to wear what were called "G-pants." They were equivalent to bikini bottoms, but still racy for the time.

There was a dinner show at 8:00 p.m. and a second show at midnight. My mother sat ringside opening night. She had sewn herself a new dress, especially for this performance. She lifted tomato juice to her lips just as we came out dancing in our opening number. She got so excited she missed her mouth and spilled tomato juice down her new dress.

We performed so many shows it was easy to forget if we were performing the dinner or supper show. If you ever forgot, you knew as soon as the curtain opened by the aroma of melted cheese. The most popular light meal of the time was a tasty dish of melted cheese sauce on toast called "Welsh Rarebit." Almost everyone ate it at the midnight show. It also was the cheapest item in the menu.

As the weeks progressed, Van and I discovered we shared a love of horseback riding. We got into the habit of going to Central Park to rent horses for an hour of riding. One evening, one of the girls from an act called "The Rosebuds" said she'd like to come along. The Rosebuds was a group of about five dancers. Each had to weigh at least three hundred pounds. So our Rosebud came along. We all had English saddles. You wouldn't be caught dead in Central Park riding Western.

You had to climb a little step to mount the horse. Rosebud climbed up, mounted her horse and off we rode. We were halfway around the reservoir when Rosebud started listing, saddle and all. She continued twisting slowly sideways until she finally hit the ground. Amazingly, she was not hurt. Van galloped off and got her horse. He turned the saddle upright and tightened the cinch. The question now was how to get Rosebud back in the saddle. We found a bench and Van helped her up on onto her horse. She went with us several times after that. And you can bet I always knew where benches were in Central Park, just in case.

We liked to dream up things to do between shows. Sometimes, if the timing was right, we could squeeze in a movie. A group of us liked to walk in the rain. So, when it would downpour, we popped our umbrellas and strolled down Fifth Avenue looking in all the windows. Sometimes we would stop at Schraft's for hot chocolate.

Those were the innocent and crazy days. I never got home until 2:30 or 3:00 in the morning. My father would get home about the same time after making his rounds at the clubs drumming up business. My mother, who was working in the wardrobe department at Ben Marden's Riviera, a nightclub in New Jersey, would be up late, too. We ate what we called a "Night Lunch," which was a Dagwood-type sandwich. I'd sleep late the next day, never getting up before noon. Maybe that's why I'm still a night owl and feel like eating late at night.

Top: You could always find me riding in Central Park. Bottom: Where's the horse?

YOKEL BOY

Yokel Boy was my next Broadway show. It starred Buddy Ebsen, Judy Canova, Dixie Dunbar and Phil Silvers. Phil had been in a lot of burlesque shows by this time, but this was his first Broadway show. This show had a large chorus of dancers so no one individual dancer got to shine. We rehearsed for weeks then headed off to New Haven and Boston before opening in New York. While in Boston, Phil took a bunch of us to a burlesque show. It was really quite tame by today's standards and a good education, because there would be a time in my career when it seemed every time I turned around I was teaching a new starlet how to do a 'mock strip' for a movie.

Phil knew everyone in the show and all the performers knew he was in the audience. They gave it their all. I can honestly say that that night they performed what I consider one of the funniest shows I'd ever seen.

There was a war scene in *Yokel Boy* in which we played soldiers who had to crawl up ramps on our stomachs. One night we rehearsed in costumes which were very hot. We rehearsed until 2:00 in the morning without eating. We were so exhausted we could barely move. Lew Brown, the producer, sat out front directing while munching on a sandwich and drinking coffee. All that couldn't happen today, but then the dancers' union was in its infancy. It was called The American Guild of Variety Artists. We didn't know anything about it, only that it cost money to join and most of us couldn't afford it. Of course, eventually it was great for dancers of that time.

We opened in New York at the Majestic Theatre on July 6, 1939 and were a big hit. The 1939 — 1940 World's Fair opened during the run and Lew Brown had T-shirts printed for us with *Yokel Boy* in big letters across our backs. He chartered busses to take us to the fair. As we walked around we were advertisements for the show. Coincidentally, Dorothy Kirsten, the opera diva, was making her professional debut at the fair. As I witnessed so many times with several people in my life, our paths would be destined to cross again.

VERY WARM FOR MAY

After *Yokel Boy* had been running a few months, I heard about auditions for a new Jerome Kern musical called *Very Warm for May*. A Jerome Kern musical sounded pretty gosh-darn classy to me, so off I went. They needed eight girls and eight guys and each would have a featured spot. That very day I got the call saying I had been chosen. I gave my two-week notice to the stage manager at *Yokel Boy*.

That night, while waiting in the wings to go on, Lew Brown charged up to me, waving my notice in the air. He couldn't believe anyone would leave a hit show. He told me he was getting ready to do another show and was giving me a spot.

"Think about it," he said. And with that I heard my cue and away I danced. When I came offstage he was still standing in the wings. As I passed him by he asked, "*Well?*" as if I'd had time to reconsider while dancing. I never did change my mind. And to my knowledge, Lew never opened another show.

Very Warm for May was staged and designed by Vincent Minnelli and starred Eve Arden, Hiram Sherman and Leif Erickson. Another performer was Don Loper, with whom I would later appear with in the film *Lady in the Dark* in Hollywood. Don designed the dress for his partner, Maxine and years later would turn his talent for fashion design into a successful career. Another member of the cast, actor-singer-dancer Richard "Dick" Quine, would make the career transition to film director and we also would work together later in Hollywood.

One of the dance numbers in *Very Warm for May* was wildly popular — on opening night it stopped the show. I had never been in a show where a chorus number stopped the show. As the song finished, we were to hold various positions until Eve Arden came out and said a line, then we were to break our poses. On opening night, Eve came on stage as planned, prepared to say her line but the audience wouldn't stop applauding. She gestured to Robert Emmett Dolan, our conductor, to start the music again. We repeated the entire number.

Again, the dancers in that show were great. They included Grace McDonald, Vera-Ellen, Walter Long, Kay Picture, Jack Seymour and June Allyson. Despite the talent and the fact that one of its songs "All the Things You Are," became an instant hit, the show itself was not a success. It opened on November 17, 1939 at the Alvin Theatre and it closed on January 6, 1940, the same day *Yokel Boy* closed. Every minute of that show was a joy. And I'm still proud to have been in a Jerome Kern show.

HIGHER AND HIGHER

Rodgers and Hart were auditioning for their new show, *Higher and Higher*. Off I went again with my tap shoes in hand. June Allyson auditioned for this one, too. So did Vera-Ellen. We all made it. Our mentor, Bob Alton, was the choreographer.

The stars of *Higher and Higher* were Jack Haley Sr. (remembered today for his role as the Tin Man in *The Wizard of Oz*), Marta Eggert, Shirley Ross, and Lee Dixon. Marta played a wealthy woman in a mansion. The rest of us were maids and butlers.

We sang one song I remember to this day. It was considered controversial at the time but Hart's lyrics were so insightful they could have been written today.

> *I'll buy everything I wear at Saks.*
> *I'll cheat plenty on my income tax.*
> *Swear like a trooper,*
> *Live in a stupor —*
> *Just disgustingly rich.*
> *I'll make money and I'll make it quick,*
> *Boosting cigarettes that make me sick.*
> *Smothered in sables*
> *Like Betty Grable's —*
> *Just disgustingly rich.*
> *I will buy land*
> *Down on Long Island*

Top: Yokel Boy – *Me in the center with Judy Canova to my right. Bottom:* Very Warm For May – *Willy Torpy, June Allyson, Louie Hightower, Eve Arden, me and Hiram Sherman.*

And as a resident
I will pan the President.
I'll aspire
Higher and higher.
I'll get married and adopt a son,
Right from Tony's or from "21."
Swimming in highballs,
Stewed to the eyeballs —
Just disgustingly rich —
Too, too disgustingly rich.

Another song which is still popular is "It Never Entered My Mind." It was the number just before the finale. I was in the wings every night so I could hear Shirley Ross sing it.

The show was going to play in Boston before opening at the Shubert Theatre in New York on April 4, 1940. At that time, the publicity people came up with crazy ways to get the names of the shows into the papers. The most oft-used publicity stunt of the time was to say someone's jewels or furs were stolen. To this day, whenever I read that a star had jewels or furs stolen I have my doubts.

Higher and Higher also featured a trained seal named "Sharky." Our publicity man dreamed up a good publicity stunt. He must have had a college cohort help him get Sharky into a bathtub at Harvard. When Sharky was discovered, the show got headlines like, "Seal Found in Bath Tub."

PANAMA HATTIE

Panama Hattie, a Cole Porter musical, teamed me with Cliff Ferre, a tall, good-looking dancer. The show, again choreographed by Bob Alton, starred Ethel Merman, Betty Hutton, James Dunn, Arthur Treacher, and Rags Ragland. Buddy DeSylva was the producer. The chorus included future film actresses June Allyson, Lucille Bremer, Betsy Blair, sisters Constance "Connie" and Doris Dowling, and Vera-Ellen (as well as celebrated dancers like Jane Ball and Ronnie Cunningham). Jack Baker and Jack Donahue, two of the male dancers in the cast, would join me later in Hollywood as choreographer-directors.

Bob asked Cliff and me to make up eight bars of tap to be inserted in one of the numbers. We became so excited we couldn't stop. Instead of eight bars we made up an entire chorus. When we finally showed it to Bob, we didn't know which eight bars he would pick. To our surprise, he liked the whole thing and used it all.

Bob chose me to be line captain so I was in charge of holding our rehearsals. If a dancer had to be replaced I held the audition. Each dancer made thirty-five dollars a week. I made five dollars extra for being dance captain and ten dollars for understudying two minor parts. Fifty dollars seemed like a fortune to me back then.

Bob was full of the devil. He had a roll call every morning and made us line up like we were in the military. He walked down the line like a drill sergeant then called someone out at random. He'd threaten, "If you don't kneel and do ten Allahs, I'll tell everything I heard about you last night." Of course, we all did the Allahs.

Higher & Higher – *Top: Me (sitting on the ground), June Allyson (top left), Vera-Ellen (top center), Maggie James (top right), Jack Hayley (center, seated), Jane Ball (far right center). Bottom: June Allyson (sitting down center), Fin Olsen, me over his shoulder and next to my right, Vera-Ellen.*

Once he had me step out. With all eyes on me he said, "I know where you went last night after the show and with whom." I had gone home alone, but he threatened to tell all. I got down and did the Allahs because — God knows — what wild story he might make up.

We all had nicknames. At this time I always wore suspenders. Bob called me "Suspenders." He called one of the male dancers "X." Once X and I were having malts at the corner drugstore. Bob spotted us. From then on I was known as "Mrs. X."

We all went up to Boston to prepare for the opening. We stayed at the Avery Hotel. One morning I was awakened by a call from the stage manager. He wanted to know why I wasn't at rehearsal. What a shock! The hotel hadn't given me a wakeup call.

I flew around the room, pulling on my clothes, bumping into furniture and walls. When I dashed into the theater no one said a word. During rehearsal no one said anything about it. In fact, no one said anything at all. All of the dancers seemed cool to me. Later I heard two of the other girls didn't get their wakeup calls and they were late, too. They had arrived just prior to me, though how they beat me, I don't know. When they showed up, Bob gave them a blast. When I arrived he didn't say a word. After rehearsal I told him the other dancers were mad at me. I asked him why he didn't bawl me out. He said, "I knew the other girls could take it. But I thought you might cry." Ever since that experience I have always had my own travel alarm clock.

As I got to know Bob, I asked him questions about choreography. How did he become a choreographer? How did he come up with his creative ideas? He told me sometimes the music inspired him. Or he'd put a pad and pencil beside his bed for ideas that came to him at night when he was relaxed. Sometimes pictures in magazines inspired him. As I reflect, I believe Bob Alton was the biggest influence on me becoming a choreographer.

The show opened in Boston then moved to the 46th Street Theatre in New York where it opened on October 30th, 1940.

Jane Ball and I were in a number with Betty Hutton. We made the gestures while she did the singing. One night Jane got an eye infection and couldn't go on, so I had to quickly teach June Allyson the whole number. The only place to rehearse was in the basement where we were unable to hear the show. We were hard at it when one of the dancers walked by and said, "What are you two doing?"

"I'm teaching June Jane's part."

"Forget it," he said, "you just missed it."

We both raced up to the stage anyway, just to be sure. You can bet we stayed out of Betty Hutton's way the rest of that night.

For years after that, I had nightmares that I missed my cue. In the dream I am fighting my way through crowds of people to get on stage and, try as I might, I can't get there. But you can bet I sure learned an important lesson that day.

Shortly after we opened in New York, Buddy DeSylva, the show's producer, held understudy auditions for Betty. I didn't audition because I didn't see myself as the Betty Hutton type. I told June she should audition. I knew Buddy liked June, Jane Ball and me because he called us "Vassar, Smith & Brown," or "his college girls." Even So, June didn't want to. She didn't think she sang well. I knew she could do it, so I literally pushed her down the aisle to the audition.

Panama Hattie – *Top: Cliff Ferre, me, Vera-Ellen and Irene Austin.*
Bottom: Me, Betty Hutton and Jane Ball.

Buddy asked to hear her sing and she did. She got the part of Betty Hutton's understudy.

It wasn't too much later that chicken pox broke out among the cast. So many dancers were out ill that Bob told us to spread out to make it appear like a big act. You can guess the rest of this story. Betty Hutton came down with chicken pox and June Allyson went on in her place. Someone from George Abbott's office saw June and recommended her for one the leads for *Best Foot Forward*. It was a new show that was about to go into rehearsal. June got the part and from that role she was signed by MGM for the film version. The rest is June Allyson history!

At this time a lot of Broadway performers were going to Hollywood. It was really an exciting time to see people who had started out in bit parts on Broadway ending up with big parts on the silver screen. Secretly, I was expecting my big call to come any day.

Vera-Ellen was the fudge maker for the cast of *Panama Hattie* and we all looked forward to Vera-Ellen's weekly batches. During that time she started "going with" one of the principal dancers, Robert "Bunny" Hightower. Vera loved hearts. So when she and Bunny married, she used hearts as the wedding theme. She wore a heart-shaped tiara with little hearts embroidered around her veil. Her puff sleeves were shaped like hearts. The neckline of her gown was heart-shaped. The cakes, all three tiers of them, were shaped like hearts. Even her diamond ring looked like a heart.

Vera-Ellen and Bunny made quite a pair. He gave her an orchid corsage every few nights. Sometimes she had two or three pinned on her jacket as she roller-skated to work with Bunny. I can still visualize the two of them skating down Broadway, Vera-Ellen dripping in orchids. Once Bunny decided to build them a boat. He began constructing it in their walkup apartment. Of course, when he got it finished it was too big to fit through the door.

A talent scout for Goldwyn Studios spotted Vera-Ellen and signed her to a contract. She gave "notice" and moved to Los Angeles. And it wasn't too long before she was making her mark. A few years later, Vera-Ellen played the lead opposite Danny Kaye in the film *Wonder Man*. We all went to see it. I got the giggles when I saw her heart-shaped neckline with little hearts on the puff sleeves.

One of Ethel Merman's numbers was called, "Make It Another Old-Fashioned, Please." One night, one of the two male dancers who did a lift with Merman was unable to go on. I replaced him with one of the other chorus boys and rehearsed the lift with him myself. He was good and I knew there wouldn't be a problem, but I thought I'd better let Miss Merman know about the switch. I went to her dressing room. I felt a little knot in my stomach. Miss Merman was a huge star by that time and not afraid to let you know if something bothered her. I knocked on her door. Her dresser opened it. I saw Miss Merman sitting at her dressing table, getting ready to go on.

"Miss Merman," I began. She glanced at me in the mirror. "I want to let you know I had to replace one of the male dancers."

She didn't respond, so I went on to explain I didn't want her to be surprised when she got on stage and saw a new dancer.

"He's a good dancer," I reassured her, "and the lift will be fine."

"Yeah, okay," she said. I left.

I found out later Miss Merman had a talk with the stage manager about me.

"What's this 'chorus girl' doing coming to my dressing room telling me about changes?" she demanded to know. The stage manager set her straight by letting her know I was the dance captain.

During the entire run of the show, Miss Merman rarely had a word for any of the girls, but she loved the male dancers. She screamed with laughter at the off-color jokes they told her.

You might be reading between-the-lines that Miss Ethel Merman wasn't one of my favorite people.

During the run of *Panama Hattie*, Irene Austin, one of the dancers, invited the rest of the cast to see the new ice show, *It Happens on Ice*, produced by the Norwegian Olympic skater Sonja Henie. Irene's husband worked for the theater and got us front row tickets. I put on my full-length beaver coat, tucked my hair in my beaver hat and off I went.

We had wonderful seats at the Center Theatre. For me, the most terrific thing about the show was a young, good-looking, athletic skater. I searched for his name on the program. It was Gene Berg. After several numbers I realized he was looking at me as much as I was looking at him. This innocent flirtation was so obvious the other girls were teasing me.

The following week there was so much talk about this flirtation that Irene asked if I'd like to go back. Of course, I was raring to go! So I got dressed. I really put quite a bit of thought into my outfit. I wanted to wear something entirely different and definitely eye-catching. I wore a different coat — a cross-fox jacket — and no hat. I headed off to a repeat performance.

There was a dresser for the ice show named May who had been my dresser in one of the shows I had been in. So when I arrived at the theater I went backstage and asked for her. It was a bit of a ruse — I really wanted an introduction to Gene. After we hugged "hello," I casually mentioned I had a crush on Gene.

"Come with me," she said as she took me by the hand.

She took me to where all the performers had gathered around, waiting to go on. I caught Gene out of the corner of my eye, but he didn't see me. May tactfully introduced me to several skaters before introducing me to Gene. Gene was very cordial, but before we had a chance to get acquainted we heard "Places!" The skaters scurried off and I ran around to get my seat which was front and center. Gene smiled at me several times during the show.

A few days later I got a call at the 46th Street Theatre where we were performing *Panama Hattie*.

"This is Gene Berg," the voice said. I didn't believe it was really Gene. I thought one of the guys in my show was playing a trick on me. But it was, in fact, Gene Berg. I found out later May encouraged Gene to see my show, which he did. She also suggested he call me. And here he was inviting me to dinner the following night.

It would have to be an early date because we both had shows. I gave him my address. I was living with my parents at the time. Our doorbell rang and I opened the door, ready to go, in my full-length coat with my hair tucked into my beaver hat, just as I had dressed the first time we spotted each other. Gene looked surprised. I didn't understand his reaction, but it was as if he didn't expect his date to be me. I invited him in to meet my folks. We went to dinner and talked with great animation. Probably he talked and I listened.

I found out he was of Scandinavian descent and had been born in Seattle and raised in California. Like me, he was an only child. He had taken tap classes as he was growing up and he had trained as a skater and gymnast. He had been in the chorus on several Sonja Henie movies. Before we dashed off to our respective theaters, he asked if he could pick me up the following night after the show to go ice-skating. I told him that even though I was from Chicago I had never been on skates. He said not-to-worry: He'd teach me.

The next night he picked me up and off we went to Rockefeller Ice Rink. The rink was closed to the public at 11:00 p.m. Then they made fresh ice and let the skaters from the ice show skate for nothing until one o'clock in the morning.

Gene rented a pair of skates for me and laced up my boots. I stood up and stepped onto the ice. Gene spent the rest of the evening trying to keep me on my feet and off my bottom. As we skated (I should say *he* skated and I stepped alongside) he introduced me to the other skaters from the show. I'd already met several of them through May, but honestly, I was so nervous about meeting Gene I couldn't recall a single name. I don't know that they remembered me, either, because they told me they were glad to finally meet me after hearing about me all week.

As we skated, I felt comfortable enough to ask Gene about his reaction the first night he picked me up. Gene confessed that he was, in fact, surprised when I opened the door. He said he had a crush on a young woman who had attended his show about a week back. She wore a beaver fur hat. Gene said he had wanted to throw a note in her lap as he skated past, but it wasn't practical. So the minute the finale was over, he slipped guards over his blades and ran to the front of the theater to search for her. But she was gone.

When May introduced me, I looked so different he didn't realize I was "The Crush." At my parents' apartment, in my beaver coat and hat, Gene connected I was the same girl. Obviously, he liked both of us girls, because he asked out the second girl, not realizing she was also the first one. But then, Gene did have an eye for ladies. Of course, you don't see these things when you're young and in love. You think you're the only one and it's destined to last through eternity. Ah, the innocence of youth!

As Gene and I became more involved, we began collaborating on dance numbers. We rehearsed the numbers in my family's front room. Then, an agent got us a job as a team, working in a short film with Will Bradley and his Band called *Boardwalk Boogie* — one of the more than 1800 "Soundies" produced from 1940-1946. Soundies were the predecessors of Scopitone and later music videos; a single-song filmed and projected on something like a juke box, only with a screen. You put a quarter into the slot and got to see a film. My feelings for Gene deepened and our romance grew. He was so good-looking and so full of life he was really fun to be around.

About that time Betsy Blair, a dancer from my show, began dating another dancer she would later marry by the name of Gene Kelly. Gene was starring in *Pal Joey*. Every so often Gene Kelly and Gene Berg would arrive at our theater to pick us up. The backstage manager would call up.

"Betsy!" he'd call. "Miriam! Your Genes are here."

Ice skater Gene Berg with partner on ice.

LET'S FACE IT!

"*Panama Hattie* is closing in New York in two weeks!" the posted sign said outside the theater. It was going on the road. The performers had to sign up for six months or leave the show at the end of its run. You can imagine, at this time in my life I did not want to leave New York.

Luckily, a call went out for a Vinton Freedley-produced show called *Let's Face It!* Of course, I showed up at the audition with bells on. I was picked!

Charles "Chuck" Walters was the choreographer. When he finished our show he was going on to do a movie in Hollywood. He said to us, "I'll never be able to think of another idea or step." Of course, he thought of many more steps and ideas since that show. He would choreograph many films at MGM before going on to become a director.

Let's Face It! starred Danny Kaye, Mary Jane Walsh, Nanette Fabray, Jack Williams, Sunny O'Day, Vivian Vance, Edith Meisner, and Benny Baker. It opened at the Imperial Theatre on October 29, 1941. Performers in that show were always thinking up fun things to do. We formed a bowling team and bowled at midnight against teams from other Broadway shows. We'd all go ice skating. By now I was able to at least stand up on ice.

Gene became as much a part of our group as I did of his. We'd go sledding in Central Park. Then we'd have snowball fights. Gene was so much fun. You didn't want to dare him, because he'd try anything. I called him "Fearless Gene."

Every day at our apartment I put my hair in curlers. Then I wrapped a scarf around it and dashed off to the theater. I had scarves in every color imaginable. I kept forgetting to take my scarves home at the end of the night. One night the girls tied all the scarves together. They used them to suspend my dressing chair from the ceiling. I had to undo all those scarves before I could sit.

Another time, a group of us decided our dressing room looked dreary so we bought some brushes and powder blue paint. We painted everything in sight. We painted the walls. The toilet seat. Even the handle on the toilet plunger. When the other girls came in the next night they couldn't believe it.

I got the job of Nanette's understudy. She had a nice part in the show. She sang a terrific song and got to dance with Jack Williams. One afternoon I got a call from the stage manager to come in early. "Nan" (as we called her; although she called herself "Nani-goat") was sick and I would be going on. This would be my first big performance. With dancing. *And singing!* My stomach did flip-flops. Jack came in early to go over the number with me and to rehearse our lines.

After a while I began to feel I could handle the part and my stomach began to settle.

"Go upstairs and try on Nan's costumes," someone told me.

No sooner had I turned around when who should walk in but Nan. I could have killed her! To have to deal with my panic — and then not get to do the show — was a real letdown. But, obviously, I got over it. Nan is one of my good friends to this day.

Danny Kaye knew a lot of celebrities. Tallulah Bankhead, a good friend, came to see the show once in a while. She always sat in front and we could count on her to

Let's Face It! – *Top: That's me center with Danny Kaye. Bottom: I'm on the far right, same show.*

PORTRAIT OF 'BEST CHORUS GIRL ON BROADWAY'

Miriam Franklin is in front-center, the envied spot in the *Let's Face It!* chorus line. She's blonde, 20, and 5 feet 5.

Long-Legged Miriam Franklin Is Never Out of a Job

Let's Face It! – *Top: Dancing with partner Fred Demming. Bottom: Magazine cover, look who made the best chorus girl on Broadway – Me!*

do something crazy to try to break Danny up. Once she read a newspaper throughout the entire show, casually flipping from page to page.

Another friend of Danny's, Ray Milland, the movie star, was at the pinnacle of his career at the time. All of us girls had palpitations when he came backstage at intermission to say hello to Danny. Danny introduced Ray to all of us. Ray decided to watch the rest of the show from the wings. You've never seen so many dancers show up so early, ready to go on for their number. I had no way of knowing at that time that Ray Milland would be the male star of my very first motion picture, *Lady in the Dark*.

At the time a newspaper called *P.M.* featured many show-biz stories. In one issue they ran a full-page picture of me in a dance pose from *Let's Face It!* I was so excited! The caption read: "Long, leggy Miriam Franklin is the best chorus girl on Broadway." For a long time afterward I was known as "Legs."

Then on Sunday, December 7, 1941 everything changed. Pearl Harbor was bombed and America declared war! A lot of the boys from *Let's Face It!* were drafted.

Gene and I had been dating for about a year by now. When we weren't on a date we were talking on the phone. We'd been together so long it was sort of a given that we'd get married. Gene was very proper and old-fashioned about it. He asked my father for my hand. They had a lengthy conversation, although I can't imagine my father had any objections. Both of my parents liked Gene. I think their biggest concern was that we might be getting married just because of the war. And that Gene wouldn't be able to support a wife. Gene had such a winning personality my father finally consented.

When Gene's parents learned we were marrying, they flew from California to New York to meet me. Gene and I showed them the town including sights I had never seen. His parents were nice to me and I liked them right away. They gave Gene and me their blessing to go ahead with the wedding.

Because we didn't have much time, we arranged to be married at City Hall. Besides, we weren't really church goers. I bought a new dress. On December 22, 1941, Gene and I went off to the Hall. June Allyson was my maid of honor. JoAnn Dean, a skating partner of Gene's, was in our bridal party. I became Mrs. Gene Berg.

It wasn't much of a honeymoon. We didn't have the money or the time. We were both working. In fact, that very night I had to work. Gene was off that night so he hung around my theater.

After the show I moved out of my parents' apartment and into a hotel room with Gene. When we opened the door to our room we saw the sink was full of ice. A bottle of champagne was chilling in the middle of it. Little cakes and other goodies were set alongside. My dear mother, God bless her soul, had done this for us.

We had been married only a short time when Gene decided to join the Signal Corps instead of waiting to be drafted. So, in March of 1942, he was sent to Fort Monmouth, New Jersey. Fort Monmouth wasn't too far from New York, so I visited him on my day off. Robert "Bob" Sidney, a dancer and future choreographer, was also in his corps. They began putting on shows and Gene began to dance again. A scout named Irving "Swifty" Lazaar, one of the most powerful agents in Hollywood, saw Gene. He wanted Gene to be in an Irving Berlin show called *This is the Army*. It was to open on Broadway on Independence Day.

Wedding portrait of Mr. and Mrs. Gene and Miriam Berg.

Gene went into rehearsals and the show opened as planned. It was a smash. It went on a national tour that ended in Hollywood. After that Warner Bros. would make a film version in which Gene would dance in an uncredited role. And then the show would travel overseas.

When the cast was getting ready to move to California, I gave my two week notice at *Let's Face It!* We all traveled on a troop train. We were told the food wouldn't be good so all of us dutiful wives brought shopping bags of food. We were pleasantly surprised when the food turned out to be very good. They even served us Buffalo steaks.

I planned to be with Gene in California until the show went overseas. Then I would move back to New York. I really thought I belonged in New York. I loved dancing on stage.

When Gene and I boarded the train at Penn Station on a freezing day in January of 1943, we had no way of knowing that a two-and-a-half year separation lay waiting. Nor did we know that Gene was destined for international stardom and my own career was about to take some interesting turns.

Newlyweds out dancing in New York.

CHAPTER THREE

Hollywood: Where Dreams Can Come True

Gene and I moved in with his parents in their bungalow in Santa Monica, not far from the Ocean. They lived in a quaint and hilly part of town where all the streets had been named for trees. Ours was called "Pine."

Gene immediately started rehearsals for the L.A. stage version of *This is the Army*. As for me, being young and excited about being in California I wanted to see the sights. My first day in Los Angeles, I put on a nice dress, a coat with a fur collar and headed downtown.

Today, Los Angeles is a sprawling city with several suburbs, but back then downtown was still a hub. I boarded a bus and headed for downtown. Almost as soon as I got off the bus I ran into Billy Daniel, a dancer friend from *Let's Face It!*

"Billy!" I shouted when I saw him, "what in the world are you doing out here?" Billy informed me he had been signed to a contract at Paramount. He asked if I would like to have lunch there and see the movie stars. I eagerly accepted.

They've made several changes to Paramount over the years, especially after it absorbed the adjacent RKO Studios. If you visit today you enter through a double arched gate. Back then, the bus let us off outside the original entrance gate made famous (or infamous) in that glorious scene from *Sunset Boulevard* when Norma Desmond (Gloria Swanson) returns to the studio to be reunited with Cecil B. DeMille.

The guard let us enter and the second we stepped on the lot I realized I was way overdressed. Everyone was in work clothes except me. I must have looked like a tourist. And when we entered the commissary I felt like one. I could hardly take a bite of my sandwich for all the movie stars. I saw Ray Milland, Alan Ladd, Dorothy Lamour and many others.

"You want to come watch them shoot *Lady in the Dark?*" Billy asked. *Lady in the Dark* starred Ginger Rogers — and Don Loper was her dance partner. Knowing Don from *Very Warm for May*, I was thrilled to be invited to the set.

As we were leaving the commissary I heard someone yell, "Hey, Franklin!" I wondered who would be calling me by my stage name. I turned to see Buddy DeSylva. "What's my college girl doing here?" he asked.

By now, Buddy had become president of Paramount, lucky me. He asked what I was doing. I told him about my marriage to Gene and my move to Los Angeles.

"Miriam," he asked, "how would you like to go to work for Paramount?"

Of course I jumped at the chance. I mean, opportunities like this don't come around every day. Buddy told Billy to take me to the Business Affairs office in about an hour. We had just enough time to go watch Ginger Rogers shoot a scene.

By the time we arrived at the Business Affairs office a contract had already been prepared. It was for seven years acting and dancing. Every year Paramount would have the option to pick me for another year, with or without a raise. I was signed for $75 a week, which was pretty good money at the time.

When I arrived home that night I said to Gene, "You'll never believe what happened to me today. It was my first day in Los Angeles and I got signed to Paramount!" It was like something you'd see in a movie.

The very next day I got a call to report to the dance department for *Lady in the Dark*. One of the dancers had been injured and had to be replaced. They didn't tell me how soon they would be shooting and I didn't dare ask. I learned the routine before lunch for fear they might be shooting the next day.

Ginger and Don were featured in this dance. It was a waltz with lots of lifts. I learned we had several weeks left to rehearse and went to the studio daily. One day Ginger and Don began rehearsing with us. The director decided the dancers were doing so many lifts it was taking away from Ginger and Don's performance. So the dancers were cut.

I was, however, in two dream sequences that made it into the film. One was a wedding procession called "The Blue Dream." I wore a strapless gown with a big skirt and a wig and tall headdress that gave me a headache. The Makeup Department put blue body paint on my shoulders, arms, back and face. No matter how hard I scrubbed at the end of the day, there still was blue makeup on the towel.

It was cold the day we shot. The sound stage at Paramount didn't feel much warmer than it was outside. To make matters worse, they blew fog from dry ice onto the set. There I was waltzing around in my strapless gown and tall headdress smeared in blue makeup. Now that I think back on it, this wasn't a very glamorous way to start a movie career!

Lady in the Dark was based on a book by Moss Hart with music by Kurt Weill. It was about psychotherapy which was pretty heady stuff for 1944, the year it was released. Though it developed somewhat of a cult following, it was considered kind of "dark" for its time and didn't do well.

Buddy DeSylva on far left. Fashion show for press, using costumes from Lady in the Dark.

UNDER CONTRACT TO PARAMOUNT

Gene received word that *This is the Army* was going overseas and we said a tearful goodbye. If I hadn't been signed by Paramount, I would have returned to New York. But I decided to stay on with Gene's parents.

When I was under contract at Paramount, most of the musical numbers were orchestrated by a wonderful musician, Joseph "Joe" Lilly. He had to spend a lot of time in the dance bungalow and became friends with all of us dancers.

One day we happened to be sitting together. He surprised me by saying, "A girl has to be careful because so many guys will try to hit on you. If you give in to them and go down that road, it will eventually show on your face and it won't be long before you will look hard and lose that innocence that makes you so pretty."

Too bad the young girls of today don't have a Joe Lilly in their life.

I felt right at home at Paramount. I loved all the creative people and the movie-making process. I'd spend free time wandering around to see what I could see.

Once I went by a sound stage where Cecil B. DeMille was shooting. A sign read: "Closed Set," but I peeked in anyway. The coast was clear so I stepped inside. Mr. DeMille saw me lurking in the background and came right over.

"What are you doing here?" Mr. DeMille wanted to know. I told him I had just signed with Paramount and was always looking in on sound stages for something wonderful that was shooting. There was a man whose sole job was to follow Mr. DeMille around and place a director's chair of appropriate height under Mr. DeMille. When the man realized I wasn't going to be thrown out, he set one of those high director's chairs under Mr. DeMille so we could talk at eye-level. I looked around for a stool to be put under me but no such luck.

When Mr. DeMille found out I was a dancer he asked if I knew his niece, Agnes. I told him I admired her work but I didn't know her. Then he asked if I knew Katherine, his adopted actress daughter who was married to Anthony Quinn. "I have not had the pleasure," I told him.

"We're ready for you Mr. DeMille," someone called out (and it wasn't Gloria Swanson). Mr. DeMille went back to shooting and I observed him working for the rest of the day.

My path would cross with Agnes de Mille's in 1979. She was choreographing a revival of *Oklahoma* that was going to play at the Pantages Theatre in Los Angeles. I was asked to teach Harry Groener a tap sequence for "Everything's Up to Date in Kansas City." Coincidentally, that was the same number my husband, Gene, sang and danced in the film. The show would go on to the Palace in New York and Harry would be nominated for a Tony for his performance. I remember going to the theater one afternoon to start rehearsal. Agnes hadn't finished her rehearsals yet. She was seated in the middle of the theater beside a lighted makeshift desk. She saw me come in and ordered, "Come here!" I thought, "I wonder if she's seen what I've done and doesn't like it." When I got to her aisle she motioned me to come to her. "Sit down," she said when I got beside her. I sat. She reached over to her desk and pulled out a bag. She handed the bag to me and said, "Have a cookie."

I would meet Agnes a second time at a dinner in 1989 in New York. She was up in age then and not walking well. I was seated across from her at a table with about eight other

Studio Still from Kitty *starring Paulette Goddard.*

people. "Do you still live at the beach?" Agnes asked me. That kind of bowled me over because I hadn't remembered talking with her about my apartment on the beach. Agnes de Mille was a sharp lady and I had tremendous respect for her and her work.

Cecil B. DeMille wasn't the only legendary director I got to know. One day while lunching at the Paramount commissary, Preston Sturges walked up to me. "I may have something for you in my next picture," Mr. Sturges told me. It was called *Hail the Conquering Hero* and would star Eddie Bracken and Ella Raines and feature William Demarest (best remembered today as Uncle Charlie in the television show, *My Three Sons*).

Mr. Sturges went on to describe my part. The picture, he told me, would open with credits. Then as they showed the final credit ("Written and Directed by Preston Sturges") they would dissolve to my tapping feet. The camera would pull back to reveal me dancing in a nightclub. I would be on screen for about sixteen bars of music. Then the camera would pan through the club to the bar and down to Eddie, sitting at the end. That would be the end of me!

I created my own routine then I rehearsed and rehearsed. Edith Head, who dressed all the stars at Paramount at the time, designed a snazzy, French-sailor inspired outfit. It was high-waisted bell bottoms that accentuated my 21-inch waist, a halter jacket that exposed my midriff and a little cap.

The day of shooting I arrived at the sound stage at Paramount. The stage had been transformed into a nightclub. Extras who played club patrons took their seats. Someone told me to take my place on the dance floor, which I did.

My dance opening the film, Hail the Conquering Hero.

The same voice yelled "Playback" — meaning play back the music — which signaled my dance and my mind went absolutely blank. For the life of me I couldn't remember what I created. So I started ad libbing and my feet took over. No one knew I was making the routine up as I went along, because I was the only one who knew it. As I danced I thought, "How will I ever record these taps?" (I'll write more about dubbing taps later.)

About that time Mr. Sturges yelled, "Cut!" I thought, "Uh-oh." But, luckily for me, he bawled out a fellow in the background. By the time we did the next take I remembered the whole routine.

After the picture was made, I found out through the grapevine that Mr. Sturges had talked to the studio heads about me. He had wanted me to play the female starring role. But Paramount wanted Ella Raines. No becoming a star there for me!

June Allyson's career was doing quite well by this time. In fact, she was on her way to becoming the top female box office draw in the country. But she didn't want to get a place on her own. By now, I had a little bit of money saved up, so June and I pooled our money and rented a nice apartment on Wilshire Boulevard in Beverly Hills.

Living with June was so much fun because she had a lot of friends, like Judy Garland, and was always going to this party or that one. This was before she married Dick Powell, so she was still a popular "bachelorette."

Back in New York, my mother and father separated for the second time. My father, coincidentally, started dating another woman named Mildred, whom I never met.

My mother came out to Los Angeles for a visit. She liked it so well she wanted to stay. June and I asked my mother to move in with us. She began cooking for us

Bing was the first to arrive at my BBQ and the last to leave.

and helping out with the cleaning. We all lived together until June's career skyrocketed. We all sat down and talked it over. June decided to hire a housekeeper and keep the place on her own. My mother and I decided to get our own apartment within walking distance of Paramount. It was a cute, little building where all the apartments faced into a central courtyard.

One day Josephine Earl, a choreographer at Paramount, asked if I'd like to housesit for her and her husband. Josephine's husband was a successful agent and I knew they owned a magnificent home. They were going away for a week and wanted someone to watch over the place. I joyfully said, "Yes!"

Josephine told me to be sure to invite my friends to the house while they were away. And then she told me to be sure to take advantage of the pool — which I did. Boy, was that living! I could envision myself living like that some day.

At the time I was working on a Bing Crosby picture called *Here Come the Waves*. I invited all of the other dancers to the house for a BBQ one Saturday night. Bing got wind of it and asked if he could come. I couldn't believe it. Bing Crosby was the biggest movie star in America at this time and here he was asking to come to my little shindig. What would *you* say if you were in my shoes?

Bing was the first to arrive along with his sidekick, Barney Radinsky. Their contribution to the party was a case of scotch.

I know that over the years Bing has been portrayed as distant and cool. But I didn't find him to be that way. He jumped right in and helped me with the barbeque.

Bing loved to laugh and dancers are the most fun-loving, yet hard-working people in the business. Bing was good at talking with most people on all levels, but I think he had a special fondness for dancers. He was so good to us.

We all had a wonderful night and I think Bing did, too. He was the last to leave.

My first lines in a movie occurred in a party scene in 1945's *Masquerade in Mexico* starring Dorothy Lamour and Arturo de Cordova. My friend, Billy Daniel, had a role in the film and was the choreographer.

Mitchell "Mitch" Leisen, the director, had an assistant who told me I should make up a character for myself. He told me Mitch thought that would make the scene more believable. I invented myself as a rich and famous lady. I mentioned it to Edith Head.

By now, Edith had become a celebrity herself for her personal style. She had a tremendous talent for knowing how to feature a person's best features and assets and disguising their flaws. Edith got me all done up with a beautiful gown. She wanted my hair up. The hairdresser fixed it to her specification.

I would work with Edith on several films over the years. She once told me, "Miriam, we should have a class where you teach our young actors how to walk."

With all this exposure, especially now that I had a speaking part, I thought I was on my way. But nothing came from *Masquerade*; the same was true of a "Musical Parade" short *Halfway to Heaven*, in which I played a hatcheck girl in a nightclub. Nor of *Incendiary Blonde* or any of the other films in which I danced, including "You Can't Ration Love" and two other "Musical Parade" shorts, *Naughty Nanette* and *Bombalera*, which starred Olga San Juan. I was one of the "Bombalera Dancers."

Then, one day, Paramount's casting director took me to meet Billy Wilder, the famed director. He was shooting a film called *Double Indemnity*. The casting director thought I'd be perfect for the part of the secretary for insurance inspector Barton Keyes, played by Edward G. Robinson. Mr. Wilder took one look at me.

"She looks too much like Barbara," Mr. Wilder said. By that he meant the star of the picture, Barbara Stanwyck. The casting director, who was quick-on-his feet, said he would have my hair pulled back and he'd put glasses on me so I would look totally different. So I got the part.

I had two lines. "Oh, Mr. Neff, Mr. Keyes wants to see you," was my first line. I would continue with "He's been yelling for you all afternoon."

I was to deliver them to Fred MacMurray in front of an elevator on a mezzanine overlooking a huge office with several desks. The scene was complicated. It was to be done in a long, continuous shot. As the camera rolled in, they pulled the desks away then the camera panned up to the mezzanine where Fred got off the elevator. I was to run into the shot, stop Fred and deliver my lines.

I had to get Fred at just right the moment so he would appear to be stopping naturally on his mark, which was under the microphone that was out of camera range. I was petrified I would stop Fred at the wrong moment and ruin the entire shot.

We went into rehearsals. The first time I did it, I stopped Fred in the right spot. I was pleased with myself until Fred told me I was moving around when I delivered my line. It must have been obvious to him that I was scared to death. He told me I should run in, stop him, plant myself, and then deliver my line.

Studio publicity shot for Masquerade in Mexico.

Top: Scene from Naughty Nanette. *Bottom: Scene from* Bombalera. *I'm standing behind the piano player while Billy Daniel plays conga for Olga San Juan.*

"Otherwise," Fred said, "your mother won't be able to recognize you."

They shot the scene and I felt good about it. Fred was so gracious to me. He even upstaged himself so the camera would favor me.

The finished picture was a huge hit and garnered several Academy Award nominations, including Best Picture, Best Actress, Best Director, Best Screenplay, Best Music, and Best Cinematography (Black-and-White). In 1992 *Double Indemnity* was selected for preservation in the United States National Film Registry by the Library of Congress as being "culturally, historically, or aesthetically significant."

Everyone told me I was good in my supporting role, but I was horrified to hear my voice. It sounded so high. After that I made a conscious effort to lower my voice. In spite of my high pitch, I thought I was on my way!

I learned early in life to set a target and aim for it. But you also have to be prepared to change your target if necessary. My target was still to dance on film like Eleanor Powell. And then fate, or destiny, or whatever you call it intervened.

I was called into a bungalow where dance rehearsals were being held for *And the Angels Sing*. Danny Dare, the dance director, explained this was a military tap routine sequence. I counted the number of dancers in the room. There were thirteen including me, which stuck me as odd because dance lines were always an even number. Then I found out why I was there.

"I'm leaving you in charge to choreograph this number," Danny told me. And that's what happened. Even though I couldn't remember the name of that picture until I started researching this book, this moment marked the beginning of a different career for me. Although I never received credit for this or any of my early choreographic jobs, without realizing it, I was laying a foundation for becoming a choreographer.

After that initial number I was asked to choreograph several others. One was a Tyrolean "Slap Dance" for Fred MacMurray and Eddie Foy, Jr. They wore short leather pants and suspenders, knee-high socks with tassels and funny, little hats with feathers. Now the tables were turned. I was the one trying to get Fred to relax. He was so self-conscious it took several days until I could get him to dance.

"I have to make a phone call," Fred would say or he'd use my favorite excuse, "my feet are too big." Or he'd light up a cigarette. Fred always seemed to be out of cigarettes. I smoked in those days, too, and he would bum from me. Fred was notorious for being tight with his money. He did finally bring me a pack of cigarettes.

Fred was a good saxophone player and, as such, had good rhythm. We inched our way through the number. Fred and Eddie were terrific in the finished number.

I ran into Fred years later. He and his wife June Haver were seated behind me at a theater. June used to joke about how Fred hated to spend money. She went on to tell me that a pipe had broken under the kitchen sink and Fred decided to save money by fixing it himself. He crawled under the sink and repaired the pipe. He turned the water back on. The pipe burst, flooding the kitchen and ruining the linoleum. June said by the time they called in the plumber and bought a new floor it cost far more for Fred to fix it.

I finally got a terrific opportunity to dance in a movie called *Duffy's Tavern*. It seemed as though every star on the lot was in this movie, including Betty Hutton, Bing Crosby, Alan Ladd, Dorothy Lamour, Paulette Goddard, Veronica Lake and a

Several glamour shots of me from the 1940s.

then-unknown named Joan Caulfield; however, most of them were not dancers per se, so the featured number I was going to do would supply the dancing. Billy Daniel, my friend who helped get me into Paramount, was also the choreographer.

They teamed me with Johnny Coy, a wonderful Canadian tap dancer. We danced to "When Johnny Comes Marching Home." Between Billy, Johnny and me, we created a scenario about love during War Time in dance. This was an exciting time for me! I would watch them build our set and think, "That's just for us."

In Duffy's Tavern, *the set was built just for us!*

The day of the shoot arrived and I figured it would go pretty much the same as others with lots of stops and starts. Wrong! Mark Sandrich, the director, wanted to shoot as much as possible in one take. If you watch the dance as it appeared on film you'll notice there were only a couple of cuts.

After "Duffy's Tavern," Mark Sandrich went on to begin production on a big Irving Berlin musical called "Blue Skies." Bing Crosby, Billy De Wolfe and Olga San Juan had been signed. They brought Paul Draper, a dancer/choreographer from New York, to play one of the male leads. They were looking for a female to star opposite him. Word went out that the actress had to be a dancer, but not necessarily a "name." I was given my first screen test with a really fine actor named Patric Knowles. Pat was a terrific help and I learned my lines inside and out. The scene ended with a kiss. He had a mustache and I remember thinking I had never kissed a man with a moustache.

I found out the hard way I didn't get the part. I read in the newspapers that they signed Joan Caulfield. Joan was a beauty — you couldn't take that away from her — but SHE COULDN'T DANCE!

Suddenly, Mark died at the age of forty-four before filming could commence. Stuart Heisler, his replacement, was not crazy about Joan, nor was Paul who didn't want a leading lady with two left feet. They began auditioning other actresses for Joan's part.

Suddenly, Paul, who also had a slight stutter, was fired. Joan was back on the film. Fortunately for all of us, Fred Astaire was coaxed out of retirement. He and Hermes Pan created some really spectacular, memorable dancing in that film.

It was widely rumored that Joan and Bing had grown close after their meeting on *Duffy's Tavern*. She later told the press she had an affair with a movie star. Although she didn't name him, it was easy to put two and two together. So I guess I didn't have much of a chance. The irony of the story is that, when they finished the shoot, they brought me in to dub the sound of Joan's taps.

Tap sounds are always recorded in pictures after the filming is completed. To dub the sounds, a dancer performs the original dance in a recording studio where there is no noise interference. Microphones are placed by their feet. All of the great dancers do their own dubbing, unless they are unavailable.

In my career I dubbed for many dancers, male and female, including Bob Hope and Bing Crosby, doing a soft shoe, and Dorothy Lamour (when she wore shoes).

Then there was Betty Hutton, who wasn't exactly on the beat for a particular dance. I asked the music people, "Should I go with what I'm seeing or fit it on the right beat of the music?" They told me to go with the right beat and it would make Betty look like a better dancer. Oh, the power of film!

Once they called me in to dub for Ginger Rogers for *The Major and the Minor*. I thought, "How could that be? That movie had already been released." They told me I was dubbing for a foreign release. They had to have a clean track of her taps because she had been talking while she was dancing. Someone else would dub her dialogue in the foreign language. I had never learned a routine by watching on a screen so it took a little doing. It didn't take long to learn the routine and record it.

To this day, I am still periodically called in to dub for a dancer. I must say I thought it was neat when a friend of mine recently called to tell me I was written up in a December 29th, 2004 article in *The New York Times*. The focus of the story was on lip-syncing, but in a section on feet dubbers, the author referred to me as "one of the best."

AN OFFER FROM COLUMBIA

I had been with Paramount for over two years when they got a call from Columbia. Columbia wanted to borrow me to dance in *Cover Girl*. As I mentioned, I am a huge fan of Jerome Kern. The music to *Cover Girl* was written by Kern and the lyrics were by Ira Gershwin. The picture was like old-home week. It starred three performers I knew from my Broadway days: Eve Arden, Phil Silvers and Gene Kelly. The dance numbers would be staged by Seymour Felix and Val Raset, although Gene Kelly choreographed his own numbers.

As if this call from Columbia couldn't be any more exciting, I was told I would dance with Gene. I was thrilled about the prospect of working with him. He danced with an athletic style, similar to my husband's.

Top: A scene from Cover Girl, *my chance to dance with Gene Kelly. Bottom: Backstage on* Cover Girl *with me, Phil Silvers, Leslie Brooks, Gwen Norris and Lucille Marsh.*

In those days studios were paid extra when they loaned you to another studio. Paramount kindly told me if I wanted out of my contract they would let me go with the full amount they received from Columbia. Columbia was paying twice my current salary so off I went.

Charles Vidor, the director, shot the dance sequence later in the filming. Meanwhile, I was in several shots with other girls rehearsing or backstage, rushing in and out of dressing rooms, that kind of thing.

The Powers-That-Be decided the number that got me to Columbia in the first place, would go to Rita Hayworth. Although I had a nice little dance with Gene, Rita got the big one.

THE JOLSON STORY

After *Cover Girl*, I was asked by Columbia to choreograph a tap number in a film about the life of Al Jolson called *The Jolson Story*. Larry Parks, a wonderful actor who was married to Betty Garrett, was cast as Al Jolson. I showed him a little step he used in one of the numbers, but my main job was to create a routine for Jolson's wife.

Ruby Keeler, the tap dancer, had been married to Jolson in real life, but Ruby wouldn't allow Columbia to use her name. In the film they named her "Julie Benson" and the role was played by Evelyn Keyes. Ruby was considered the first female movie tap dance star so this movie was special to me.

An assistant choreographer told me that in the story, Julie was to dance down a long flight of stairs to "Liza." After she takes about three steps she is gripped by fear and almost falls. At that moment Jolson, sitting in the audience unbeknownst to Julie, stands and starts singing the words to her song. This reassuring gesture is enough for Julie to overcome her panic and continue with her dance.

I was given a sound stage and a staircase that, I believe, was nearly twenty-feet high. I also had a soundtrack which included Jolson's voice, since Jolson recorded all his songs. I went to the studio and began creating the number.

I didn't see anyone else for several weeks until I got a call that the legendary Harry Cohn, Head of Columbia, was coming to see what I had done.

Chairs appeared from nowhere and ashtrays were set out. The door opened and in strolled Mr. Cohn, followed by the director, the assistant director, the producer, Evelyn Keyes and many others I didn't know. But one man I recognized immediately gave me quite a jolt. It was none other than Al Jolson himself!

No one made any introductions. They all just shuffled into their chairs, lit cigarettes and looked in my direction.

"Let's see it!" someone yelled out.

I got into position at the top of the staircase. The music started and I danced my way down. If you've seen the film, you know there are a lot of bounds and leaps. Down and down I leapt. The number finished. Silence. You could have heard a pin drop.

"They hate it," I thought. "That's why no one's talking." I searched the faces for some sort of reaction. Then I realized each and every person was looking to Mr. Cohn. Mr. Cohn said something to the group. This opened a floodgate of buzzing and gesturing, none of which I could decipher.

The Al Jolson Story. *I was the dance double for Evelyn Keyes (inset). Everybody thought she was really dancing and she didn't do one step!*

Mr. Cohn motioned me to come closer to him.

"Evelyn," he instructed, "stand beside her." Evelyn got out of her chair and stood next to me. More buzzing.

"Would you 'double' Evelyn?" Mr. Cohn finally asked me.

"Of course," I said trying not to sound too eager. "Then she won't have to learn this routine."

There was talk about the costume they would make for me. It was to be exactly like Evelyn's and I would wear a red wig. Then everyone in the group got up and left. Except Mr. Al Jolson who walked up to me and said, "They all thought the number was wonderful. I noticed nobody bothered to tell you and I thought you should know."

Years later an author who was writing a book on Jolson called me for any stories he could use. So I told him how kind Mr. Jolson had been to me. He responded with, "You're the first person who has anything nice to say about Al Jolson."

After several weeks of rehearsal they finally shot the number. Evelyn was in two close-up shots during the number but I did the rest. I have friends who also know Evelyn who have watched the film. And even though they know it's all me they still can't believe it.

After filming I went in to record the taps. But when they played the taps along with the film they thought they interfered with Jolson's singing so they didn't use them.

The Jolson Story became Columbia's first real blockbuster musical and the "Liza" number was a big hit. I did every bit of the dancing, but Evelyn took the bows. I didn't even get a film credit.

A few years ago, Tad Tadlock, a choreographer friend of mine, let me know she was lunching with Evelyn. I told Tad if she had the opportunity she might mention she knew the gal that doubled her in *The Jolson Story*. Tad called me after the lunch.

"Evelyn remembered you well, Miriam," she said. "After she saw you leaping down the stairs (in the studio) she was glad she didn't have to do it." Tad went on to say, "She said fifty years later it was about time she thanked you."

GENE GETS A CONTRACT AT TWENTIETH CENTURY-FOX

The war ended and Gene came home. It had been so long since we'd seen each other I was excited as well as anxious. We got reacquainted quickly. Gene moved into the apartment I shared with my mother.

It isn't this way now, but back then a wife was expected to focus on her husband's career. And so my perspective shifted to Gene's career. Not that I minded. Nothing thrilled me more than seeing my husband succeed.

Johnny Darrow, a Hollywood agent, knew about Gene's talent from *This Is the Army*. He called shortly after Gene got home. At that time Twentieth Century-Fox Studios didn't have any dancing male stars, so Johnny thought Gene had a good chance of a contract. He lined up a test. Johnny knew I had read scenes with the newcomers to Paramount. He thought I might be able to put together a routine

The Nelsons expecting, 1947.

that would show Gene off to his best advantage. Gene and I found a scene that worked well and then we choreographed a number for him.

I went with Gene to Fox to read the few girl lines. I was as nervous as Gene. I wore a little tie. My heart was beating so hard I hoped no one could notice the tie jumping. I kept putting my hand up to cover the tie.

After Gene and I did the reading, Gene danced. I stood off to the side, watching proudly as he demonstrated his talent. Fox was so impressed they signed him to a contract. They didn't, however, like his last name. Gene and I came up with several options. We decided on "Nelson," which was Gene's mother's maiden name. And so "Gene Nelson" was born.

With a contract at Fox, Gene and I felt financially secure enough to start a family. We moved into a one-bedroom apartment in Santa Monica. My mother stayed in the apartment near Paramount. After furnishing our apartment, there wasn't much money left. Gene and I often had company in that tiny apartment. Some of them were actors or actresses with whom he worked, like June Haver, and I most often served spaghetti.

There was an Italian deli down the block and a wonderful woman who worked there taught me how to make spaghetti. She gave me fresh basil and oregano from her garden. The spaghetti was good and it was cheap. We were saving money for our baby who would soon be born.

Nine months passed quickly. As the delivery date drew closer, June Haver threw me a baby shower. I was awakened in the middle of the night on May 9, 1947 with labor pains. They were coming every five minutes which wasn't what I had been told. I had heard the initial pains would be at least a half an hour apart. From there, the gap was to slowly decrease, like thunder in an impending storm: Fifteen minutes ... Ten ... Five ... Three. That would allow ample time to get to the hospital. We called the doctor.

"Come to the hospital immediately," he said.

Gene raced around and pulled the car up in front of our apartment. I got in and we sped away. I was petrified I might have the baby in the car and "Fearless Gene" would attempt to cut the cord.

But we made it with plenty of time to spare. I delivered our beautiful son, Christopher, at 10:30 the following night. He was seven pounds, ten ounces and twenty-one inches long. At first, probably because of the sedation, I didn't realize I had delivered him. The nurse told me I had delivered a beautiful boy and I said, "No, I haven't."

I was wheeled back to my room after the delivery. I had a groggy conversation with Gene that was lost when I drifted into a deep sleep. He recounted our conversation after I'd regained consciousness.

"How'd it go?" he had asked me as I lay there on the gurney.

"The first act was great," I told him. "But the second act was lousy!"

Fox cast Gene in one musical, *I Wonder Who's Kissing Her Now*, in which he danced with June Haver; but the other films he did were small acting roles in *Gentleman's Agreement*, *The Walls of Jericho* and *Apartment for Peggy*. Gene was considered to appear opposite Betty Grable in *Mother Wore Tights*, but looked very young at this time. I think because of that, Dan Dailey got the part and nearly all of the other Fox dance roles.

Top: Baby Chris' Birthday – left to right, Miriam, Candy Withers, Chris and grandmother, Lenore 'Chrissie' Berg. Bottom: Little Chris and Mom (left), Big Chris and Mom (right).

I must say — although I could be accused of being partial – Gene was a terrific dancer. In spite of his talent, he was only at Fox for one year when they didn't renew his contract.

About that time, Gower Champion was directing and choreographing a revue at the Las Palmas Theatre in Hollywood called *Lend An Ear*. Gene was signed for a role. Carol Channing was in it and she was a sensation. The show was such a success it went to Broadway.

By this time a few chinks had begun to develop in our marriage. I don't want to sound like I'm defending Gene, but you can't imagine the kind of pressure women place on a young, athletic, attractive movie star to stray. One woman even had the audacity to bring a pie to our home. As I mentioned earlier, Gene was already kind of vulnerable because he had an eye for women.

I certainly wasn't the kind of wife to keep her husband on a leash. My motto was "Look, but don't touch." But Gene developed a relationship with a dancer from *Lend an Ear* that crossed over my boundaries of acceptability. We separated. Then Gene went to Broadway with *Lend an Ear*.

Gene called me one day and asked me if I would come to New York to try and make our marriage work. I decided to go. My mother took care of Chris. Once I got to New York, Gene and I decided to make a go of it. We found an apartment. I flew back to California to get Chris, then flew him to New York. Our family was together again.

Gene got a lot of praise and attention for his performance in *Lend an Ear*. I loved being back in New York again, and the time I got to spend with my father. We lived happily like that for most of that year. And then, a talent scout for Warner Bros. saw Gene in the show and signed him to a contract and we all flew back to Los Angeles.

THE WARNER BROS. YEARS

We borrowed money from Gene's parents and combined it with the money from Warner Bros. to buy a house. Nowadays, a home in Burbank would cost over a half a million dollars. Back then we found one for the exorbitant fee of fifteen thousand. I decided to go back to work so my mother moved in with us to look after Chris and we hired Ardie, a wonderful African-American woman, as a housekeeper.

Gene wanted me to be an assistant choreographer for LeRoy Prinz, the Dance Director at Warner Bros. LeRoy told me had several assistants on his payroll and couldn't afford another. "Why don't you dance in the picture?" he suggested. "You'll make a salary and then, in Gene's next picture, we'll put you on as head choreographer." So, that's what we did.

The movie was called *The Daughter of Rosie O'Grady*. Gene finally got to show off his dancing skills and acted with Gordon MacRae, June Haver and an unknown named Debbie Reynolds. Debbie was very funny. On the breaks she'd play baseball with the guys. She also was involved with Girl Scouts so we had to buy her cookies.

After Debbie became a star she invited me to her home in Burbank. She had just installed a pool. The top step read "Abba Dabba." She told me she built the pool with the money she got from the sale of that record!

The first number Gene did in *The Daughter of Rosie O'Grady* was called "A Farm Off Old Broadway" which, naturally, took place on a farm set. Gene did a dance that included a cartwheel over a wheelbarrow. I wheeled the wheelbarrow and danced a bit role. Several other girls, called "Farmettes," danced in the background. This would be the first of many films Gene and I would work on together at Warner Bros.

Chris with my mother 'Nana' at June Lake.

Warner's laid Gene off after *Rosie O'Grady*. As was the custom, they had six weeks to decide if they would pick up his option for another year. We weren't sure if they would, so Gene and I decided to spend the six weeks in a beautiful little town up in the Sierra Mountains called June Lake. We took our son, Chris, who was three or four at the time. June Lake had only about a couple hundred people and it took me back to those wonderful times in Glenn, Michigan. We rented a small cabin.

We did a lot of fishing. Gene would clean the fish and I would cook them. My mother came up for a visit. My father even came out from New York for a short visit. Then we got a call that Warner's picked up Gene's option and he went on salary. We headed back to Los Angeles for his next picture.

When we got home, Gene began filming "Tea for Two" co-starring Doris Day. He would also be the choreographer — and I would be an assistant. The picture reunited Gene with Gordon MacRae. By now the Nelsons and the MacRaes had become friends. We would spend many happy times together.

Publicity photos while working at Warner Bros.

Billy De Wolfe, who was also in the movie, gave everybody nicknames. He dubbed Doris Day "Clara Bixby." She's been Clara to me ever since. Gordon was called "Norbert Kunkle" and Gene was called "Melvin." He called me "Anastasia Gonzalez." When I asked him why, the answer was, "Because you look so Latin." I haven't seen too many blue-eyed, blonde Latinas in my life.

Gene and Doris did several song and dance numbers together. Gene and I would create the dance and I would teach it to Doris. Doris had studied tap, so I had fun working with her. She was able to hit-the-ground-running as they say. We came up with one really complicated step that I use to this day.

In those days Doris lived close to the studio and we'd often go to her house for a terrific lunch made by Alma, Doris's mother. I especially loved Alma's German potato salad. Afterward, we'd take a dip in her pool.

Doris had two big poodles. One of them, named Smudgy, loved it when people swam. He would race down the diving board and jump into the pool with his legs sprawled. It was quite a sight to see, Smudgy the poodle doing a belly flop. He'd swim to the stairs, climb out and do it all over again. The other poodle, Beanie, just sat there and barked.

On the far side of the pool was a cabana. It sat away from the pool by about three feet, separated by a concrete walkway. Doris climbed onto the roof of that little house and dove into the pool. She was quite the daredevil! I thought Doris and Gene made a good dance couple because she also was fearless.

"Cuddles" Z. Sakall was in many of Doris' movies and this was no exception. His darling wife brought him lunch every day in a picnic basket. They went into his dressing room to eat.

The next picture Gene did with Doris was called *Lullaby of Broadway*. It also featured "Cuddles" and Billy De Wolfe.

The credits for the picture say the musical numbers were created and staged by Al White and Eddie Prinz, but, as Doris writes in her autobiography, Eddie didn't dance. Gene and I created several routines for that picture. During the finale, Doris and Gene were to dance down a long staircase. Doris wore a long gown during the rehearsals to get used to dancing in a full-length dress.

Gene made up a step going down the stairs backwards. You couldn't really see where you were going until you got there. If you see the number it looks easy. And that's testimony to the skill and artistry of a good dancer. But it was far from a simple dance.

I had danced several crazy dances in my own career up until now. Many included jumps off platforms. But this dance scared me. I could never do it up to full tempo. I would carefully put one foot down, turn, then put the other one down. After Gene and I created the routine, we taught it to Clara.

When we got to the going down backwards part, I showed her how to do it my way. As she learned the routine we'd speed it up. By the time we'd gone over it several times she didn't have any trouble doing it at tempo. It wasn't until after they'd shot the scene that I told her of my own fear. She was shocked she could dance something I couldn't. She included this incident in her own autobiography. She called it an act of "unforgivable treason," but I guess she got over it since Doris and I are friends to this day.

Top: Publicity still of Chris and Gene dancing. Bottom: Chris and Mom trying out the studio's ice rink. The rink was built for the film By the Light of the Silvery Moon.

Studio publicity photos.

Top: The Nelson's taking Gordon and Sheila MacRae for a ride in their new car. Bottom: Marge and Gower Champion and the Nelsons at a Hollywood Premiere.

One Sunday afternoon, Gower decided to take a picture of the 'Mouse Pack' girls, looking like it came out of Vogue *Magazine. Left to right: Patty Edwards, Marge Champion, Janet Leigh, and Me.*

THE MOUSE PACK

During this time Gene and I were also spending a lot of time with Marge and Gower Champion. We formed a group we called "The Mouse Pack," referring, of course, to "The Rat Pack" of Dean Martin, Frank Sinatra, Peter Lawford, Joey Bishop and Sammy Davis, Jr.

The Mouse Pack included Tony Curtis and Janet Leigh, who were dating when we first formed the group; Blake and Patty Edwards; Bob Wells, the songwriter who (with Mel Torme) composed "The Christmas Song," also known as "Chestnuts Roasting on an Open Fire" and his wife, singer Lisa Kirk; actors Jim Lanphier and Max Showalter, who I had worked with in *Very Warm for May* and Gene had worked with in *This is the Army*, under contract to Fox at the time as "Casey Adams"; Fox made him use that name which he hated. Other people floated in and out of the Pack like Lee Remick, Gordon and Sheila MacRae and Richard "Dick" Quine, who was also in *Very Warm for May*. He became a film director and we would later do two films together. Dick would have several tragic circumstances related to guns in his life. His first wife, actress Susan Peters, permanently paralyzed herself with a gun during a hunting accident and Dick would then tragically take his own life by gunshot.

Songwriter Sammy Cahn and his wife Gloria were also occasional members of the Mouse Pack. Sammy would go on to be nominated for more than thirty Academy Awards for writing classic movie song lyrics like "Three Coins in the Fountain," "High Hopes," "Call Me Irresponsible," "Come Fly With Me" and "Love And Marriage." It was my privilege to witness his creative process for more than the thirty years I knew him.

"I just wrote the funniest song," Sammy told me one afternoon. "There were no rhymes until you got way into the song, but it seemed to work." He sang the number to me. It was "Be My Love," the song that was later made into a huge success by Mario Lanzo. Or maybe it was the other way around? There were many times in my life I'd hear a terrific song for the first time after it was released and I'd think, "Where have I heard that before?" Then I'd remember hearing Sammy singing it.

The Mouse Pack got together on weekends to cook and swim. We frequently went to the Champions' house on Woodrow Wilson Drive, off Sunset. I was always in charge of the salads. Marge would be in charge of the roast. If we had a barbeque, Gower and the guys would watch it.

We always sat down in front of the television, eating off TV trays, so we could watch *Your Hit Parade*. We sang along to "So Long for Awhile" and finished with a farewell salute at the television.

Marge and Gower threw an engagement party for Janet and Tony. Janet had worked on a film for billionaire Howard Hughes, owner of RKO, and he had a bit of crush on her. By now Mr. Hughes was quite reclusive. They invited him to the party and he did attend, however, sitting by himself and not "mixing."

Sometimes the focus of the day would be car washing. The guys would wash cars while we girls cooked. Janet said she couldn't cook but she was the best cleaner-upper I ever saw. I would no more lay down a dirty spoon before Janet would grab it and wash it.

The Champions moved to a new house at 9137 Cordell Drive in Beverly Hills. It was the house Ronald Reagan and Jane Wyman had built and lived in until they separated. One day, Gower mentioned the wall that went up their driveway needed a coat of paint. The Mouse Pack pitched in and painted the wall.

Somebody brought a bottle of champagne and a small jar of caviar to one of our Sunday get-togethers. We liked it so much we decided we would chip in and buy a big tin of good caviar and champagne for the following Sunday. Gower put the caviar on cracked ice. He decided it didn't look fancy enough so he made a psychedelic design on the ice from food coloring. We ate every bit of the caviar then went to the movies. It was a serious film, but we all had the giggles. I wonder why?

Once in a while The Mouse Pack dined at Gene's and my house in Burbank. We had one of those twirling barbeques that were popular at the time. Gower was tending the steaks one night. He was being dramatic and spun the steaks. One went flying! I was the only who saw it. He picked it up, put it back on the BBQ and gave it another spin. "No one will ever know which one it was, including us."

Our friendship with Gordon and Sheila MacRae also grew during this time. We had a lot in common. Gene and I had Chris and they had Meredith, Heather, Gar (shortened from Gordon) and Bruce. Meredith would grow up to become an actress herself, including her role as Billy Jo in *Petticoat Junction*.

Like so many of us back then, Sheila loved throwing parties. The MacRaes had a one-story, rambling house with a pool up in Laurel Canyon. Sheila would spend time in the kitchen, cooking with their housekeeper, Mamie.

Sheila had studied theater and acting. In fact, she met Gordon playing summer stock in Upstate New York. A lot of the MacRaes' friends were actors, too, like Rod Steiger, Jeff Chandler and Jack Carter.

After dinner we played charades. As you can imagine, actors are good at charades. I especially like playing racing charades, where one person sat in the doorway between two rooms of opposing teams. One member of a team would run to that person to get the question, then run back to their team and act it out so their team could figure it out before the other.

Sammy Cahn made up the questions one night. Sammy played a trick on us. We kept guessing and guessing, trying to figure out the question. It took a while before we realized there were no such things as what he made up.

Sheila had a crazy "bit" she used to do for fun. She played a "Southern Belle" with a thick drawl. When she was offered a drink she'd refuse.

"One mint julep won't do any harm," she'd say in her Southern drawl. She sips it until finished. "Well, maybe one more couldn't hurt." She proceeds to get smashed. She was so good at it Gordon thought it might be funny for her to do it in his next act. Later they would form a hugely successful act — one of the top acts in Vegas — and would ask me to choreograph and stage.

During this time Warner Bros. sent Gene on a publicity junket with his dancing partner, Virginia Gibson. I can't remember if they were publicizing "Tea for Two," "Painting the Clouds with Sunshine," or "She's Back on Broadway." But I remember vividly another actor they sent along was Ronald Reagan. Ronnie was publicizing a picture about a baseball player called *The Winning Team*. I got to go along; his wife Nancy did, too.

We traveled across country by train. I never could sleep well on a train. Perhaps it had something to do with that experience of the small girl so many years ago. When

I was able to sleep, I'd awaken in a new town. Warners' representatives would meet us at the station. A bouquet of roses was generally presented to the ladies to the pop and flash of the local *paparazzi*. We were driven to the best hotel in town as though we were visiting royalty. Then we'd have breakfast with members of the media.

The rest of our days went pretty much the same. We'd usually meet with town dignitaries. Then we'd visit the local Veterans' or children's hospital where we'd circulate from one bed to another. I remember conversing with one man, in particular, who had lost his legs in the War. As he told me about his experiences, tears welled in his eyes. My eyes got misty, too. I turned to the man beside him and talked with him for a few moments to compose myself. When I turned back to the legless man he seemed to be all right, too. Many of the children had been crippled by polio. Some were in body casts. Faces like the veterans and especially the children have stuck with me all these years. It's horrendous what some people have to endure.

After a day of these types of events we'd return to the hotel to freshen up. We'd change into dress clothes then go to a large dinner. I didn't always have much of an appetite, but I couldn't politely refuse to eat. I think I gained eight pounds on this trip.

The first sound we heard every morning was a knock on our wall.

"Come on, Nelsons," our future President would call. "Let's go." Off we went. When we got to Missouri we stopped in Springfield, where we were told we would dine with the President. President Truman, that is. I was pleased to have a private dining experience with him. As it turns out, several hundred others were dining with the President. The breakfast was in the lower level of an auditorium. After breakfast we took part in a large parade for the 35th Division reunion. President Truman had been a captain in World War I.

Ronnie and Nancy rode in an open car. Gene and I rode in another. We smiled and waved on the entire route, up and down the main street of Springfield. I soon understood why Queen Elizabeth developed her signature wave, side-to-side rather than up and down. It wasn't as tiring. My mouth got so dry in the Missouri heat my lips began to stick to my teeth. We all followed President Truman who led the parade. He wasn't driven; he walked. The entire route! He was a feisty little man.

That night, Gene and Ronnie were going to do a show where President Truman was the guest of honor. President Truman was seated onstage along with several other dignitaries. I thought, here they are, performing for the President of the United States, and the performer had their backs to him! Even then I was staging and producing.

Ronnie was the emcee. He and Nancy had a cute bit where he asked her to make a speech. She'd tell him she couldn't. "I'll coach you," he'd offer with reassurance. He whispered in her ear.

"I'm so delighted to be here," Nancy repeated.

Ronnie whispered something else. Nancy would repeat it for the audience. They went on like that for a while so the audience got the gist. And then Nancy began adding "and my handsome, wonderful husband" to about every other sentence. The audience loved it, knowing those words had been crafted by Ronnie.

During that same show, Ronnie happened to look into the wings, where I stood in my most formal of formal gowns. Without blinking an eye, he turned to the audience and said, "You've all met Gene Nelson. I think you should meet his lovely wife,

Miriam." I reluctantly came out onstage to applause. I was pleased to be able to show off my pretty gown.

Ronnie and Nancy returned to Los Angeles prior to the end of the tour. I ended up in the show alongside Gene, and he and I stole their bit.

Those were such happy, innocent times. Gene and I had created a dream life. Everything seemed to just get bigger and better. Nothing could have prepared me for the big, heart-breaking event that was about to occur.

CHAPTER FOUR

The Beginning
of the End

It started innocently enough. Gene had been teamed with our friend Gordon MacRae for a fourth time in a remake of a 1936 Eleanor Powell musical, *Born to Dance*.

Three Sailors and a Girl had a simple story line, so typical of the early 1950s. A Navy submarine docks in New York and three sailors (a singer, a dancer and a funny guy) go ashore. They meet a talented unknown actress and pool their efforts to make her the star of a hit Broadway musical. Sammy Cahn, who was a good friend of Gene's and mine, wrote the music.

The role of the girl went to the MGM musical star Jane Powell. Jane had a screen image of being the wholesome sister-type. Years later she wrote an autobiography (that I discovered while researching this book) entitled *The Girl Next Door and How She Grew*. After what was about to happen, I could never look at Jane Powell again and see a wholesome naïf.

While the story line for *Three Sailors and a Girl* was simple and carefree, the real-life drama unfolding behind the scenes was complex and painful. It wasn't long after rehearsals began that Gene and Jane developed a mutual attraction.

They say the wife is always the last to know. In this case, I was the *first*. I grew suspicious about the time Jane brought a cake to the house. I asked Gene if he was having an affair and he admitted he was. It's probably not an understatement to say I was devastated. I told him to get out!

Warner Bros. tried to keep the story out of the news. But a story that salacious is hard to keep quiet, especially when two celebrities are involved. The whirlwind of gossip and innuendos eventually gave way to tremendous media attention. Hedda Hopper, a Hollywood gossip columnist, called one day. I received a phone call from another famous gossip columnist, Louella Parsons.

"Is it true what I hear about Gene and Jane?" Louella asked.

I know Louella had made many enemies over the years. But I didn't hate her for the call. She was a journalist, after all, just making sure her copy was accurate. In an odd way, I respected her for calling. She wasn't printing on hearsay; she was checking facts. I told Louella that, in fact, Gene and I had decided to separate. I tried to find a way to get it out without assigning blame.

Hedda and Louella weren't the only people to call. Our friends from The Mouse Pack all called. Sammy and Gloria Cahn called. Friends from around the country called to express their shock and sympathy. Two of the most shocked and supportive people were Gene's parents. They just couldn't believe it.

Jimmy Cagney called me, too. Gene and I invited Jimmy and his wife to dinner after the making of *West Point Story*. I liked him very much.

"What's gotten into that guy?" Jimmy wanted to know. He said he was going to have a talk with Gene. I knew it would never happen, but it was a comforting show of support. I even got a call from Jane's husband, Geary Steffan. We got together and offered each other a shoulder to cry on.

In Jane's autobiography, she wrote that after Gene decided he wouldn't marry her after all, she realized she had needlessly hurt a lot of people, including Geary, me, and our children.

Sheila MacRae was a true friend during this time. She called Gene one day and said she wanted him to talk to her. He came over to her house. He sat on a stool in front of the fireplace as they talked. She said he never mentioned that he was in love with Jane. He told her he and Jane were going to get an act together and play The Palace.

When I filed for the divorce, Sheila went with me to the Los Angeles County Court House. We dressed down so we wouldn't call attention to ourselves. It didn't matter. The media got wind of the story and met us at the court house. When Sheila and I saw the photographers — we didn't call them paparazzi back then — we started running. They chased us down a hall that came to a dead end. "Look," one of the photographers said, "we don't want to bother you. Just let us take a picture and we'll leave."

It was the most difficult photo I ever took. How *do* you look when you're filing for a divorce from your husband and the father of your child? I didn't want to look angry and I didn't want to look hurt, yet I didn't want to look happy. It was a pretty somber event for me.

My life took a radical change after Gene and I separated. I stayed in the house with my mother and Chris. Gene moved out. It was lonely, yes, but the hardest part was telling our darling son. How do you explain something like this to a six-year-old? It was the worst thing I ever had to do. I must have been in shock, because I can't remember a word of what I said. And then there would be months of intense emotions: anger, resentment, fear, grief and depression. It was not easy for me, someone who liked being in control of her emotions.

I felt so fortunate to have my mother living with me during this difficult time. She was there for me immediately and never judged or blamed me. She just listened and listened. My mother was a gentle, loving woman who always gave people the benefit of the doubt. I never heard her speak ill of anyone. I know it wasn't easy for her to watch me go through this. She had to witness firsthand my devastation. I think it's safe to say she hated Gene for it. She never forgave him for what he did to Chris and me.

My mother was able to care for Chris when my emotions got the best of me. I don't know how people go through such difficulties without the support of family.

They say during a crisis you learn who your friends are. I know I certainly did. Usually, when a celebrity couple separates, the friends go with the one that is the most famous. But all of our mutual friends — every single one — continued to be friends with *me*. That's not to say they didn't have contact with Gene or that they didn't sympathize with him and the pain he must have endured. But I think it's safe to say their primary loyalty was to me. Even Gene's skater friends stood by me. In fact, I still attend their annual Christmas party.

Marge and Gower, in particular, were wonderful. They tried to keep me busy. Gower even asked me to give them tap lessons. Imagine — Marge's father was Ernest Belcher, a ballet instructor who started Marge dancing at the age of five months. She and Gower were one of the greatest dance teams at that time. And here they were, asking me to give them tap dancing lessons to keep me busy. You can't buy friendship like that.

Another time Marge and Gower were making a guest appearance on a CBS show called *Lux Video Theatre*. Their episode was called "A Bouquet for Millie." There was a shot in a courtroom scene done to music. Flowers had to fly in on a certain beat and hit the judge.

"Nobody can throw the flowers on the right beat," Gower told me, which certainly couldn't have been true. "Why don't you come over and we'll have them hire you?" I think I made about one hundred dollars for hitting the judge on the right beat. It was the easiest money of my career.

In spite of moments like these, I must say my inclination was to retreat into the safety of my home. But my wonderful friends wouldn't allow it. Everyone from The Mouse Pack kept calling and insisting I come back to the Sunday parties. I finally found the strength and did go back. Of course, Gene was no longer a part of the group.

Hollywood is notorious for spawning divorces. But Gene and I were the first couple to separate in The Mouse Pack. I think it was more than a little disorienting to everyone. The next couple to separate would be Janet and Tony. That really put a damper on our Sundays. But when Marge and Gower divorced in 1973, we were all devastated. They were the group's mainstay.

Bob Wells and Lisa Kirk were the only couple to stay married. I thought it was because Lisa spent so much time in New York. They remained married until Lisa passed away in 1990.

Lisa was another friend who was good to me after the separation. I decided to go to New York to get away and to see my father. When Lisa heard about it she said she wouldn't let me stay in a hotel.

"I have an apartment on W 57th Street," she said. "Stay as long as you want." I met my father at Sardi's Restaurant one night for dinner. I think he was almost as upset about the breakup as I. Sure, he felt bad for me, but he also was losing his movie star son-in-law. Having a daughter who was married to a celebrated dancer made for great storytelling. I was sharing my tale of woe with my father when another good friend from The Mouse Pack — Paula Stone Sloane — came up to me. Paula, the daughter of the character actor Fred Stone, was an actress and also produced several Broadway shows. She happened to be in New York and was dining in the same restaurant.

"Miriam, what're you doing in New York?" Paula wanted to know. She hadn't heard the news which kind of surprised me because I was certain everyone knew.

"You're not staying in that apartment by yourself," she insisted when I told her what happened. "Get your things and come to my apartment." She and her husband, Mike, had a lovely apartment on Park Avenue. So I moved in with them. That experience reinforced how important it is to surround yourself with caring people during difficult times. They can provide you with another set of listening ears and can offer helpful advice. After I told Paula the whole sad tale, it didn't take her long to tell me what she thought I might do.

"Get a new image," Paula encouraged. She told me to go out that very afternoon and get a new hairdo and buy new clothes, different than I had been wearing. "Become a new Miriam!"

Off I went with credit card in hand. I had my hair lightened from ash blonde. Then I made a trip to Saks Fifth Avenue. I bought two new pairs of shoes, an attractive suit and a bottle of perfume. This was not characteristic of the old Miriam. That Miriam was frugal. But the card was still in Gene's name and I guess I had a bit of an axe to grind. Gene almost had a stroke when he got the bill!

I toyed briefly with the idea of changing my name back to Franklin. But I didn't really want to because people knew me as Miriam Nelson. And I liked Nelson, because it seemed to fit me. Besides, I figured, it wasn't even Gene's real last name. It belonged to his mother's side of the family and I was very fond of Gene's mother.

It's funny how your perspective can change over time. When I was going through this difficult period all I could see was loss. It wasn't until later — years later — that I realized a lot of good could come from the pain and suffering.

The shattering of my old life opened me up to begin to see life in new ways. The rose-colored glasses definitely had been lifted. When I got back to Los Angeles, I began seeking answers to some of life's bigger questions. Why do people do what they do?

As soon as I awakened to the idea that I didn't have all the answers, it seemed as though everyone I knew or met was exploring some new and different type of religion or spirituality. Sheila MacRae was a Christian Scientist. Doris Day was another Christian Scientist. I attended some of their services. One of the speakers was Doris's friend, composer Martin Broones. He was married to Charlotte Greenwood who was a terrific legomania dancer and played Aunt Eller in the film version of *Oklahoma* with Gene. Marge Champion went to the Unity Church and I went to one of their lectures.

But it was my hairdresser who introduced me to a new way of thinking — Religious Science of the Mind — that would resonate. I attended a class with her. I liked it so much I began attending services and taking more classes. What I was learning made a lot of sense to me. It wasn't some kind of pie-in-the-sky religion where you based all your hopes and fears on some Omniscient Man sitting on a throne up in Heaven. It was hands-on, practical information I could use to change the course of my life.

Religious Science of the Mind is often confused with Scientology. I don't know enough about Scientology to tell you how they are different. I can only tell you what I know about Religious Science of the Mind.

Posing by my pool with my dog, Happy.

A basic belief of Religious Science of the Mind is that the Kingdom of God is within and we experience the Kingdom to the degree that we become conscious of it. Religious Science of the Mind believes in the power of the mind. Through our thoughts, we are forming our own destinies.

Spirituality was not the only path I journeyed down on my search for answers. I also tried psychology.

In the mid-1950s, people who saw psychologists or psychiatrists were "nuts" or "fruitcakes." Seeing a mental health professional was considered a sign of weakness. It never made sense to me to stigmatize a person for seeking information about oneself. It saddens me to hear people in some parts of the country still feel stigmatized for seeking help. Over the years I saw some of the most talented men and women destroy themselves, either instantly by suicide or slowly through alcohol, drugs or dangerous living.

I believe as we learn about ourselves — through spirituality, psychology and whatever means, even dancing — we uncover our deeper beliefs and thoughts about ourselves. So often our thoughts are negative. We believe things that aren't anywhere close to the truth. By becoming aware of this negative programming we can become liberated. We can set a new course for our life — one that leads us to mental and physical health — and abundance. (You see why I am a natural believer of Religious Science of the Mind.)

In spite of the stigma of the times, I summoned my courage and asked around to find the best psychologist in Los Angeles. It wasn't long after that I began seeing a helpful man named Dr. Barker.

The first time I arrived at Dr. Barker's office, I had to confront my preconceived ideas about what a therapy session would be like. I think most of my information had been based on movies (like my own *Lady in the Dark*). I was relieved when I learned Dr. Barker didn't want me to lie on the couch. I sat across from him and we talked like two normal adults. We didn't go into my childhood. As I wrote earlier, I had a happy childhood. I don't think there was much there that had contributed to my current situation.

Dr. Barker helped me to objectively view my current challenges. I had a husband who betrayed me and walked out on his beautiful son. We had achieved the kind of life that most people can only dream about and here he was, tossing it out. It didn't make sense.

Dr. Barker told me my reactions were normal. He suggested the divorce had to do with Gene and issues he had to work out in his own way. Fairly quickly, Dr. Barker helped me to get on the right track. He suggested I read some books. Nowadays, self-help books occupy several shelves at the bookstore, but back then they were few and far between. I read these books voraciously, searching for many answers.

One of the things that weighed on my mind was how I would make money to support my mother and my son. I was getting a little money from the mandate the court issued Gene, but there wasn't anything left over for extras. Dr. Barker told me to get the Friday issue of *The Hollywood Reporter* and *Variety*. They always had every television show and movie that was going to be done. I was to underline everyone I knew who had a show or a job coming out. I had to call every one of them and tell them I wanted a job. I wanted to be a choreographer, but I would have taken anything. I followed his advice and made those phone calls. Let me tell you, that was one of the hardest things I ever did.

Acting silly.

I continued attending sessions with Dr. Barker, but decided it was time to leave when he began telling me about *his* problems.

Another good thing that happened during this time was that most, if not all, of my friendships deepened. Doris "Clara" Day is another person who became a fast friend during this period of my life. Clara had a marriage herself that had ended badly so she was sympathetic.

Clara lived in Toluca Lake, about five minutes from my home in Burbank. I'd get a call from her out of the blue.

"Come on over," she'd say. "Mom just made your favorite German potato salad." Her mother was a German lady named Alma Kapplehoff and I was crazy about her German potato salad. Or Marty Melcher, Clara's husband at the time, would say, "I just sliced a watermelon. Come on over."

One time Clara called and said, "Marty and I are heading to a dinner party. Get on your best duds and we'll pick you up." I didn't feel right about going to a party without having been invited by the hostess. Clara said hundreds of people would be going, so it wouldn't matter. I still didn't feel right, horning in, and I expressed that on the phone.

"Some day you'll be invited to a party," Marty interjected. "And you'll take us." That lightened my mood, so I went.

After that initial party Clara kept saying, "You've got to start going out." She knew I was very reluctant, but kept trying to persuade me.

One time I went with Marty and her to Martin Broones' for dinner. They had invited King Vidor, the famed director, thinking they could fix us up. He was my dinner partner.

King Vidor was very nice and, as you can imagine, interesting. A contemporary of the pioneering director D.W. Griffith, King had been in the film business since almost the beginning and had directed ZaSu Pitts, the silent film actress, in several films. He had also recently directed *The Fountainhead* with Patricia Neal and Gary Cooper. But at twenty-five years my senior, he seemed much too old for me.

Doris and Marty had a circle of friends, similar to The Mouse Pack, who went to their house for parties on Sundays. Doris invited me one hot Sunday and I decided to go. After lunch the men started playing volleyball in the backyard. Doris had a tummy ache so she and I retreated to her upstairs bedroom. We gazed out her window at all the guys playing volleyball.

We watched them hit the ball back and forth over the net for quite a while. They were drinking lemonade from a bucket. When the bucket was half empty, Marty filled it from the hose. I figured it was pretty watered down.

"Which one do you want?" Clara asked. I was so startled I came back with, "which ones are available?" Clara pointed out the ones who were married, or those who had a girl. That left about five who were eligible.

"How about that one?" I asked, pointing to a tall, dark and handsome guy.

"He's an up-and-coming executive at CBS," she responded. He had never been married.

"I'll take him," I shot back. His name was Jack Meyers. The party started winding down and everyone went home.

CHAPTER FIVE

Share Happily and Reap Endlessly

One day in 1953, while I was in the midst of my divorce from Gene, Sheila MacRae invited me to lunch. She also asked Jeannie Martin (who was married to Dean at the time), Gloria Cahn (who was married to Sammy), Marge Chandler (Jeff's wife), Joy Orr (the stepdaughter of Jack Warner and wife of Bill, who ran the television department at Warner Bros.) and Paula Blythe, who was married to a prominent businessman.

The lunch had been arranged to cheer up a mutual friend whose mother was dying. As if that weren't bad enough, her husband was cheating on her. We were going to talk about cooking, sewing, books — anything to lift her spirits. We all arrived except our guest of honor. We waited lunch and still she never showed.

We finally decided to go ahead and eat. Someone mentioned there seemed to be a lot of people who needed help. We decided then and there to do some good. That simple thought would generate millions and millions of dollars over the next fifty years, which just goes to show the power of intention!

We started tossing out ideas. Someone suggested we collect magazines and take them to the Old Soldiers' Home. And that's what we did. Sheila MacRae's father delivered them for us.

The holidays were coming and we decided to bring holiday cheer to needy families. We got our butchers to donate turkeys and our grocers to donate all the fixings. We also got toy stores to donate toys. We put together baskets and had them delivered to names and addresses we got from Social Services.

Word got around about our group and other women, mostly wives of celebrities or stars themselves, started asking if they could join. Over the years, celebrity members would include Anne Jeffreys Sterling, Mary Ann Mobley, Marge Champion,

Liza Minnelli, Eydie Gorme, Janet Leigh, Lucille Ball, Natalie Cole, Elinor Donahue and many more.

Then we sort of stumbled onto a group of boys who would become our true mission. Someone heard about The McKinley Home for Boys in the Valley. Many of the boys had no families or their parents were unfit so the courts had taken them away. We went out for a visit. The home needed so many things.

We found out the Board of Directors was sitting on some money. We shamed them into fixing up the dormitories. Another building was so run down it was unusable. The Board had it cleaned up and painted.

We girls thought it might be nice if we became surrogate mothers to the boys. We visited once a month for lunch. Each gal headed a table and got to know "her" boys. We brought the boys cookies and other goodies. We threw parties and showed movies. We brought games and sporting equipment. We had clothing donated. One boy was very tall. He had a hard time getting clothes to fit, so Jeff Chandler and Forrest Tucker (who were each 6'5") gave him suits.

The boys needed some form of transportation to take them to the doctors and dentists, so we finagled a station wagon for them. We took turns driving. As you can imagine, some of them needed psychological help and we provided that, too.

Within a year we had grown to about twenty girls. We decided we should be a real club. We appointed Marge Chandler as president and Gloria Cahn as treasurer. We made lists of possible names for our newly formed organization.

It was Sammy Cahn, the talented lyricist, who came up with our name. He said it should be "Share Happily and Reap Endlessly," known by the acronym SHARE. Sammy also suggested we might host a dinner party and show to raise money. He volunteered to write an opening for the girls to sing and he suggested I should stage it.

Our group made for good press. As one clipping stated, "All Hollywood wives don't lounge around their swimming pools and count their minks. One group of show business spouses has organized a charity club."

We made a deal to take over Ciro's Night Club for one night. Ciro's, located on the Sunset Strip (now the location of The Comedy Store) was one of the most popular clubs in Los Angeles at that time. We decided to call the event a "Boomtown" party. To us, Boomtown meant oil wells and Texas money. We thought it would be fun to have everybody come in Western clothes.

Jeannie Martin talked Dean into starring along with Jerry Lewis. We charged $35 a couple. We were afraid no one would come. We sold out!

Sammy came up with a show opener as promised and I staged it. The girls and I began rehearsals. Gloria Cahn had been a Goldwyn Girl and Marge Chandler was an actress, but most of the other girls had never been on stage.

I had just used a Western-style fence for a big show with Gordon MacRae at NBC. The studio was kind enough to let us borrow it.

After dinner at Ciro's, the lights went down and the girls took their places on the stage behind the fence in a blackout. The lights came up and there was warm applause from the husbands, families and friends in the audience. The girls sang their song as they leaned on the fence, swinging their western hats back and forth and sometimes bobbing up and down.

No one expected much since the girls were mostly amateurs. They looked so professional they were a huge hit! We "blacked out" to thunderous applause.

Dean and Jerry agreed to do our second show but by the time the date rolled around they were in the midst of their well-publicized disagreements. Jeannie Martin talked Dean into being our emcee without Jerry. Until then, Dean had never worked alone. Jeannie told me he stayed up half the night trying to come up with funny things he could say.

The night of the show arrived. I taped a show order to Dean's mirror and some other ideas.

Debbie Reynolds and Alex Ruiz would perform a number called, "Tequila," from the film, *Pepe*. The hit song was staged by Alex Romero, a dancer and choreographer at MGM. Debbie and Alex wore serapes and Mexican hats that were so huge you couldn't see who was under them.

During the number, Debbie and Alex drank Tequila (actually, water) from gourds. By the time they were finished there was quite a bit of water on the stage. I had written on Dean's list that the stage would be wet after the number, so if he thought it would be funny, he could come out mopping the floor. I had set a mop backstage. Of course, Dean came out with the mop and cleaned up every bit of water. He was so funny working alone — I think it gave him a lot of confidence.

The third year we moved to the Coconut Grove in the Ambassador Hotel on Wilshire Boulevard. The Ambassador no longer exists, but back then it was pretty swanky. With two shows under their belts the girls were getting braver. I decided they should venture out onto the stage so I staged a Western number. We rehearsed for weeks.

Gloria Cahn sprained her ankle the day of the show. Gloria was one of my better dancers so, naturally, I had positioned her in front. The only one who could replace her was me. We had a run-through prior to the show. It was my choreography and I had rehearsed for weeks, but I couldn't dance it. When we had rehearsed I faced the girls and did the routine on the opposite feet to mirror them. Now I had to dance it the opposite direction. I took myself off and reversed the routine in my mind. During the show I was nervous because the girls in the second and third rows sometime followed the girls in front, so a mistake could have been disastrous. However, I managed to get through successfully.

We were constantly looking for new ways to raise money. At one of our SHARE shows we tried having an auction. We got department stores, art galleries, the LA Dodgers, the studios and all kinds of businesses to donate goods and services that we could auction off. Sometimes we got interesting donations. In 1956 Desi Arnaz paid $2,000 for a toy French poodle. The auction was such a success it became part of our annual tradition.

In 1958, I got a crazy idea. I thought it would be fun to have a professional stripper "take it off" for money. Of course, it had to be done with class. I immediately thought of Gypsy Rose Lee. I tracked her down. She was in New York and was unavailable. Someone suggested Lili St. Cyr. I called her and explained my idea. Lili liked it, but decided she couldn't do it because her act had a voyeuristic element to it. In her act, she'd strip and get into a bathtub as if being secretly observed by onlookers. She never looked at or acknowledged the presence of the audience. So, she begged off.

Many other strippers were suggested, but I needed someone with class. Then our luck improved. Gypsy Rose Lee's schedule changed and she was coming to Hollywood.

I called Gypsy and explained the number. She thought it was a great idea and we made plans to get together. I spent quite a day with her. We went to different stores in Beverly Hills that agreed to donate clothing and accessories. We found her a leopard print bathing suit. "I think this will work fine," Gypsy told me. "I'll just cut the legs up higher and the front down lower."

SHARE – Virginia Cook, Gloria Cahn, Vera Gordon, Me, Jackie Gershwin, and Joni Erenberg.

Sammy wrote a special song for Gower Champion to sing to Gypsy. Gower thought the entire thing would be a hoot! One afternoon, he popped in on our rehearsal. As I mentioned, for the most part the SHARE girls are not pros. And when they got together they loved to talk. Talk, talk, talk!

"I could never work the way you do," Gower told me on one of our breaks. "I don't have the patience. It's like holding a bowl of Jell-O without the bowl."

The afternoon of the show Gypsy asked me where to get a glass of water. She said she wanted to take one of her "piddle pills," so her stomach would be flatter by show time.

The lights came up on Gower and Gypsy at a table set for two. The audience recognized Gower immediately, but Gypsy wore a large hat and faced away from the audience so no one knew her identity. Gower sang something like, "lovely lady of the evening." When the woman turned and the audience saw it was Gypsy, you never heard such a scream. As the stripper music played, Gypsy got up and did her famous walk. By then the audience knew this was to be an auction and the room was positively electric.

Top: SHARE on stage '63. Me, Sheila MacRae, Audrey Wilder and Gloria Cahn. Bottom: SHARE on stage Special material number with new lyrics to Sondheim's "I'm Still Here!" Joan Benny, Gloria Franks, Anne Jeffreys, Me, Janet Leigh, Joni Horowitz and Ruth Berle.

Top: My solo in the 'Boomtown' Show. Bottom: We didn't have an overhead camera, à la 'Busby Berkeley,' for our show. I had a mirror lowered on stage at an angle so the audience could see the routine in the mirror.

The hat was the first article of clothing that was auctioned. It went for $770. Gypsy continued walking and stripped off her gloves. Jack Lemmon bought them for $250. Gypsy auctioned off her jewelry and then stripped off the dress. It went to Jack Warner for $2,500. Gypsy now stood there seductively, yet with utmost class, in her bathing suit. After a bit of teasing, auctioning began on the bathing suit. Sammy Davis got it for $700.

"I'll need a screen to stand behind while I take it off," Gypsy said. It had been pre-planned that Dean Martin, Eddie Fisher, Tony Martin and Gene Autry would make

Dean Martin, Gower Champion, Gypsy Rose Lee, and Paul Weston.

a half circle around her. They would face the audience, except for Eddie who faced Gypsy. This got a good laugh. Gypsy turned Eddie around so he faced the audience. Then Gypsy took pity on him.

"What the hell," Gypsy told Eddie. "You can watch." She turned him back. Another scream!

We hid a negligee on the bandstand behind Gypsy that she put on over her bathing suit. She flung a duplicate bathing suit over the screen so it looked like she had stripped out of it. She strolled out from behind the men, dressed in a negligee, and tossed the suit to Sammy.

Gypsy Rose Lee was sensational!

Within a few years, because of their connections, the SHARE girls had enlisted the top entertainers in Hollywood: Dean Martin, Phil Silvers, Dan Dailey, Milton Berle, Sammy Davis Jr. and Frank Sinatra to appear in the show. Nelson Riddle would conduct the orchestra. I wanted a show worthy of all this talent. We moved to the Moulin Rouge Nightclub in Hollywood which had begun as Earl Carroll's in the Forties and now is owned and used by Nickelodeon. The building had a larger stage and higher ceiling than the Coconut Grove where we would have room for risers and various levels.

The theme for one of our early shows at the Moulin Rouge was "Mish Mosh." The idea was that every girl wanted to do a different kind of show so that's what we did: a sort of smorgasbord of numbers.

For our opening number, I passed around a piece of paper and pencil and asked the girls to write down anything special they could do. One girl said she excelled in hula hoop, another put down she could stand on her head, another could sing and one was an excellent shopper! I asked if anybody thought they could walk on a ball. No one could, but several volunteered to learn. The only girl who managed to stay up was Joni Erenburg.

Joan Benny (Jack Benny's daughter) came out with a violin and played her father's theme song, "Love in Bloom." (Jack was actually backstage playing the violin as badly as he could). After about eight bars of this ear-piercing screech, Jack walked out on stage, took the violin from Joan and bashed it over her head. It got a great laugh.

I wanted to finish the opening with something big. The biggest thing I could think of was an elephant. I was put in touch with a man who agreed to bring me an elephant. For nothing! When the man asked me how many tons I wanted, I stopped cold. Then it dawned on me, I might need to find out how much weight the stage would take. I wound up with a medium-sized elephant, but he sure looked big on that stage.

Marge Champion was the one who rode out on that elephant. When Marge heard I was going to have an elephant, she called me at home. She had ridden an elephant in a movie (*Jupiter's Darling*) and had terrific memories of a big musical number with many elephants.

All through this part, Ginny Mancini and Gloria Cahn kept doing tap dancing crossovers. Each time they crossed, two more girls joined them until finally all the girls were in a tap dance kick line which finished with a kick line. Janet Leigh was in the line. I remember telling her, "It's too bad you became a star, Janet, you would have made a great chorus girl."

Another year I thought it might be fun to do three segments in our show: Burlesque, Vaudeville and Minstrel. I wanted Phil Silvers to head up the Burlesque portion because he came out of burlesque, Milton Berle would head up the Vaudeville section, and I thought Dean and Sammy could do the Minstrel show.

Frank Sinatra could do anything he wanted!

I went to Sammy Cahn to get his input. He suggested I choose one theme. I thought we could have the most fun with a Minstrel show. He offered to write a special material number.

I asked a writer at Paramount if he would write a script. He finished it and, to my chagrin, I thought it was awful. I called Milton Berle and asked for his help. He said he had a library full of Minstrel jokes and a writer to help put a script together.

After a few days, Milton called me to come read the script. I thought it was terrific. It had a silly little bit that set up "A Dance That Stops the Show," written by Sammy and Jimmy Van Heusen. In it, Dan Dailey would take the stage and tell Dean about a group called the S.F.R.T.D.T.S.B. Dean would be puzzled.

Dean Martin: What the hell is the S.F.R.T.D.T.S.B.?

Dan Dailey (Amazed that he doesn't know): 'The Society for Re-
introducing Tap Dancing to Show Business!' Furthermore, how
do you think you're going to get through a minstrel show without
laying down some iron?

Dean Martin: SHARE has always been cooperative and, besides,
what do you need?

Dan Dailey: It isn't what I need, but what the show needs. If I can
just have some gals and an orchestra, I will demonstrate.

Some of the girls who were better tap dancers were chosen to dance with
Dan.

I cast Milton as the "interlocutor." The interlocutor is the man that sits in the
middle of what were called "end men" (which were basically comedians). The end
men would be Dean and Frank. The entire script was sensational and we couldn't
wait to get started.

"Let's call Dean and Frank," Milton said, "and see if we can go to Frank's office
and read through it."

"Why can't Frank come over to your office?" I asked Milton.

"Oh, we can't do that," Milton said. "Frank is the 'Chairman of the Board,' so we
have to go to his office." I said, "but you guys *appointed* him Chairman of the Board."
I guess they were stuck with it because Milton and I traipsed over to Frank's office.
Dean, Frank and Milton read through the script. Of course, these guys added their
own touches. When I heard them read through it, I knew I had a winner.

After weeks of rehearsals, we moved into the Moulin Rouge. We used four rows
of risers with 30 girls on them. It looked impressive to see them on the risers. They
all had tambourines. The girls were supposed to stand up after a joke, shake the
tambourines above their heads, hit them and sit down. The first time we tried it, it
looked pretty ragged. Milton stood in the back watching and after it was over he
came rushing down the aisle.

"Miriam," he said, "aren't they supposed to hit those tambourines at the same
time?"

I don't know what possessed me, but I said facetiously, "Yeah, how about that?"

By show time, they all hit them in unison.

Dean had a pile of tambourines by his chair. Every time he shook the tambou-
rine and then hit it, his hand went right through (the tambourines had break-away
paper over them). He would hold up his hands and say in his own inimitable fashion, "What are you going to do with hands like these?" He went through the whole
stack before the show was over.

I wanted the girls to play banjos for one number. They were good sports. They
cut their fingernails and took lessons from Perry Botkin, the best banjo teacher in
Los Angeles. As we were learning, someone mentioned that Kirk Douglas played the
banjo. He was called and said he would play with the girls but he needed brushing
up. I took Perry to his house one day, and he helped him learn the song.

Sammy Davis said he would lead the girls in a cakewalk finale. We came up with a routine that included blackface. Milton Berle and his wife, Ruth, who was a SHARE member, bought several kinds of black face makeup and experimented with it at home. Milton taught the girls how to apply it. The night of the show we planted Sammy in the audience. As the girls started to go into the cakewalk Sammy jumped up from his seat and came rushing down the aisle.

"Hold it! Hold it!" he yelled. He got up on the stage.

"I've been sitting here all night long and you haven't blacked up yet," he said. "How can you do a Minstrel show without blacking up?"

The girls stood in a straight line across the stage facing the audience. Sammy began singing a song that had been specially written for the number. The song had geographical locations that sounded like body parts. "First we'll make up Lake Erie," Sammy sang and the girls put makeup on their ears. Another line included "Great Neck" and they blacked up their necks. Then he sang about "Chicago" and they made up their cheeks.

The girls applied the makeup without a mirror, so at the end there was a line something like, "turn around, look at your partner's face and fill in the space," which they did. They all backed up, put on straw hats and white gloves and went into the Cakewalk with Sammy leading. It was a showstopper!

We had some of the best reviews for this show. *The Citizen News* declared "Broadway never had it so good." *Life* magazine ran a full page photograph of all the girls in black face. As you can imagine, the blondes looked pretty funny!

On our 25th anniversary of SHARE, I wanted to do excerpts from the best numbers we had done. I called Sammy Davis to ask what he thought about repeating the blackface number. "I don't think the timing is right politically," he told me. I agreed, so we did not reprise anything from that very politically incorrect show.

One show featured the Rat Pack which consisted of Dean Martin, Frank Sinatra, Joey Bishop, Sammy Davis, Peter Lawford and Tony Curtis. They made their entrance — drinks in hand — by wheeling out a bar. They sang a number with special lyrics written by Sammy Cahn. At one point Dean picked up Sammy Davis and handed him to Frank: "I'd like to present you with this award from the NAACP."

Tony later walked across the stage in his shorts without saying a word. That cracked up the audience.

During the auction, Frank surprised everyone by coming out in a mink coat with a rhinestone tiara on his head and dangle earrings. He made a great model and raised a lot of money on that coat.

Sammy Cahn wrote another song, sung by the Rat Pack along with at least ten other male superstars, like Gary Cooper, Kirk Douglas and Louis Jourdan. I had these fellows crammed together in a small room backstage for about 15 minutes before the show. By then they had had a few drinks and were acting silly. They were a bunch of Peck's Bad Boys, and crazy me, I kept trying to get them to rehearse. The whole thing reminded me of *A Night at the Opera*, the Marx Brothers movie where they were all jammed into a little state room on a ship.

We knew we had to have cue cards for the lyrics, so Janet Leigh, Anne Jeffreys, Jo Stafford and June Hutton (called the "Idiot Card Girls") held up the cards. Half the time the guys would sing the words and the other half they made up their own words.

The Moulin Rouge had a turntable in the floor that took up almost the whole stage. When the curtains were closed, half the turntable was backstage. I lined up all these fellows on the turntable backstage. I worked it out so I knew where they had to be when the turntable took them out front. As the song played, the turntable would revolve so that the star who had a one-liner would be at the right stationary microphone. For instance, at certain points during the song, Gary Cooper would take one step forward, say "Yep," then step back.

Back behind the curtain, the guys didn't want to stand still. I must have looked like a crazy person to them. I literally took them by the shoulders and pushed them into place. I remember shoving Louis Jourdan into the right place and shouting to the stage manager, "Roll the turntable!" Out he went. After he was whisked away I thought, "that was LOUIS JOURDAN." I had a big crush on him ever since I had seen him in *Gigi*. This was my introduction. I think Louis Jourdan had one of the most mismanaged careers in the business. He was such a talent and so handsome. He should have been much bigger!

During the "Aftershow," audience members would bid on celebrities who attended to do some sort of performance. I cannot tell you how much money those impromptu performances made for our charity. Someone bid one thousand dollars for Judy Garland and Gene Kelly to sing "For Me and My Gal." I also recall someone bidding to have John Wayne sing. And he did! Another person bid one thousand dollars for Lucille Ball to dance "The Boogaloo."

"I'll give two thousand not to," she quipped.

When the original bidder increased the bid to twenty-one hundred dollars, Lucy got on stage and danced. In 1962 someone bid for Juliet Prowse to dance. I'm talking big bucks! Juliet just finished adlibbing a terrific dance when I heard Sammy Cahn call out.

"I bid one thousand dollars for Miriam Nelson to dance." I wished the floor would swallow me up! But I had to do it because it meant another thousand dollars for our group. On my way to the stage my wheels were spinning.

"What will I do?" I thought as I headed for the stage. To this day I can't remember what I did. All I remember is hearing the wonderful drummer, because he was so with me. No matter what I did he was right there. That kept me going.

We SHARE girls were lucky to have the wonderful comedian, George Burns, for several shows. Whenever he committed to doing a show he went at it wholeheartedly. Every day he'd call with an idea. It got so when I was in rehearsal and the phone would ring, one of the girls would grab it and yell, "Miriam, your boyfriend is on the phone."

One time George and Jack Benny did a "Burns and Allen" sketch. Jack played Gracie. He wore a black beaded gown, high heels, a wig and lots of make-up including false eyelashes. When George and Jack (made up like Gracie) made their entrance, the audience just howled. Then George and Jack just stood there, staring at each other. As long as they held this pose the audience kept screaming and clapping. They finally went into the sketch. George had rehearsed Jack to perfection. They did a hilarious sketch, but it never topped that entrance.

Another time George had an idea to have Jack Benny and John Wayne do a vaudeville-type number. John ("Duke" as everyone called him), said he'd never rehearsed so hard in all his life. George was relentless. George, Jack and Duke came out in tuxedos and straw hats. Duke was in the middle. They sang a song with lots of gestures, did a little soft shoe and then Duke stepped forward and sang, "The Shadow of Your Smile."

When Duke came offstage, I stopped him and said, "Listen to all that applause you're getting."

"That just shows you what the Big C will do," he told me. The world had just learned he had cancer.

George did a soft shoe routine with the girls one year. He didn't want to bother learning a new number so everybody learned his. Over the years I watched him on television dance his soft shoe with celebrities like Ann-Margaret and Carol Channing. It tickled me to see him always performing the same routine.

Some comics are funny onstage, but not in person. Whenever I went to a dinner party and George was there, no matter who was there, I would always position myself near him. George was *always* funny. He is sorely missed, but I'm sure everyone's happy he lived to be one hundred.

For the 1964 SHARE show, I thought it would be fun if we had a Circus theme. We borrowed great clown costumes from NBC. They were white with big red polka dots and a wire around the middle to make them look fat. They had little pointed hats and round noses the size of ping pong balls.

As I always do before a show, I began my research. I looked for crazy things clowns do in a circus. Joni Erenberg (she's now "Joni Berry") and I went to visit a retired clown in Orange County who gave us many clown bits.

I also knew that Red Skelton would come up with many ideas. I made an appointment to see him at CBS. I wanted to know how all those clowns got out of that teeny little car.

"I'm not sure your girls would want to get into that crazy position," Red told me, "because bodies are stacked on top of the other." A couple of his friends were in the dressing room, including Jackie Coogan, so Red said, "I'll show you."

Red had Coogan lie on the floor, then he had another fellow lie in the opposite direction on top of him, then reversing it with another fellow lying on top of him. It crossed my mind, "what if somebody opened the door at that moment?" It looked pretty rude.

There was a trap door in the stage floor at the Moulin Rouge. I came up with a way to work it into our routine. I had about ten girls, dressed as clowns, come out carrying boards. They hammered and nailed them together to build an outhouse. The last part was the door, which had a half moon on it.

When the outhouse was finished, one of the girl clowns walked up to the door but before she opened it, the door opened. Out came another girl clown carrying a Sears Roebuck catalog. The door shut automatically. The clown tried opening it, but before she could, another girl clown came out. She carried knitting needles and yarn and from the length of her knitting it looked as though she'd been there a while. This went on about ten times. All of a sudden, everything was drowned out by the sound of a racing motorcycle engine. The outhouse door sprung opened and out raced Janet Leigh on a motorcycle. As she rode offstage, you heard the sound effect of a terrible crash.

I thought I couldn't do a Circus number without some trapeze work, so as part of my research I found somebody who could teach the girls how to swing on trapezes.

I found a wonderful man who came to the rehearsal hall and hung what *he* called a "trap." Many girls volunteered to try it, but we chose Sheila Madison (actor Guy Madison's wife), Joni Erenberg, June Hutton and Janet Leigh.

When I cooked up this idea, I never dreamed how far these girls would go. They learned the most amazing tricks!

Four trapezes, each with five metal rungs, were hung in a row across the stage. They swung out over the orchestra pit and back. We also had "pullers," which were girls who stood on the stage and held a line tied to one end of the trapeze. The girls had to coordinate pulling the lines so the girls on the trapezes would be going forward and back at the same time. If they jerked a line, the girls could flip off. That wasn't too easy, either.

The trapezes had wrist straps attached to the top rung. At one point, the girls put their hands through the loop of the strap, which tightened, and put their other hand on the bottom rung of the ladder. As they swung out over the audience, they lifted their feet from the ladder and shot them out toward the audience. It was spectacular when you saw it, especially because our audience knew these girls were not professionals.

In the last week of rehearsal, we were rehearsing a trick called a "crab." The girls were tucked up with their faces shooting down toward the audience. Then they had to unwind, letting their feet down first, and get into a straight hanging position so they could come down.

Janet Leigh gave us all a good scare. As she came around she overshot the bar. She kept going over until she was hanging with her arms behind her instead of in front. It was impossible for her to undo herself. I witnessed all this from out in the audience.

"Janet, hang on!" I yelled. I must have been jet-propelled because I don't know how I got on the stage so fast. I stood under her.

"Swing out," I told her, "and when you're over the stage, let go and I'll catch you." I wasn't sure I could catch her, but I thought I might at least break the fall. By golly, she did what I asked. She let go and came careening down onto me. We both landed on the floor in a heap. After a moment of silence, I finally spoke.

"Are you O.K.?" I asked.

"I think so," Janet responded. "Are *you*?" We got up and tested our limbs. Nothing was broken. The worst thing that happened was Janet's arms were sore for days. I don't know how she found the courage, but trouper that she was, she went back up there and actually did the show.

The routine started with special lyrics to "Be a Clown." We then went into a clown dance and all the crazy crosses I had compiled leading us to four girls going out on a ramp in front of the orchestra in these big, fat costumes to David Rose's "The Stripper." The costumes had Velcro so they could get out of it easily. They stripped out of them. They threw their little hats at the audience and finally pulled off their noses and threw those out into the audience, too.

While this was happening downstage near the audiences, the trapezes were being lowered over the stage. Then the girls went back up on the stage and became "The Trapeze Ladies." The pullers, who were still dressed as clowns, lifted them up so they could reach the bottom rung. They then were able to flip themselves up into a sitting position on the bottom rung. The trapezes were raised back up. The pullers started to pull them and the girls went into their routine.

Two days before the show, Joni cracked her rib doing one of the tricks. I knew I had to get a professional to replace her. I called a dancer friend, Michelle Boyer, who had worked for me many times. She said she would try. She learned all the movements and the counts before she ever went up on the trapeze. She didn't want to go up too often because she didn't have time to go through what the other girls went through. They had developed blisters on their hands that turned into calluses. The girls who were not dancers were in awe, as I was, that Michelle could learn it and perform it as fast as she did.

Vera Gordon, Jeannie Martin, Gloria Cahn, Dean Martin, and me.

Dean Martin, who emceed our show for seventeen years, had a running joke that came out of a skit entitled, "The Martins At Home" or "I'm Not Doin' the Show." He and Jeannie were on stage in two comfortable chairs when the lights come up.

> *Dean:* I'm not doin' the show.
> *Jeanne:* Like I told you! You'll do like I told you!!!
> *Dean:* There must be a way out.
> *Jeanne:* There is — Death! Or divorce!
> *Dean:* Two chances — slim and none.

But it did actually happen. Not the "Death" option. Dean and Jeannie broke up and Dean stopped doing the show. We got the husband of Altovise Davis, another SHARE member, to be our emcee. This brilliant performer was Sammy Davis, Jr. Sammy emceed the show for several years.

After a few years of our help, the McKinley Home for Boys had grown self-sufficient. We began putting the money we raised toward our new cause: children's mental retardation.

Back in the late Fifties, someone brought to our attention that retarded children (now identified as "Down's Syndrome") were getting little or no help. The children

SHARE award – Left to right: Mayor Tom Bradley, Nancy Reagan, Me.

weren't even allowed in public schools because their I.Q.'s were too low. Without sufficient support, mothers would give their children up to the State to be raised in institutions or they would keep them secluded in rooms, or worse yet, in closets. We found an organization in downtown Los Angeles called The Exceptional Children's Foundation that was devoted to helping these children and their families. We went down to find out more.

They told us they were trying to put together a program so mothers could bring in their children for evaluation. If they could come up with the funds, they wanted to provide additional services. With our help, they eventually were able to put together a school. They taught these children to do all the everyday things we take for granted, like comb their hair. They also provided them with art and music classes.

We girls felt really good to be helping such a worthy cause. When John F. Kennedy was elected President in 1960, he and his mother talked about his retarded sister. That made a huge impact on the public, perceptions began changing and it made it that much easier for us to raise money.

We hadn't done a Western theme in a SHARE show for a long time, so in 1971 I started putting ideas together. By now we had moved to the Santa Monica Civic Auditorium. I wanted the girls to twirl lariats. Monty Montana was about the best lariat twirler in the world. I called and asked if he would teach the girls. We made a lunch date at a restaurant way out in the San Fernando Valley, near his home.

Monty was a real cowboy in the old-fashioned sense. I had seen him in films and Rose Bowl parades, but wasn't sure I'd recognize him. Boy, you couldn't miss him! He showed up in the most beautiful cowboy clothes, boots and a ten gallon hat.

Monty couldn't have been nicer. He called me "Miss Miriam," which tickled me. He had such cute sayings like, "Let's all bunch up and go some place." I told him about SHARE and how the money we raised was used to help children. He said he was looking forward to working with the girls. When he left he gave me a phone number. I told him I already had his number.

"This is the number for the barn," he told me. "It's kind of where I'm living now."

"You live in a barn?" I asked.

"My wife and I are having a little problem," he said. I told him I'd heard of putting a husband in the doghouse, but never in the barn!

It wasn't long after this first meeting that I went out to the ranch to ride one of his horses. I must say I was surprised by how nice and large the barn was. A trapeze bar hung in middle. Monty worked out on it, doing chin ups, every day. I had never seen so many boots in a row, all shined up like mirrors.

I noticed a picture from *Life* magazine hanging on the wall. Monty proudly told me he had ridden in the inaugural parade for President Eisenhower. He had approached the President and asked, "Mr. President, can I lasso you?"

"Sure," Ike said.

He made all the secret service agents stand back and Monty lassoed the President.

Monty had many expensive and beautiful horses that were stabled in the barn. His favorite and best trained was "Rex." He told me whichever horse was his favorite at the time he named Rex. He took me over to Rex and made an introduction.

"Rex, are you pleased to meet Miss Miriam?" Monty asked that beautiful horse.

Rex nodded his head "yes".

"Can she take you for a ride?" he asked.

Rex nodded "Yes."

"Will you throw her off?"

He shook his head "No."

I couldn't believe it! Then he revealed the trick: "If I stand *here*, the horse answers one way. If I stand *there*, the horse answers the other way."

He saddled a horse for me and I took him for a ride. What a smooth ride, like being in a rocking chair, unlike the horses I used to rent. I hardly had to touch the horse to get him to respond.

Monty brought several ropes to the SHARE girls one day. I had no idea how many girls would pass muster. To my surprise eight girls learned to do it very well. They included Rosemarie Stack (Robert's wife), Janet Leigh, Altovise Davis and Joan Benny.

Rosemarie got so good she could circle her body with the lasso and make it go up and down. Some of the girls could jump in and out of the circle. I've always been amazed by what those SHARE girls could do. Someone once asked how I got them to do so many difficult things. "I don't tell them it's hard," I responded.

We rehearsed for three months. Monty came to many rehearsals. He showed up alone when he first started coming. Before long a "Miss Ellie" began to show up with him. She was a nice lady who wore cowgirl clothes. They eventually got married and Monty built another house and big barn out in Agoura.

We pre-rehearsed that Janet would be in the middle downstage and at some point

Left to right: Amy Nelson, my assistant, Dale Evans, Roy Rogers, and me, while filming a television special of the Korean Children's Choir. Dale had forgotten her western jacket and had to borrow mine for the filming.

she would get the rope tangled around her. At that point, Monty would ride Rex out on stage, lasso Janet and pull her off. This got a big roar from the audience.

The act finished with Monty in the center of the stage. He made a big circle with his rope. It kept getting bigger until it circled him and the girls as they moved in alongside the horse. He let it drop to the floor. The girls formed a straight line alongside him. The horse bowed. The girls bowed the same as the horse. Monty pranced off stage. The girls followed him off like prancing horses, to thunderous applause.

Several years passed before I saw Monty again. While reading the paper one morning I was saddened to see Monty and Miss Ellie were divorcing. "She got a high-powered lawyer and was going to rake him over the coals," the article went on to say. She wanted the house, the bar — and even Rex.

"I always wanted to have Monty to dinner," I told my husband. "Maybe now would be a good time." I called Monty and told him I was sorry to hear the news. I invited him to dinner.

"Could I bring Miss Marilee?" he asked. He arrived with an attractive young lady. She, too, wore cowgirl clothes. We had an enjoyable evening. Shortly afterward I got a package in the mail. I opened it to find a dish shaped like a cowboy hat. Inside was a beautiful invitation for Monty's and Miss Marilee's wedding.

We drove out to the Valley one June day to a beautiful country club. Most of the guests had already arrived. I never saw so many gorgeous cowboy suits and cowgirl dresses. I think Jack and I were the only ones dressed in civilian clothing. A big arch of flowers, shaped like a horseshoe, stood on the side lawn where the wedding would take place. A small group of musicians was playing romantic cowboy songs. Every cowboy I ever saw in all those movies back in my theater in Chicago was there. Roy Rogers and Dale Evans sat in front of us. Slim Pickins sat beside us.

The preacher, dressed in a black suit with a string tie, looked like he was out of a cowboy movie. He carried a Bible under his arm. When he took his place under the arch, the music struck up a lively beat. Suddenly, from over a knoll, came the thunder of horse hooves. A horse-drawn stagecoach, decorated beautifully, came up and over that knoll. It stopped behind us. Four lovely bridesmaids were helped out and then they escorted out the bride. The bridesmaids adjusted the bride's long train. The musicians struck up another galloping song. I heard more hooves coming from another direction.

Monty, dressed in a white, Western version of tie and tails, came galloping over another hill, swinging a lariat over his head. He looked gorgeous. He pulled his horse up to a screeching stop, tossed the lariat at Miss Marilee and missed! Monty Montana never missed. He told me later he was so nervous that when he threw the rope he forgot to let go. He gathered up the rope, dismounted, placed the rope over Miss Marilee and pulled her in to him. You never heard such a roar of laughter. The wedding march started and they walked down the aisle together with the rope around her waist.

"I couldn't have staged anything better in my wildest dreams," I told Monty as we got to him in the reception line. He beamed.

In trying to integrate the stars into the SHARE show, I continually tried to come up with a theme — an overall idea. One year I thought it might be fun to use *A Chorus Line*, which was playing at the Shubert Theater. I wanted to do a take-off on it so I got a ticket to the top row of the balcony. I arrived with a tape recorder hidden in my big bag because you're not allowed to tape a show. When the lights went down I set my recorder out and taped the entire show.

After the show, I went backstage to say hello to a friend, Don Correia, who did a wonderful number in the show called, "I Can Do That." I told him what I planned on doing and whispered to him I had taped the whole show. He said, "Why didn't you tell me? I could give you the whole script," which he proceeded to do. (By the way, several years later Don married Sandy Duncan.)

In case you live on Mars and have not seen the show or film version of *A Chorus Line*, the premise is that dancers are auditioning for a spot in the chorus of a show. I thought it would be fun to see the SHARE girls and established stars playing the parts of struggling dancers vying for parts in the SHARE show. I asked Harry Crane, a top Hollywood writer and friend, what he thought of my idea. He not only encouraged me to go ahead with it, but he came up with some wonderful ideas.

Al Mello, who was our rehearsal pianist for twenty-seven years, got the song book of *A Chorus Line* and we started picking and choosing what we would use. I learned the first dance from *A Chorus Line* from one of the dancers in the show at the Shubert Theatre so I simplified it for the SHARE girls.

One of our members is married to the famous writer, Larry Gelbart, who originated the television show, *M*A*S*H*. I asked Larry if he would write material for these stars — and he was such an angel! He brought his portable typewriter to the rehearsal and said, "I'll be right here if you need any more dialogue." Everything he wrote was hysterically funny.

Me with Larry Gelbart. He SHAREd his talent with us, writing a SHARE Show.

We covered the back wall of the Santa Monica Civic stage with mirrors, just like in the original stage version of *A Chorus Line*. At the opening, the choreographer talks to the people on stage from out in the audience on a microphone. I got Earl Holliman to play the part of Zack the choreographer.

Earl was terrific. He got onstage and talked the dancers through the dance that was quite complicated. It was a constant stream of words in dancer's jargon, with a lot of "5, 6, 7, 8" and he never missed a beat.

The dancers faced upstage, away from the audience, and then Earl said, "Face away from the mirror and let's do it from the top. 5, 6, 7, 8."

The SHARE girls turned forward and did a dance. At the end, Earl said, "Okay everybody, go get your pictures and resumes and bring them back on stage."

Janet Leigh didn't leave the stage. Earl tells her to go get her picture. She tells him she has it with her. She pulls out a tiny snap shot.

"That's a very small picture," Earl said.

She said, "I have a very small agent."

Dancers, holding photographs in front of their faces, ran back on stage and formed a straight line. My assistant, Bob Street, walked down the line collecting the photographs. When they lowered the pictures there were "faces" (interspersed with several of the SHARE girls) that were recognizable immediately, like Lucille Ball, Johnny Carson, George Burns, Liza Minnelli and Milton Berle.

"Would the redhead step forward, please?" Earl asked.

Lucy stepped out. "No, the *other* redhead," he said referring to Madelyn Rhue, a SHARE girl. Then Earl asked several of the star dancers why they wanted to be in a SHARE show.

When Lucy was finally called out of line, Earl asked her why she wanted to be in the show.

"Well," Lucy said, "I've seen many SHARE shows and always admired the girls. I want to be part of it." Earl asked her how old she was. You never heard such skirting around the issue of age, like, "Let me see, my sister is two years older, and that would make me, well, two years younger than my sister." She had a dozen excuses why she couldn't answer the question. She finally just said, "Oh, shit," and walked off stage.

Steve Lawrence, me and Johnny Carson.

When Earl called Johnny Carson out of the line he said, "Why do you want to be in the SHARE show?"

"My wife spends hours and hours rehearsing for this show," Johnny said. "I thought the only way I would get to see her was to be in the show."

Then Earl asked Johnny what he did.

"I'm funny," was Johnny's response.

Earl said, "Okay, *prove* it." With that everyone else went off the stage, *The Tonight Show* theme played, and Johnny came out on the ramp and did a whole monologue.

Later in the show, songwriter Paul Williams, who was a short man, came running out apologizing for being late for the audition. He said every time he tried to get out the door, his canary kept picking him up and putting him back.

I used the mirror number from the Broadway show. It was done on Broadway by one girl, so to make it different I used our four best dancers: Sammy Davis' wife, Altovise; Howard Keel's wife, Helen; Steve McQueen's wife, Neile; and Dolores, wife of producer Joseph T. Naar (*Starsky and Hutch*). I had eight mirrors that were moved in different patterns so that the girls could dance in and out of and even around them. Even though only one girl did the number in the original show, it was very effective with four.

The night before our big show in 1974, Sammy Davis, Jr. and Altovise had a disagreement and I heard he wasn't going to do the show. I called Sammy, hoping I could patch things up. He sounded very down on the phone.

"I just can't do it, Miriam," he told me. "Maybe next year."

With Milton Berle. He's holding me down to finish his joke.

Here it is, the night before the show and I don't have an emcee. I sat there racking my brain. Who could I get? Then the husband of another SHARE member came to mind. Joanna Carson was married to Johnny. I went to Joanna and told her my sad tale and asked if she thought Johnny would do it. She said she'd invite me over for dinner to ask him.

We ate dinner on little tables in the den. We talked about all kinds of things while I worked up my courage to ask him. Finally, I said, "Johnny, I want to ask you a favor."

"I *thought* this was a mysterious dinner," Johnny told me.

I explained the situation with Sammy.

The first thing he said was, "I can't sing like Sammy."

It struck me funny. I told him we needed an emcee, not a singer. I threw in that Frank Sinatra was singing for us, thinking that might help to persuade him if he knew Frank had volunteered. Johnny thought about it for a moment and then he said, "I guess I can do it. What time do you want me there for rehearsal tomorrow?"

I could have kissed him.

We all showed up the day of the show for rehearsals. I made a list of the running order of our show for Johnny. When he came in, I went over the list. "Do you want me to make notes or do you want to?" I asked. "I don't need notes," Johnny told me. "I'll remember everything."

I was impressed with the fact that he *did* remember everything — even special things about the performers. He pulled out a piece of paper from his jacket pocket and said, "I've written down a few jokes I could tell in case you need more time for the girls to change their costumes."

He was terrific!

I believe this also was Henry "Hank" Mancini's first year of conducting. Like so many artists, Hank really didn't have a choice. He *had* to do the show. His wife, Ginny, was also a member of SHARE. Hank did the orchestration which was quite long. For a joke he said, "Here's your orchestration, Miriam" and he threw it out accordion fashion. It went all across the stage. Hank conducted many SHARE shows after that.

The time came to rehearse Sinatra's number with the orchestra. Sinatra walked toward me with his hand on his throat and shaking his head. He told me he had a sore throat and wasn't sure he could go on. He was going to the doctor and would call and let me know. In the meantime, his conductor would rehearse his music. An hour later I got a call. It was Frank.

"I'm sorry, Miriam, but the doctor absolutely won't let me sing." It seems like I just got one problem resolved and here was another doozy! Frank's number was an important part of our show.

The number had a Chicago nightclub setting. I had a special material song written called, "Frankie's Place." It was to be sung by the girls that would bring him on stage. Frank would close his portion of the show singing, "My Kind of Town, Chicago Is," which was important because Jack Benny was going to come on directly after, singing "My Kind of Town, Waukeegan Is," and then go into a sketch about his home town.

I went into my little room at the Santa Monica Civic and started going through my little black book. When I got to the "L's," Steve Lawrence jumped out at me. Mind you, the show was that night! I called Steve and explained what happened. He said he'd come down. Steve saved me from having a heart attack, I'm sure. By the time he got there, dinner had already started.

The orchestra pit at Santa Monica Civic Auditorium is very deep and unbeknownst to all our guests having dinner, the whole orchestra, conducted by Hank Mancini, rehearsed Steve Lawrence doing a couple of Sinatra's songs and then "My Kind of Town, Chicago Is." It sounded so far away that I think the guests thought they were listening to Muzak. Of course, the girls had to hammer into their heads that instead of singing "Frankie's Place," they would sing "Stevie's Place."

The moment for the opening of the show arrived far too quickly, but we all took our places. Steve Lawrence finished "My Kind of Town, Chicago Is." He had only about an hour to rehearse, but he was wonderful. He was followed by Jack Benny who sang "My Kind of Town, Waukeegan Is." The audience roared with laughter. Jack told the audience about his home town. As he talked about the town butcher, Lorne Greene, wearing a butcher's apron and holding a meat cleaver, crossed from one side of the stage to the other, and they exchanged good mornings. Then he told a story about the town druggist. Rock Hudson was to do the same thing — just cross over and say "Good Morning." Rock messed his hair up, came on like he was drunk and made his cross over. I couldn't believe my eyes. I think it even threw Benny for a moment. When Rock came off to my side of the stage, I said to him, "Whatever possessed you?"

He said, "I thought it would be more interesting if I played the druggist as the town drunk."

At that point a staircase was pushed out onstage with a red light hanging on it. Who should be standing on top of that staircase in a flimsy negligee? No other than Lucille Ball. She had one leg exposed. Lucy had great legs. Jack continued talking

I won the toss to receive the award from President Ronald Reagan and First Lady Nancy, on behalf of SHARE.

about the town and Lucy just kept assuming sexy poses. As the staircase and Lucy were pulled off, Jack sang the end of "My Kind of Town." The audience loved it!

In spite of all the problems, it turned out to be a wonderful show. I think I slept for two days after that! I wasn't physically tired as much as mentally exhausted.

While President Reagan was in office he gave awards to about twelve charitable organizations that made significant contributions to the country. Prior to the end of his second term in office, we were notified he would bestow the honor on SHARE. We were thrilled! A SHARE representative would receive the award from him at a luncheon in Washington.

We discussed who should accept the award. We considered sending the President or the Chairman of the Board. The members finally decided Gloria Franks and I should go because we were the only founding members who were still active. We later found out that, while two could attend, only one could get up and receive the medal from the President. The only fair thing to do was to flip a coin for it. Gloria and I flipped. I won.

A.C. Lyles has been an executive at Paramount Studios for many years. They even named a building after him. He is married to SHARE member, Martha. A.C. and Martha said they would go to Washington, too, because A.C. had been a liaison between Hollywood and the White House.

Off we went to Washington and checked into a hotel. "Would you like to tour the White House?" A.C. asked. We did. Because of A.C.'s prominence, we had the White House all to ourselves. A.C. had made several visits to the White House and was a good host. He showed us the Oval Office and pointed out the new carpet which was also oval. A.C. pointed out a lot of the President's appointed staff. As we walked down the hall we heard the patter of little feet. We turned to see a dog followed by Maureen Reagan, President Reagan's daughter by Jane Wyman. Maureen didn't look up as she strolled by. I debated whether to say hello. I thought better of it because several years after Gene and I had divorced, Gene had dated Maureen. We continued on the tour that included everything but the upstairs bedroom. We ate lunch in the restaurant in the White House. It was a dark-paneled room that looked like the inside of a small ship.

The next day we arrived back for the luncheon. A small group of military musicians played some nice contemporary music. A military man walked up to each of us ladies, put his arm out and escorted us into a large room.

The medal recipients were asked to come into the room where the luncheon was going to be served so we could rehearse. It was a sea of tables with pink tablecloths and a huge centerpiece of pink peonies. They had stand-ins for President and Mrs. Reagan. They stood on top of a platform. The "President" would say something, shake our right hand while handing us the medal to our left hand. We would then shake Nancy's hand and go off to our designated table.

We waited with the main group until lunch was announced. I was seated at Nancy's table. She couldn't have been more charming. She was the perfect hostess. "Are you still producing and choreographing the SHARE show?" Nancy asked me. I told her I was. She asked about the SHARE members she knew. I wasn't sure if she remembered being on the road with Gene and me during those early Warner Bros. days because she never mentioned it. Nancy talked to the entire table about her "Just Say No!" campaign against drugs.

After we finished our fancy lunch, President Reagan rose and welcomed everyone. He made a nice speech about the wonderful volunteers and how much good they had done. He then asked the awards recipients to rise. We all got into line in the positions we had rehearsed.

When I got to Ronnie, the audience was applauding so loud I couldn't hear what he said. I think I giggled some sort of response, but I doubt he heard me. As I shook Nancy's hand I think she said, "Congratulations." When I looked up I was surprised to see about eight photographers on a platform cattycorner at the end of the room. They had been so quiet coming in I hadn't noticed them. They photographed the whole thing.

As we said good-bye, I was handed a White House cookbook (which I have used many times over the years). We went out to the front lawn where several cameramen were videotaping us. We were asked to do interviews. My cameraman told me he was going to ask questions and I should just talk to the camera. We were standing on the grass and I was in heels so I had a hard time keeping my balance.

"Are my feet in the shot?" I asked the cameraman.

"No," he told me. "Just from your waist up." I took off my shoes and did a short interview in my stocking feet. A.C. asked Gloria and me if we wanted to wait a few minutes to watch the President take off in his helicopter. As we waited, Vice President George Bush walked by and said hello to A.C.. He was much taller than I expected. Ronnie and Nancy eventually came out, shaking hands and waving to everyone as they walked to the helicopter. When they got to the top of the stairs, they turned and waved again. They ducked inside, the door was closed, and up and away they went. A.C., Martha, Gloria and I flew back to Los Angeles that afternoon with our medal.

SHARE has come a long way since the days when we were anxious to charge $35 a couple. Our audience still wears Western clothing for our "Boomtown" parties, but now they pay $500 a ticket. Along the way we've raised over forty million dollars to help children in need. Finding SHARE (or was it *SHARE* finding *me*?) was just what I needed to heal after my marriage dissolved. Over the past 50 years of creating shows, I have honed my writing and directing skills. And having something this important in my life has given me strength, happiness and great fulfillment.

CHAPTER SIX

Television –
When it was "Live"!

Back in 1953, as I was gaining the strength to start a new life, I decided to "work out" to get back into shape. I wanted to take tap-dancing classes just to get myself going. I found the best teacher around was Louis DaPron. I showed up one night and stood in the back to watch Louis and his class run through some of the routines they had already learned.

When he was ready to start something new, he had me come down front. I think he was trying to make me feel more at home in the class.

"What're you doing these days?" Louis asked as we were dancing.

"Not much," I answered.

"Would you like to go to work?"

"Yes!" I practically shouted. After class he told me about a call he'd received from CBS asking him to do a show. He couldn't do it because he was headed for Las Vegas to work with Donald O'Connor. He said he would call the producer and recommend me.

I had made so many phone calls seeking a job. Though everyone was very nice and took my calls, they didn't have anything for me at that time. They told me they would keep me in mind for the future. And now, here I was being asked if I wanted a job by someone who didn't even know I was looking. It is my belief that this job possibility came to me because I put myself "out there" and had done everything I could.

When it rains, it pours. Doris called that night and said, "We're going out to dinner tomorrow night. Jack Meyers will be your date."

Poor fellow — he had never seen me. And he didn't realize *I* had seen *him*.

We had a lot of fun at dinner. Jack and I seemed to get along okay, despite the awkwardness of being on an arranged date. To create a common interest, Clara told Jack I might be working at CBS.

"When you get there," Jack said, "we'll have to split an apple." I thought that was a bit flip, but even so I expected the phone to ring within a couple of days after dinner. It didn't. So I wrote it off.

Jack didn't call, but producer Ben Brady did. He asked me to come to CBS the following day for an interview.

I awoke bright and early for my interview and dressed in my best suit. I got in my car and drove to CBS on Beverly Boulevard and Fairfax. I looked up at the four-story white building with the big CBS eye, took a deep breath and stepped inside. The receptionist directed me to Ben's office.

After the interview, which only lasted a few minutes, Ben said "You're hired." It was only then that I learned I would be choreographing *The Red Skelton Show*. I had been hired for only one episode, but I didn't care. I would get my own full screen credit! After the interview I went to the business office to sign my contract. As I was leaving I noticed Jack Meyers' name on one of the doors.

When I met Jack I thought he had been flippant. Now I was the one feeling a bit flippant for starting my first job. I opened the door and stuck my head inside. Jack was seated behind his desk. I think he was a bit taken aback by the sight of me.

"Let's split an apple," I said. I closed the door behind me and ran down the hall.

I stepped outside and looked up at the big eye gazing back at me. It was one of those special, miraculous moments when you can see your life full of possibility. I realized for the first time in my life I was truly on my own. I felt an inner strength welling up inside of me. Future articles would no longer read "the wife of Gene Nelson ..." or "the former wife of Gene Nelson..." Instead, they would say "Miriam Nelson, choreographer!"

THE RED SKELTON SHOW

The first number I had to choreograph for *The Red Skelton Show* took place in a drugstore. Red was a soda jerk. I was given a script.

"Don't show the script to Red," I was instructed. "We want to give him the script close to show time so he won't have time to change it." (Keep in mind that this was in the days when television was *live*.)

I hired dancers to do a jazzy jitterbug with Red. I didn't get Red right away, so I got a dancer to dance in for him so we could rehearse.

I got a call the morning we were to shoot the show.

"Red Skelton has just fallen through his shower door." They didn't know how badly he had been hurt but they asked me to redo the choreography in the event he couldn't use his right arm. Or his left arm. Or, if he couldn't dance at all. After I worked out three new versions with the dancers, Red arrived at the studio. He was unscathed so we were able to use the original choreography.

I was given a script for the next show. It was at that point I realized they were keeping me on. Red was to be tied to a stake. They wanted a wild Indian dance. I started the number with a dancer flying into the shot. He would do this by springing from a platform onto a trampoline offstage, then jumping into the set. The first time we rehearsed, the trampoline hadn't arrived.

Jack Benny (on stage), Ralph Levy (standing at stage) and Jack Meyers talking to young boy.

"The trampoline isn't in yet," I called up to the director. The stage manager, who was very conscientious, almost had a stroke. It was his responsibility to see that the trampoline was there. We did get the trampoline but after that, the stage manager didn't speak to me for several shows.

Come show time my Indian dancer was on his platform waiting to spring onto the trampoline and into the scene. This routine was to begin as soon as a commercial had finished. Just prior to starting the number we got word that Red ran over the allotted time with his opening monologue. The number would have to be cut. The dancer was upset because his mother in New York wouldn't get to see him.

One day Red came into the rehearsal hall. He noticed a booklet on the piano called *The Daily Word*. It was a Christian booklet of thought-provoking ideas with suggestions of ways to think or behave during the day. I had read it faithfully since my divorce.

"Who does this belong to?" he called out. I told him it was mine.

"I read it every day, too," he continued. Then he pulled a Mezuzah from his pocket. From another pocket he pulled out a crucifix. Another pocket held a rabbit's foot. He said, "You can't be too careful." I really cracked up.

I learned a lot about comedy during the year I did that show. Not only was Red hysterical, but all the top comics of the time were on the show.

The next show had a baseball theme. All the dancers dressed like kids and acted like they wanted to get into a game. They tried to see the game through a peephole in a fence. I had them start the number by peering out through a knothole. Then they would come downstage and sing a baseball song and then go into the dance.

At dress rehearsal, which was the day of the show, the producer asked me why the performers were singing to the audience. "They should be singing to each other," he said. This was my first job and I certainly wasn't about to disagree. So I looked for a place to rehearse the dancers. By now the rehearsals halls were taken. Danny Kaye was in one hall and Carol Burnett was in another. So I took the dancers up on the roof. I rearranged the number to the producer's liking. It went off without a hitch. Three shows down!

Red played several recurring characters on the show. He played a tramp, a senator, a drunk, a cowboy. Each had its own theme song, approximately eight to sixteen bars of music, which would repeat. One musical number with the tramp and dancers had to be full-blown. With one eight bar phrase repeating, the theme music sounded repetitious. I heard a melody in my brain I thought could be added. I don't read or write music but wanted to write it down so I could remember it. I went to the piano and found the right notes. I sketched a keyboard on a piece of paper. The first note in my head I called the number "one." I counted in my head up and down from that initial "note" for the subsequent notes until I had it all written down.

David Rose was the composer and conductor of the show. David had written many well-known tunes like "The Stripper." A few years earlier he had married, then divorced, Judy Garland and dated a friend of Judy's who was also a friend of mine — June Allyson.

I handed the paper keyboard to David. "What's this?" he asked. I told him about my melody and that he was welcome to use it if he thought it would work. I explained my system for composing music. He laughingly started to decipher my code.

"Number one is a B," David said. "Six is a G." He went to a piano and played my melody. He liked it so well he didn't change a note. Then he orchestrated it. Let me

34　DAILY NEWS, MONDAY, DECEMBER 5, 1955

Marlene Dietrich and Michael Todd at opening of "Oklahoma!" They've been a twosome.

Charlotte Greenwood, distinguished comedienne, kicks up one of her famous heels in theatre seat.

Behind Hollywood's Silken Curtain

By FLORABEL MUIR

HOLLYWOOD, Dec. 4.—Marlene Dietrich is cast in one of 40 so-called cameo roles in "Around the World in Eighty Days," which Mike Todd is producing. This means she'll be on the screen about two minutes.

But, if seeing is believing, she's been working on the movie long enough to have made quite an impression on Mike's heart. They've been dating all around town and Mike isn't one who falls easily.

Mike and Marlene were among hundreds of cinema headliners who attended the recent opening of "Oklahoma!" here after special equipment for the movie finally was installed in Grauman's Egyptian Theatre. Todd is gambling a fortune on the movie depicting the round-the-world trip of Phineas Fogg. Marlene plays the operator of a dance hall in San Francisco to which comes the traveler, played by David Niven. In the same two-minute scene are Frank Sinatra as a piano player, Red Skelton as a drunk, and George Raft as a bouncer.

Gene Kelly escorted his daughter, Kerry, to the opening and it was a big thrill for her. It was her 13th birthday.

her first premiere, and the first time she'd been out with Dad after dark in formal garb. Her mom, Betsy Blair, is abroad making a picture.

Gene Nelson, still estranged from his wife, Miriam, came with Piper Laurie when his team dating since his romance with Jane Powell ended when she married another guy. Gene and Miriam still are good friends and she's usually around to handle his choreography problems when he does a TV show. Miriam attended the opening with Jack Myers, a CBS executive.

Charlotte Greenwood, the great comedienne, made one of her rare appearances and kicked up a heel for the photographers. Liam O'Brien—he's Edmond's brother—and Florence Allen were not as sad as they seem in the foto. She's a friend of Liam's and not in show business.

Florence Allen and Liam O'Brien

Miriam Nelson and Jack Myers

Gene Kelly escorts daughter Kerry to her first premiere on her 13th birthday.

Gene Nelson, still estranged from his wife, Miriam (foto left, above), came with Piper Laurie who laughs at one of his gags at Cocoanut Grove after premiere.

Isn't life funny?

tell you, I was more excited to hear the whole orchestra play my eight-bar composition than I was to see the number!

The Red Skelton Show was my "summer stock" of television. By that, I mean I learned a lot during those episodes. After that, not much bothered me, like when I had to rearrange something, or a number was cut because the show ran long, or I had to make up a new routine because the show was running short.

One day while I was rehearsing Jack Meyers poked his head in my door. "Do you want to split an apple?" he asked.

I thought, "My God, I'm going to have my first date!"

Despite our slow start, it didn't take long before Jack and I were "going steady." People don't go steady anymore. Back then, it meant you were committed to seeing only each other.

SHOWER OF STARS

Shortly after *The Red Skelton Show* I got a call from Nat Perrin, another producer at CBS. He said they were putting together a new show called *Shower of Stars*. The premiere episode was to star Betty Grable, Harry James and Mario Lanza. Mr. Perrin wanted me to choreograph it. I was very excited!

He called me after he had offered me the job. He had met with Betty Grable. She had a choreographer she had worked with on many movies and wanted him for the television show. Mr. Perrin met with the choreographer.

"He was off the wall," Mr. Perrin told me. "And I didn't understand a word he said."

So, Mr. Perrin made *me* an Associate Producer in charge of the production numbers. "That way," he explained, "he wouldn't have to deal with the other choreographer."

Betty was a huge star; even so, she was nervous. This was her first television show and, again, television was live. There were *no* cuts, and *no* opportunity for a mistake. Once the show started, it didn't stop until it was over. Everyone involved with the show got together for our first meeting.

"I don't want to show my legs," Betty announced. We all about fell off our chairs. Betty had been the most popular pinup girl during World War II. Her legs were known around the world. At one time her legs had been insured for one million dollars.

"Why not?" someone finally asked.

"Because that's what they're going to expect," Betty said.

Along the way, I learned that the best way to please an audience is to give them what they want. Everyone else involved with the show knew that, too. We had a lengthy meeting about Betty's legs. It sounds kind of silly now, but we went back and forth. *Should* we show Betty's legs? Should we *not* show them? While we were debating, the costume designer sketched a fabulous, glitzy costume. There were many feathers on it, but her legs would be visible. Betty agreed to wear the costume. She did the number and, of course, her legs looked terrific.

Mario Lanza had a big vocal number. They decided he would lip sync to a prerecorded track. The show was wonderful, but the critics jumped on the fact that

Mario did not sing "live." Of course, today *everybody* lip syncs, but back then it was a new concept for television.

Chrysler, the sponsor of *Shower of Stars*, decided to do a big musical show each month. Red Skelton was the emcee of one of the initial shows called "Golden Records." I was asked to stay on as the permanent choreographer.

The Andrews Sisters were guests on that show and, at that time, they were not talking to each other. It was quite an accomplishment to talk them into doing the show. Red introduced them during dress rehearsal.

"And now here are the Andrews Sisters," he began, "coming to you from Stages 34, 35 and 36." We all knew what he meant by this inside joke. Even the Andrews Sisters laughed.

During one of the shows, Chrysler wanted to introduce their new push-button transmission. I staged a number where you saw a hand turn the key. Then the hand pushed the button so the car was in first gear, then second, then third, then reverse. I staged the dancers to match all the gears. They even danced in reverse. We didn't know when we put it together that it was considered a commercial. The dancers got a whopping extra amount of money for that routine.

FORD STAR JUBILEE AND JUDY GARLAND

I am a huge fan of Judy Garland; I think I saw every picture she ever made. So I was thrilled when CBS hired me to choreograph Judy's first television appearance on *Ford Star Jubilee*. There would be one other performer, David Wayne, a musical group and twelve male dancers. Judy would perform several numbers from her movies.

I went to CBS and the pianist, Dick Priborsky, and I began to lay out the arrangements. Jack Cathcart was the composer and conductor. He looked at what we had done, then went home to begin the orchestration.

Judy asked for five weeks of rehearsal which was unheard of at that time. Ten days was about as much as I was ever given on a big musical for TV. But Judy was such a huge star her request was granted. Judy and the dancers were to start rehearsals on a Monday about the middle of August. Monday came and the boys arrived, but Judy didn't.

I got a call that Judy wouldn't be in for a couple of days and perhaps it would be a good idea to get a girl to dance in for her so I could begin. I hired Joanne Dean, my ex-husband's skating partner, who had worked for me many times.

One number we were going to do was Judy's "Get Happy" from the film *Summer Stock*. Remember, these were the days before video and DVD so I couldn't rush to the local store and rent a copy of it. But I got lucky because a couple of the guys had been in the movie. They were a great help to me.

In a movie you can stop and start as often as you like; it's never done in one continuous shot. You can cut from one part of the dance to the next with a completely different look. The audience never questions how the dancers got there. But to make the number work for television I had to change it in a few places.

The first week came and went — without Judy — so I started working on our next number: "Swanee." Every day I was told Judy would be coming in tomorrow. Tomorrow would come and go, but still no Judy.

David was anxious to get started on his number, which was a solo, so I decided to work with him. He was to perform a sequence from a series of stories by Don Marquis called, "Archie and Mehitabel," about an actor cat. David was a joy to work with — such talent!

Finally I was told Judy would definitely be in, but she preferred working at night. We all changed our schedules to accommodate her. I had never met Judy in person and was a bit excited. When the door opened and Judy walked through it, I was shocked. She was so big! This was during one of her heavy phases, but no one had told me. I quickly told Joanne, who was tiny, to pull her shirt out to make her appear larger.

Judy was accompanied by her chauffeur and bodyguard. He also carried her liquor and ice.

"Judy," the director said, "I'd like to introduce Miriam Nelson, our choreographer."

"I can't wait to see what you've been doing," Judy told me. I introduced Judy to everyone then we showed her the choreography and staging for "Get Happy." She seemed to be pleased, but had a question. "Why did you change it?"

"It has to be a continuous routine," I told her. It took a great deal of explaining that she couldn't stop and appear in another spot. We finally got over that hurdle and I showed her the routine for "Swanee." She accepted everything I did and then went to the piano and started singing. What a joy!

What followed were good days and bad days (or should I say "nights"). On the good nights, after rehearsal, Judy called "Villa Nova," a celebrity-favorite Italian restaurant on the Sunset Strip and asked them to stay open. We would go and between uproarious laughter we'd eat pasta, pasta and more pasta. Nobody liked laughing more than Judy and she made us laugh, too.

Judy's girls, Lorna and Liza, came to rehearsals once in a while. Lorna had to go to the little girls' room one time. She was still too young to go on her own. Judy was in the middle of a song so Joanne took her. She told me she was very nervous about it, thinking, "My God, what if I dropped Judy Garland's daughter down the toilet?" At that time I had no way of knowing that one day I would be staging an act for that little girl.

We finally arrived at show time. Ten minutes before we were to go on the air Sid Luft, Judy's husband, came running into the control booth. He told us Judy had locked herself in her dressing trailer and wouldn't come out. We all went into a panic. Someone jokingly said, "Get the organ music ready." That was a reference to live shows, when the organ player would fill in for missing performers or any other catastrophe.

So there we were, about to go on air with Judy locked in the bathroom. Of course, we all knew what had to be done. Sid broke down the door. Judy was partially ready. Her wardrobe people and dresser literally threw her into her opening costume while her makeup was applied and her hair was finished. The floor manager took her by the hand and led her out into her opening position. Without a second to spare we were on the air: "It's *Ford Star Jubilee*, starring Judy Garland!" the announcer exclaimed.

A series of curtains opened to reveal Judy off in the distance. Judy had pre-recorded the first two songs in the show, thank God! She started singing to the music and vocal track. She walked slowly toward the camera singing until she hit her downstage mark, where she finished her song. She started her opening dialogue as printed on cue cards, then after a couple of sentences she began to ramble.

The director asked frantically, "Have you got *any* of this dialogue in your script?" Judy was being folksy and carrying on far too long. It probably never occurred to her we were on a schedule and had to be off the air in an hour.

She wore a beautiful floor-length coat and was cinched into it within an inch of her life. When she finished her dialog, it had been planned for a dancer to walk in and remove her coat, revealing Judy in her "Swanee" costume. The dancer would hand her a hat and cane, then Judy would turn to another set of cameras revealing the "Swanee" set behind her. Because she was rambling, the director cued the dancer to go on and take off the coat. He did. The director shouted "Music!" Judy went into her "Swanee" number. I think she performed the number by rote.

She had a sequence of dialogue with David and I know he didn't know what she was saying part of the time. They went into the "Trolley Song." By the time they got to David's solo, the poor man was not as good as during rehearsal. I know he was too worried about Judy to concentrate on what he was doing. He pulled it off like the pro he was, but I know he could have been better.

Every commercial break someone would grab Judy, throw her into her next costume and set her in her next position. By the time the show was over, all of us in the booth were wrecks. I don't think Judy really knew what she had done during the entire show.

There was a party afterwards and by then she seemed to be in pretty good control of herself. We all laughed a lot. Judy told me she had never worked with a woman choreographer before and she was terribly worried about it. She thought I would have her dance like some "damned ballerina." But she was very happy with the movements I gave her.

Whew!

By now, Jack and I had been dating for about two years. Periodically we would talk about marriage. I was gun shy. And I loved Jack, but I wasn't ready to become that involved. One night Jack came right out and delivered an ultimatum: "Miriam, I want to get married, or I think we should break up."

The thought of breaking up hurt terribly, but I couldn't bring myself to get married yet. I chose the latter and Jack and I stopped seeing each other.

THE EDDIE FISHER SHOW

The last *Shower of Stars* show I did was conducted by Gordon Jenkins. He told me he was going to do a show at NBC featuring Eddie Fisher and would recommend me.

The Eddie Fisher Show was to be done from the Hollywood Bowl. Eddie was courting Debbie Reynolds during that time. When we moved to the Bowl, Debbie dropped by to visit him. Between rehearsals they acted silly and played tag. One time, Eddie jumped into the lagoon in front of the stage fully clothed. The lagoon no longer exists, but then it wrapped around the front the stage. Fountains of water and lights would shoot up through the pool of water. Eddie could have killed himself jumping into that lagoon because of the possibility of electrocution. The things a guy will do to show off for a girl!

Something I didn't know about Eddie Fisher until I started working with him was that he couldn't hear the downbeat of the music. Eddie Samuels, his conductor, stood by the camera as they were shooting. Samuels pointed at Eddie when he was to start singing.

One number opened with the dancers frozen in place. The music was "vamping" so that Eddie could start singing on the fourth downbeat. His voice was the cue to start the dancers on their number. During rehearsals Eddie never started on the same beat twice. He would start on 2 ¾ or 3 ¾. This made the dancers nervous because they were never sure when they would have to start dancing. Eddie came in on the right spot. The entire routine came off right and no one was any the wiser.

I guess it didn't matter that Eddie couldn't hear the beat. He had such a glorious voice. He sold millions of records, more than any other singer during that time.

THE COLGATE COMEDY HOUR AND GALE STORM

I guess NBC liked my work because they hired me to do several episodes of *The Colgate Comedy Hour*. In one show, Gale Storm stood on a platform, singing about waiting for a train. The lyrics were written so that we learn she is waiting for a huge Hollywood star to arrive. The suspense builds as to who the star might be. They had sound effects of a train pulling in to a station and would shoot steam under the camera.

Imagine the audience's surprise when it turns out the Hollywood star is a chimpanzee that jumps into Gale's arms. Gale held the chimp during her song. I watched her singing from the booth. All of a sudden, Gale got a strange expression on her face. When the show was over Gale told us during the number she felt something warm on her stomach. You guessed it! The chimp had "let go" all over her beautiful gown! Trouper that she was, Gale kept singing and the viewing audience never knew.

Oh, the thrill of live television!

DINAH SHORE

Dinah Shore had done a series of fifteen-minute shows for Chevy. They were so successful they extended them to one-half hour. I was assigned to choreograph. Peggy Lee, Kay Starr and Patricia "Pat" Morrison were also on the show.

Pat did a number that included a waltz with a male dancer. He was to do a lift with her. During rehearsal she pulled me aside.

"Can you keep a secret, Miriam?" she asked. She then told me she had just found out she was pregnant and no one, not even her husband, knew. She preferred to do the number without lifts. Of course, I cut them.

The four ladies were to do a finale together. The director let me in on another secret. He told me he was going to have fun watching to see which lady wore the most spectacular dress. At the first dress rehearsal only one lady wore a beaded gown. The next

That's me with the high kick in front of the stairs.

dress rehearsal all the dresses were more elaborate, except for Dinah's. She played it down. Then came the show. Dinah was dressed to the nines. She outshone them all.

"See the USA in Your Chevrolet," Dinah sang. And she ended with her famous kiss that she would throw to the audience: "*Mmmwhaaaa.*"

PETE KELLY'S BLUES

In 1955, Jack Webb (of "Dragnet" fame) starred in a movie called *Pete Kelly's Blues* and decided to produce a television special out of it. All the stars from the film were to be in it, including Peggy Lee, Ella Fitzgerald and Janet Leigh. I had to choreograph a number for Janet and Jack Regas, my assistant at the time. We used a number from the movie called "The Pete Kelly Hop" and went into rehearsal.

Janet would be traveling overseas after the show, so she got an inoculation (in those times, various shots were needed for foreign travel). Immediately, she had a bad reaction and had to back out of the television show. At first, the number was cut.

With Jack Regas in Pete Kelly's Blues.

Then they decided I should do it. Jack and I had danced on a lot of shows together, including *The Peter Potter Show*, so we were able to put in more complicated steps and flashy lifts. I wore a beaded dress in the style of the 1920s. It weighed a ton!

I gave my all during dress rehearsal, which I later discovered was a bad idea. I didn't have enough time to get my strength back before we did the show. This was still when television was live and we were to perform it in one continuous take.

I stretched out on the couch in my dressing room and put my feet up on the wall. Peggy Lee walked by and told me she had just seen the rehearsal. She told me I should take something to help me get back my strength. She said she had a vitamin that would give me energy. She gave me a big pill and a cup of water. I downed the pill, not really knowing what it was.

"Show Time!"

Before the number began, I stood beside the conductor with my back to the audience. The conductor had his own monitor so he could watch what was happening on stage. I could see my back in his monitor which struck me as funny.

"I'm sorry I have to turn around," I thought, "because I won't be able to watch any of this." As I began to move, I could feel the pill sloshing around in my stomach. We finished the number with Jack picking me up for the last pose. I thought the red light on the camera would never go off. When it finally did, I ran to the aisle, the closest place to sit, and collapsed. I could barely catch my breath. I sat there with my head down for a long while. I'm sure anyone in the live audience must have thought I was dying.

When the pill finally did dissolve, I was on a high for several hours.

THE ED SULLIVAN SHOW AND GORDON MACRAE

One day Gordon called to ask if I could teach him a Highland Fling. He was going to sing a Scottish song on *The Ed Sullivan Show* in New York. Gordon was of Scottish descent, but he wasn't a trained dancer. He wanted to do the crossed sword dance and was going to go all out with this — kilt and all!

I'd never done a Highland Fling, but I knew I could figure it out. I'd seen enough of them. So I gave Gordon a little routine. We pretended canes were swords. I laid them in a crisscross fashion on the floor. We danced in and out of the spaces created by the swords. Gordon caught on amazingly fast, but we only rehearsed for a few hours. Since *The Ed Sullivan Show* was the biggest show on television, I figured we'd rehearse the rest of the week.

"What time do you want to work tomorrow?" I asked at the end of the day.

"I can't rehearse tomorrow," he told me. "I'm leaving for New York in the morning." All I can say is Gordon MacRae had guts! I watched the show at home in Los Angeles. I couldn't believe how well he did it.

It was while working on these shows I heard Jack Meyers was dating Joan O'Brien, a pretty girl who sang with the Bob Crosby Band on *The Bob Crosby Show* at CBS. Joan, like me, had been married once before and had a son. Eventually they got married and had a daughter they named Missy. But this wouldn't be the end of my relationship with Jack Meyers.

ON A *WAGON TRAIN* WITH BETTE DAVIS

In 1959, Bette Davis was signed to appear on the successful TV drama, *Wagon Train*. She was to play a woman traveling cross country with a troupe of can-can dancers. If this worked, they would do a spin-off and Bette would have her own series. I got a phone call. Soooo . . .(Have you noticed that I mention "Phone Calls" often, as they always seemed to be the beginnings of so many career opportunities?)

In the episode I worked on, the story was written so that one of Bette's dancers becomes ill and she has to go on in her place. I created a little dance routine and went to Bette's house in Beverly Hills to teach it to her. I parked in the driveway of what you could describe as a mansion, tucked my tape recorder and music under my arm, and walked up the steps to the impressive house.

I rang the doorbell and, to my surprise, Bette opened the door herself. She greeted me warmly. I began to feel at ease right away. We went into her den. In my memory, the room was so large we didn't even have to clear the furniture.

I taught Bette the first step without music. I couldn't remember seeing her dance in any of her movies, but she wasn't too bad. She picked it up pretty fast. I set my recorder on a table. I pushed "play" and we began dancing to the music.

As we rehearsed, we seemed to be growing kind of buddy-buddy. After a few hours we took a break. Bette got some cold drinks from the kitchen and then lit a cigarette. For some reason it struck me funny – Bette Davis smoking — and I began to laugh.

"What's so funny?" Bette asked.

"You don't smoke like you do in the movies?" I said.

"You mean like this?" Bette responded. And with that she twirled her arm in concentric circles as you've seen so many times. I busted out laughing. I think that really broke the ice. All of a sudden, Bette surprised me by talking about men. She told me about her recent breakup with Gary Merrill.

"*Men,*" she scoffed. "They want you to be strong, and then when you are, they don't want you anymore." I thought that was one of the most interesting things I'd ever heard. Then we went back to work and finished the dance.

She asked if I'd like to go for a swim. I think she might have viewed me as a poor little choreographer. I didn't want to offend her by telling her I had a pool of my own, so I politely declined and left.

They didn't have a schedule for shooting yet. They said they'd call when they did so I could get a group of girls and teach them the routine. By the time they called I was working on another show. I told them I would teach the routine to my assistant and have her take over for me.

My assistant called me frantically in the middle of one of my rehearsals.

"We're in the middle of recording the music," she began, "and Miss Davis wants it half as slow as I know *you* want it." At half-time the can-can would have looked like it was in slow motion. Why Bette wanted it half as slow I'll never know. I saw her dance it up-to-tempo and she was fine.

"Tell the conductor to record at Bette's tempo and after she leaves to record it at the proper tempo." I hung up and called the producer. I let him know it was impossible to dance the can-can at a slow tempo. I told him Bette would not look good

Pulling my hair out with Bette Davis in Wagon Train.

dancing in slow motion and he might want to let her know it. The producer told me not to worry. He would take care of it. The producer told Bette what I had said and she danced it up to tempo. That's an old trick I use once in a while. If some stars think they won't look good, they'll listen.

RED BUTTONS

One of the craziest numbers I ever had to stage was for Red Buttons on *General Electric Theatre* on CBS. Red played an imaginary character named "Tippy-Top." Tippy-Top existed in the mind of a six-year-old boy who was unhappy because his parents were breaking up.

In the scene, Tippy-Top was in a park, trying to cheer up the boy. I went to the park to look at the playground equipment to get a few ideas.

The music had to be prerecorded, so I met with Shelly Manne, the famous drummer who had his own nightclub in Hollywood, Shelly's Manhole. We had quite a recording session. I hadn't had the opportunity to try out different ideas so I had to make it up as I went along. I did crazy things on the recording stage so he could catch them with the drums. I pretended to run up the teeter-totter. I'd stand in the middle, make it sway back and forth, then slide down the other end. I'd hit an imaginary tether ball, pretending it went around in a circle and hit me on the back of the head. Then I ran into a sprinkler and pretended the water chased me around in circles.

In the scene, because of these shenanigans, the boy was supposed to start laughing. Then Tippy Top would assure him his family problems were going to work out all right. He'd tell the boy he had to leave because another boy "didn't have a friend in the world" and he needed Tippy Top.

We began shooting the scene and Red was wonderful. He played it for all it was worth. When he came to the end, where he told the boy he had to leave, the boy started to cry. He cried so hard all of us behind the camera had tears in our eyes.

"Cut!" the director finally called. The little boy's father walked in, took him by the hand and walked him away where he could bring him back to reality.

"How on earth could your boy cry like that?" I asked the father later that day. The father told me, "He thought about the little boy that didn't have a friend in the world."

That little boy grew up to become a very famous director — Ron Howard.

LEAVE IT TO BEAVER

For a while it seemed every television show I worked on, like *The Donna Reed Show* and *Leave It To Beaver*, had something to do with a school play.

Beaver Cleaver's school was putting on a show. One musical number consisted of all the children being flowers and animals. I had the flowers dance and the animals hop around the stage. I think Beaver was a mushroom. The kids didn't always remember too well, so during the shoot I called out instructions.

"Poppies come down front," I'd shout. "Squirrel run across!" "Everybody turn around." When they saw the rushes they all laughed because of my voice on the film.

I sounded like a school teacher giving direction. They talked about leaving my voice on the tape because they liked it so much. After that, whenever I was on the lot Jerry "The Beaver" Mathers would sing the school song when he saw me.

With Elinor Donahue at her book signing. She had written a cookbook and asked me for a favorite recipe that she included in her book.

ELINOR DONAHUE

During this time, my ex-husband, Gene, was teaching a course in tap dancing. He called me one afternoon to tell me he had accepted a job and asked if I could temporarily take over his Monday night class.

Elinor Donahue was one of his students. Elinor played Betty, one of the daughters on *Father Knows Best*. When they did a school show on the television program, she asked me to stage the number.

I met with the producer who told me the idea of this episode. Betty and another girl would compete for the lead in the school show. Betty would tap dance. He wanted a dance number for the other girl. It was to be an Americana type of number. I suggested she wear a cowgirl outfit. He thought that would be great. I worked with the other girl when Elinor was shooting and with Elinor when she wasn't shooting.

I was also cast as the teacher running the competition. My dialogue consisted of announcing the names of the competing children. I announced "Betty," but she wouldn't appear. Robert Young, who played Betty's father, was to speak up from the audience that he would find her.

This wasn't my first encounter with Robert Young. Several years prior, I was walking down a street at Warner Bros. with a group of people. Robert spotted someone he knew in our group and stopped to say hello. We were all introduced and Robert told us a funny story. We all laughed and laughed. Then he said something else that wasn't quite as funny, but I still laughed and laughed. Then Robert said something else that was sort of serious and I laughed and laughed. Everyone looked at me kind of funny since it was obvious I wasn't even listening. Of course, I grew embarrassed pretty quickly. I was smitten by Robert Young.

I'm quite sure Robert didn't recognize me as this same giddy young woman. Thank God! But I did surprise myself to still feel that same giggly feeling doing my dialogue with him.

During the shoot, as the cowgirl did her number I noticed Elinor watching from the side. She had tears in her eyes. This wasn't part of the script. The tears were real. I told the director I was concerned about her. He told me Elinor gets so involved in her work she probably thought the other girl was going to win the contest even though she knew from the script that she would win. The director was so sympathetic to Elinor, he did take the crew aside. He told them when Elinor finished her number they should applaud loudly so she would be reassured.

GARY CROSBY AND RUDY VALLEE

For the most part, I enjoyed my television jobs. Every once in a while I pulled my hair out. The most frustrating experience happened on a show where I staged "Play a Simple Melody" for Gary Crosby and Rudy Vallee. Gary had made the original record with his father, Bing. Ralph Levy, the director, wanted Gary and Rudy to do it vaudeville-style with straw hats and canes. Gary walked into the room and spotted me.

"Oh, no," he said. "There's a lady choreographer and she's going to make me dance." I did make up a routine for Rudy and him. I didn't have Rudy yet, so I played his part. It involved some walking steps, a little work with a cane and then they would take off their hats on a certain word and put them back on. When Mr. Vallee finally came to rehearsal we showed him the routine.

"It looks terrific," he said. "But it would help me a great deal if you would write this all down so I can study it over the weekend."

It's pretty hard to write when and how to take off your hat, but the show secretary said she'd help. It took a while to go through the dance and describe every step and beat. The secretary typed it up and gave it to Mr. Vallee. I had never done this before, but I thought, "If it works for *him*."

Monday morning we were back in the rehearsal hall and I was anxious to see how Mr. Vallee would fare. He didn't know one step or a single move! He couldn't even walk and sing at the same time. I kept simplifying the number. I expressed my concerns to the director.

"Make him do it!" the director kept saying. That's pretty hard to do. And I didn't want to make him look foolish. So I kept simplifying the routine until he could manage it. Gary, who had learned the original routine, had to come down to Mr. Vallee's level.

Some years later I was being interviewed by Skip E. Lowe on a local Los Angeles television show.

"Who was the most difficult person you ever worked with?" Skip asked.

"Rudy Vallee," I blurted out. I don't usually put people down. It isn't good business. But I thought I didn't want to work with him again, anyway.

LUCILLE BALL

Undoubtedly the biggest television star of all time was Lucille Ball. It was my good fortune to do two of Lucy's shows.

One episode involved Lucy on a blind date in a Greek restaurant. Howard "Howie" Morris played her date, a shy man until he hears the Greek music and pulls Lucy onto the dance floor. They were to dance something called a Handkerchief dance, only they would use a tablecloth.

I didn't know what the Handkerchief dance was, so I called a Greek restaurant in Hollywood that I knew had dancing. I told the owner what I wanted to do. He said he didn't have professional dancers. They were just men from different walks of life who liked to dance. I didn't care. I wanted to learn the dance. I went for dinner and then the show began. These fellows were terrific! After they danced I was introduced. They taught me how to do some of the dances. They were so good I hired some of them for the show. I also suggested they hire the restaurant musician who played the Greek sitar. They did.

We started rehearsals. We weren't rehearsing for more then ten minutes when Lucy came in. Lucy was known for being very hands-on.

"Let me see what you've done," Lucy asked. Truthfully, I hadn't done much more than have a cup of coffee. I asked if she'd give me a little more time. She did.

Lucy was on top of everything that had to do with her show. She came in several times during the day to be sure she was happy with what I was doing. She evidently was pleased because she didn't change a thing.

The next time I worked for Lucy involved a number with Danny Thomas. Danny, like Lucy, wanted to see the number right away. By then Lucy had developed trust in my work.

"Leave her alone," Lucy told Danny. "We don't need to heckle her. She'll do just fine."

In one part of the show Lucy was supposed to be waiting outside an employment office, not realizing the office is holding dance auditions. She watches the girls come and go. Two girls come into the waiting area. One complains she doesn't know the "step." The other girl offers to teach it to her. They thought it would be funny if I played the part of the woman who didn't know the "step." So I did.

In the skit, Lucy stood behind us, watching me learn the "step." Of course, before long she's trying to do it. By mistake Lucy's taken into the wrong office. She auditions and beats me out for the job dancing. Even in the fantasy part of my life I didn't get the part!

CHAPTER SEVEN

Movie – Odd Jobs and Great Jobs

The life of a choreographer is not like working for a corporation, where you work nine-to-five for the rest of your life. It is made up of a series of jobs for different companies. If you're lucky enough to get a weekly television series or a movie that takes months to shoot, you know you'll be able to pay the rent. I was lucky enough to have done both. And in-between those jobs, I did commercials, staged nightclub acts, political rallies and various other odds and ends.

Today choreographers have wonderful agents and managers, websites and the Internet to connect them to prospective employees. In the Fifties, some choreographers were under contract to the major studios as "dance directors," but the rest of us usually found out about jobs through the "Grapevine." To sustain a career in the performing arts, I learned early on how important it is to get "out there." I can't tell you the number of times I got a call because I had worked with someone and he or she gave my name to someone else. One job led to another. I would tell this to any young choreographer, actor, writer or filmmaker. I'm not discounting the importance of talent, but talent can't compensate for connections. You need to be seen and have your work seen. I did have an agent, but most of my jobs came through friends and people I had worked with who liked me and my work: Marge and Gower Champion, Sammy Cahn and Blake Edwards, to name a few.

At the beginning, I did all sorts of odd jobs. Warner Bros. sent Elsa Schreiber, the great acting coach, to coach Gordon MacRae on *Oklahoma*. I met her while they were making that movie because of my friendship with Sheila and Gordon. Sheila and I read all the other parts while Elsa gave Gordon pointers on the details of film acting.

The Cahns

at the Springs

THE MORNING AFTER!

Dearest Miriam:

Gloria and I both would like it very much if
you would just drop everything and come sit in
the sun with us! (That's for openers!)

Now as to your Talent!!! Let us say that many
people have talent, but how many of us (myself
included) have the graciousness, gentility and
humility to go with the talents! Just you my
dear Chum, Just you!!!

I know how terribly hard you worked and how much
you gave of yourself and at what a cost! I just
wanted you to know that many many people are more
than aware of that contribution. You are a marvel
and we all love you!!!

I could go on and on and perhaps would, bu' I most
likely would be crying long before you were. Just
believe that Gloria and I consider ourselves most
fortunate to know you as a Great Lady and a Great
Talent!!!

                              Much love and sincerity,

                              ammy.

We're Waiting!!!

ELSA SCHREIBER

After that, Elsa called and asked me to read parts with several other actors she was coaching. One day, she asked me to read with a young actor Warner Bros. had sent her. He was fresh from the Actors Studio approach to acting (a realistic style that used "sense memory") in New York and was going to appear in his first picture. It was a period piece, set in ancient Rome. After we did the reading, Elsa was asked to go to Europe and work with Gregory Peck. She advised the actor to pay me to continue working with him when she left to help him look and act convincing in his toga. (I think I made ten dollars an hour!) His character was elegant so I had to help him with his posture.

I drove to his tiny apartment in Hollywood. I knocked on the door. He opened it and stood there in his blue jeans and a t-shirt drinking a can of beer. We went to work and I taught him to how to put on his cape (we used a sheet), how to drink out of a goblet and anything to create a convincing "classic" look. Although he worked hard, the role was a bit of a "stretch" for him. He was never totally convincing. The picture was *The Silver Chalice* and the unknown actor was Paul Newman.

PAUL NEWMAN

I worked with Paul again in 1963 on *A New Kind of Love* as the film's choreographer. Paul starred in the movie with his wife, Joanne Woodward. Maurice Chevalier was also in the film and I created one number with dancers. I also taught the "Twist" to Eva Gabor. Miss Gabor was known for her curves and her femininity, but she couldn't get the Twist-y motion in her hips. To simulate the movement, I stood behind Eva and moved her hips back and forth, à la the "Twist." I try to get a dancer to feel in their body how a dance should feel. But even that didn't work for Eva. She was unable to get it on her own.

Just before they yelled "action" they started the music and I got behind Eva. She would say, "Vind me up Darlingk!" I would twist her hips, in essence winding her up. Then I jumped out of camera range and they began shooting.

One day when I was working with Eva, Paul came up to me. By now he had been in many films and was a big star. Even so, he remembered me.

He said, "I did improve, didn't I?"

ZSA ZSA, EVA AND MAGDA GABOR

I had known Eva prior to this film. Elsa Schreiber had once asked me to do some scenes with Zsa Zsa Gabor, Eva's sister. Elsa was trying to get her to enter a room with a particular attitude in keeping with her character. She kept giving her instructions, but Zsa Zsa wasn't getting it. Finally, she had me demonstrate. I entered the room as she wanted.

"Now I get it," Zsa Zsa said. "You start on your left foot."

Zsa Zsa and her sisters, Eva and Magda, were working on a nightclub act for Vegas. She asked me to come to the Beverly Hills Hotel where she was staying and help her with her lines. Although the sisters performed together, they never rehearsed together. After a couple of days, the sisters came in and watched. Eva and Magda liked what they saw. Each of them wanted me, too. All three wanted me at ten a.m. Pretty soon, these three sisters were in the midst of a tug-of-war over me. Zsa Zsa put a quick stop to it.

"*I* discovered her!" Zsa Zsa snapped at Eva and Madga.

JACK PALANCE

Long before Jack Palance won his Best Supporting Oscar for *City Slickers*, I got a call from his publicity man. He wanted me to help out with a magazine layout Jack was doing to promote his next movie. This was a war story where he would have to jump off a tank, carry a wounded soldier and be very agile. So I became the wounded soldier he practiced carrying different ways until he found a way to lift me up and throw me on his shoulder fast. I was surprised to find while talking to Jack, how much he knew about ballet companies and names of the dancers. To look at Jack that day and the photos they took, one would think he was a dancer.

BLAKE EDWARDS

Blake Edwards was already a friend of mine from The Mouse Pack when he called and asked me to choreograph a musical film entitled *Bring Your Smile Along,* that he was doing at Columbia Studios. Blake would go on to direct many wonderful films, including *The Pink Panther* movies, but, back in 1955, this was his directorial debut. There was to be a musical number with Frankie Laine and Keefe Brasselle. Frankie also would do a number with a group of dancers.

The first day of shooting, Dick Quine, another director, showed up. I knew Dick from Broadway and he occasionally attended the Mouse Pack parties. Dick and Blake had co-authored the screenplays of several musicals at Columbia released in 1952-3 (*Rainbow 'Round My Shoulder, All Ashore* and *Cruisin' Down the River*) and were good friends. During the first day of shooting Dick, who was a big cut-up, climbed a ladder on the wall and onto the catwalk. He hovered up near the ceiling and would periodically drop a care package at Blake's feet. A scene might go terribly wrong.

Plop. A packet of aspirin. A verbal altercation with a performer.

Tink. A can of band-aids.

It was all so hysterically funny.

Blake nicknamed me "Myrtle." I asked him how he came up with Myrtle. He admitted he didn't know. He said I didn't look like a Myrtle. That job was the beginning of a long association with Blake Edwards, about which you will read more. Every encounter was fun.

Keep Your Balance, Palance!

By LOUIS BERG
This Week Movie Editor

What's this? Grisly-faced Jack Palance doing ballet steps? Yes, it's true, and there's a good reason.

In the big pictures here you see him practising ballet leaps — and in the insets, you see him putting his ballet technique to work in his role as a wildly charging infantryman in "Attack!"

Palance is a former boxer who won 18 of his 20 professional fights before he decided that his features were battered enough for tough-guy movie parts. But to perform strenuous roles on camera and on cue takes more than a battle-scarred profile. It takes rhythm and timing and muscular control. Ballet dancing seemed to Palance a logical way to train.

He took his lessons in leaping from Hollywood choreographer **Miriam Nelson.** Do you reckon this is something the Army should look into for basic training?

BATTLEFIELD RESCUE: Ballet training helped Jack perfect timing for this sequence in "Attack!"

BIG LEAP: Jumping into a rubble-strewn ruin is a waltz — with dancing technique   **STEADY: Keeping upright atop tank in combat calls for ballet poise**

A *PICNIC* WITH BILL HOLDEN AND KIM NOVAK

Later that year, I worked on (what was to become) one of the most important films in my resume. *Picnic* came along and, like Dorothy, we all went to Kansas. By "we," I mean William Holden, Kim Novak, Rosalind Russell, Cliff Robertson, Susan Strasberg and Arthur O'Connell. Columbia hired Josh Logan to direct the film adaptation of William Inge's Pulitzer Prize-winning play about Labor Day in small-town America and the stranger (Holden) who shakes things up.

This project would be the film debuts for both Cliff Robertson and Kim Novak. Cliff had appeared in *Picnic* on Broadway, in the role Bill Holden was playing on film. Both of these talented young actors would go on to stardom and Kim and I would work on two more pictures together after *Picnic*.

We all met at the airport where photographers were waiting to snap a few photos, especially of Bill Holden, our biggest star. He looked every bit the part in his suit and tie. When *Picnic* was made, he was at the pinnacle of his career. They didn't get much bigger than Bill Holden.

I took my seat on the plane alongside Cliff. We discovered we were both Virgos, so that gave us a kinship. It says in the books, Virgos are neat and tidy. We're the peacemakers of the world, often times we pursue careers in the arts. I always feel comfortable with other Virgos.

The plane took off. Once we were up in the air and the plane leveled off, Bill walked by carrying a garment bag. A few minutes later he walked past from the other direction, dressed in a jumpsuit. Before we landed in Kansas he changed back into his suit and tie. He obviously was used to traveling.

I was hired to teach Kim and Bill to dance. They would be filming all day and I would get them in the evening, when they were both tired. That wasn't the only challenge I encountered. Kim was painfully shy and inhibited, not a good thing for a dancer, and Bill didn't want to dance, so I had to deal with that. I also dealt with rehearsal conditions in Hutchinson, Kansas, which were unusual, to say the least. We rehearsed at a jukebox joint surrounded by bar patrons.

Fortunately, the dance number was fairly simple. It had to be sexy, but didn't have a lot of movements. I danced with Bill for a while then I had him dance with Kim. After a few nights of rehearsal Kim and Bill became more comfortable dancing together.

Freddy Karger was in charge of music. Years later Freddy would marry Ronald Reagan's ex-wife, Jane Wyman. Freddy tried to dream up things for us to do while the rest of the company was shooting. He found out there was a good movie house in town. We went to the first showing, which was about eleven in the morning. At the end of the movie the lights came up and we realized we were the only people there.

Freddy asked me to meet him the following morning in the hotel lobby. He had planned another adventure, but he wouldn't tell me where we were going. He got a company car to drive us outside town to the Carry Salt Mines. I was told the only way into the mine was down a tiny shaft. I'm not so sure I would have gone if I'd known ahead of time, because I'm claustrophobic.

Freddy and I squeezed into that tiny elevator along with our guide. The door closed and instantly I wanted out, but it was too late. We started descending. There were openings in the walls of the elevator and we could see the sides of the shaft as we dropped. My palms started getting sweaty and I distracted myself by nervous chitchat.

We finally reached the bottom and the door slid open. I was never so glad to get out of an elevator in my entire life. But my relief was short-lived. Tracks ran into a dimly lighted tunnel as far as I could see. A coal train, just like the ones I had seen in movies, was waiting for us. I reluctantly got in.

Visiting Bill Holden on the back lot.

"Keep your heads down," the tour guide yelled, "because the ceiling is low." I hate tight spaces so much I can't even get into an MRI machine. And here I am going lickity-split through this tunnel with my head down for fear if I lift it up I'll have it whacked off. I kept my eyes closed.

All of a sudden the train slowed and we emerged into a brightly lit cube that was about twenty-five feet square. It struck me funny to see a Coke machine. This area had originally been solid salt they had blasted out and removed on the little train. I was amazed to learn that the first time they opened the mine they had a dinner there for local dignitaries. Tables, chairs and food were brought down in that little elevator.

They were drilling a hole for dynamite. I didn't want to be around to see them blast. We got on the train and rode back to the elevator. I didn't want to get back into it, but I was many feet underground and there was no other way out. I got in and we started our ascent.

As interesting as this trip was, I breathed a sigh of relief when that elevator door opened and I touched terra firma. I licked my lips and was surprised to taste salt. They presented me with a diploma for going down into the salt mine.

Another day Freddy and I had nothing to do. So Freddy wrote a terrific melody and we both wrote lyrics. We called our song, "Picnic." It was all apple pie and three-legged races, just like the film which had Bill's character in a three-legged race with Susan Strasberg.

Our film group had dinner at the hotel one night. They put us in a private dining room and served us a feast. The group consisted of Josh, Freddy, Bill, Rosalind, Cliff and me. Kim was invited, but she refused, as she did every night. She said she'd rather have her food sent up to her hotel room. I got to know Kim better on a subsequent movie and I asked her why she didn't join us.

"I never felt I had anything to contribute." I thought that was so sad. She missed out on such fun and interesting times.

An upright piano stood in a corner of the room. After dinner, several of us got up and entertained. I remember, in particular, Rosalind Russell sang a crazy song. Freddy and I decided we'd spring our song on the group. We were secretly hoping it would get in the picture. Freddy went to the piano to play and we sang our song. I thought we did a gung-ho job, but they didn't pick it for the movie.

One afternoon I rode out with the cast to watch the filming. It was a hot-and-dry Kansas morning and we all began talking about what we'd like if we had our druthers. Someone said she wanted a tall, cold mint julep. Another said a big dish of ice cream. I said I'd like a big chocolate malted milk. About a half hour later a driver came over and handed me a chocolate malted milk. It was from Bill Holden. He had sent the driver back to town to get it.

We heard about a restaurant in a small town about fifteen minutes away called "The Chicken Shack." Our little group decided to try it. We had just polished off mounds of mashed potatoes and platters of fried chicken and were looking forward to homemade apple pie when the room got oddly still. We looked at each other with uncomfortable glances and then our waitress came up to us with a worried look.

"You might want to postpone dessert," our waitress advised us. "We've just been told we're under a tornado watch."

We didn't even lick our fingers. We high-tailed it back to the hotel. I guess none of us wanted to be alone, because we gathered at Bill's suite on the fifth floor. We were told to leave our windows open a crack in case a tornado hit to keep the glass from shattering so we opened them as far as they would go.

Two windows were side-by-side, separated in the middle by a frame. No sooner had we opened the windows than Bill raced across the room and dived out one them. He grabbed the frame and swung back through the second window. I already was a little jittery and when I saw Bill leap out the window I thought he was committing suicide. I was so shaken up I started to cry. He gave everyone in the room heart failure. I went back to my room, shaking all over. Bill didn't realize this little stunt would upset us so much. He made the rounds, apologizing.

Several years later Bob Thomas called to say he was writing a book called *Golden Boy: The Untold Story of William Holden*. He had already interviewed two people, including Josh, who witnessed that crazy stunt. Josh told Bob to call me because I had also seen it. I related the story as best as I could. My story is the version Bob used.

I realized Cliff Robertson was as crazy as Bill when he secretly told me the two of them were going to parachute out of a plane the following day. We were staying close to an Air Force base and Cliff and Bill had worked it out with some pilots to do this stunt. I never breathed a word of this, but somehow the company found out about it. Thank heavens, they forbid it. There's an awful lot of money at stake on these actors. If, for any reason, they can't finish a picture it costs a fortune to replace them.

Finally, after all this adventure, the day arrived to shoot the dance. We gathered for breakfast. Bill — the daredevil who didn't blink an eye about jumping out hotel windows — said he didn't think he could get through the dance without a drink. He sent out for a bottle of scotch. He asked Kim if she could use a drink.

"By all means," Kim said. He asked me, too. I didn't need or want a drink, but I said with a kidding tone, "make mine champagne."

We drove out to the river where we were going to shoot. They put the word out they could use the townspeople to be background to the scenes. Filming was such a big event that about two thousand people showed up.

There were several picnic scenes, including a pie-eating contest and the one where Kim is crowned as the beauty queen "Neewollah" ("Halloween" spelled backwards) coming down the river in a boat. Now we were ready to move into the dance sequence.

Stairs were leading to a plot of land beside a small stationary dock that extended out over the river. James Wong Howe, our brilliant director of photography, had the wonderful idea of decorating the dock with colored lanterns. It added such atmosphere!

The sequence started with Bill dancing on his own, sort of showing off for Susan Strasberg's character. He tells her he wants to teach her a dance he learned in Los Angeles. He claps to the beat of the music. Susan tries to do it, but she can't clap on the beat. From off-camera you hear the sound of clapping. Cut to Kim, standing at the top of the stairs, clapping in time with the music. Kim steps down on the beat. Then she claps. She continues stepping and clapping to the beat.

In the movie, Susan couldn't clap on the beat, but in real life, it was Kim who had trouble keeping time to the music. During rehearsals I stood off camera and called out to her.

"Step. Clap. Step. Clap." To make matters worse, every time Kim reached the bottom her heels sank in the dirt and she would lose her balance. She said, "No one could do this without losing her balance."

"Keep your weight on the balls of your feet," I told her. She took her shoes off and made me put them on and prove it could be done. Of course, being a dancer I kept my weight up and my heels didn't sink. Someone in the crew had the brilliant idea of scraping away some dirt, putting down a board, and then sprinkling a little dirt on top. This way Kim's heels wouldn't sink in the dirt. Even so, the scene was a challenge.

When we started to shoot, I crossed my fingers. Just as we got to the part where Kim was to begin her clap-step routine, the sky turned dark. It was such a shock because moments earlier the sun had been shining to beat-the-band. We expected a downpour but the strangest thing happened. It began to hail! I knew hail from my childhood in Chicago and my years in New York, but I had never seen anything like *this*. Hail the size of golf balls came pelting down. We all raced to our trailers. We sat in Bill's trailer, listening to the sound of golf balls pounding on our roof.

"I think it's time for that drink," Bill said. All he had were Dixie cups. Apparently, he hadn't realized I was kidding about the champagne, because he pulled an enormous bottle from a bucket of ice. I went ahead and had my champagne.

Someone came up to the trailer and told us to sit tight because the storm was expected to pass. But those golf balls kept hitting the roof of the tin trailer. After about an hour and a few glasses of champagne the hail stopped and we heaved a sigh of relief. And then it rained. Not just rain. It poured *buckets*. The crew began laying out wooden planks because the rain had turned the dirt into mud. Someone knocked on our door. We were told we'd have a meeting back at the hotel. One-by-one they carried us gals to the cars.

At the hotel, Freddy and I were told that we could go home. Mother Nature had won. We were going to shoot the dance sequence on the back lot at Columbia at a later date. Freddy and I flew home the next morning.

A few weeks later I got a call from the studio to go to the Columbia back lot out in the San Fernando Valley. I got there and couldn't believe what I saw. The set looked exactly like the spot in Kansas, complete with a little river. There were stairs and the floater and all the little oriental lights. They even had solid ground at the bottom of the steps for Kim to stand on. Why we ever went to Kansas in the first place is beyond me.

We rehearsed a few times and were ready to shoot. The director told me to stand by the camera and yell, "step, clap …" until Kim reached the bottom step. Of course, in the film soundtrack my voice was replaced by the sound of music and hand claps.

Just before they started to shoot one of the close-ups of Bill and Kim dancing I noticed a piece of Kim's hair sticking out. I didn't see Helen Hunt, the hairdresser, so I went over and smoothed it down. I had just walked out of the shot when I heard the director call, "action!"

I knew Helen pretty well. We had worked together on *Cover Girl*. Even so, she blasted me.

"You don't belong in the union and you aren't allowed to touch Kim's hair!" she snapped. Each union has its own rules. I learned long ago I wasn't even allowed to move a chair. "That's another department" was the classic line.

We shot that dance sequence well into the night. After the movie was cut together, George Duning, the conductor and composer, was inspired to write a melody called "Picnic" that he superimposed over "Moonglow." It was a haunting melody and added greatly to the scene. To this day, when I get into a conversation about *Picnic*, people seem to remember, in particular, this dance sequence. It has been referred to as the best-remembered love scene of the 1950s.

On August 7, 1996, I read an article in the *Los Angeles Times* about *Picnic*. It was being re-released.

"Even before they meet," the article claimed, "you just know that when Hal and Madge see each other that the mutual attraction will be galvanic. Indeed, their encounter later that evening when they danced to 'Moonglow' has become one of the movie's classic moments of sexual magnetism, the most graceful and sensual of mating dances."

How about that?

I ran into Cliff at a charity dinner a few years ago. He threw his arms open and we had a big hug. He said, "I always wanted you to know something." He told me Bill said he hated to dance and didn't want to do that scene. That was, until he saw this "gorgeous blonde" they hired to teach him.

How about *that?*

I was shocked and deeply saddened when I learned Bill died. They found his body in his apartment on Ocean Avenue, in Santa Monica, just a few blocks from where I was living at the time.

A *HIGH TIME* WITH BLAKE EDWARDS

I worked with Blake Edwards at Columbia a second time on *He Laughed Last* (1956). My third picture with him was *High Time* (1960), which he directed for Fox. That picture starred Bing Crosby, Fabian, Richard Beymer, Nicole Maurey and Tuesday Weld. My good friend Sammy Cahn (who else?) wrote the lyrics and Henry Mancini wrote the music. It was a jazzy fantasy about life in college.

Blake asked me to come up with an idea for the opening of the film, where everyone is checking in to college. I worked with Tom and Frank Waldman, the writers, to come up with ideas as to how everything could be done to a musical beat, such as opening and closing drawers, pulling back a shower curtain, and other rhythmic "business."

Blake told me he also wanted one big number that would require a lot of dancing. He wanted me to dream up a lot of crazy ideas. He would spare no expense. He asked me to go on location near San Francisco so that every night he could check to see how the number was progressing. There would be many dancers in the number, but I only used three as my "skeleton crew" to work out the steps.

I had worked out several bits, including one with toe dancing bears. Blake kept saying, "Keep going. Dream it up!" When he was finally satisfied with the entire number, he asked me to go back to Los Angeles, and present my ideas to the unit manager so he could make up a budget.

When the unit manager put together a budget, he told Blake it was much too expensive. Blake, however, told him he would shoot the number as I had designed it or not at all. The studio said "not at all."

So, Sammy and Jimmy Van Heusen wrote another song to replace it that didn't require any props or scenery. Sammy asked me to go to the bungalow at the studio to hear the song. I needed to stage it for Bing Crosby and Fabian. When I got there Sammy ushered me in. Jimmy was on the phone.

"How are you, baby?" I overhead Jimmy coo into the phone. "What are you doing later tonight?" he asked in a sexy, romantic voice. Sammy rolled his eyes at me. There was a pause. Then Jimmy said, "I'll call you later." He hung up. He dialed the phone again. "How are you, baby?" he asked. The conversation was a repeat of the one he just finished. Sammy looked at me and shook his head. Jimmy went through this telephone ritual a third time and was beginning to start it over again when Sammy interrupted him.

"Come on, Jimmy," he said. "I want to do this number for Miriam so she can get back to work." They performed the song. It was terrific. As I was leaving, Jimmy picked up the phone and dialed. "Hello, baby," I heard him coo as I walked away.

While we were working on *High Time*, Richard Beymer told me he had an opportunity to audition for another movie. He had to show them that he could do a few dance steps so I worked with him as did several other dancers from the movie. We were all excited on the day he went over to audition. We couldn't wait until he got back.

When he came in with a big smile on his face, we knew he got the part. It turned out to be the role of Tony in *West Side Story*.

Publicity photo taken during my paid lunch with Clara Bixby and Rock Hudson.

DORIS DAY AND *PILLOW TALK*

I previously wrote how my friend Doris Day helped me with my love life. She had found me Jack Meyers, whom I dated until he forced the issue of marriage. But Doris didn't stop there. She called during the filming of *Pillow Talk*.

"I got you a part in the movie," Doris told me, "so we can have lunch together and get paid for it." I played a pregnant woman. The part was fun; I had a nice lunch with Doris, and I even "got my picture took" with Rock Hudson!

A *VISIT TO A SMALL PLANET* WITH JERRY LEWIS

After acting in *Pillow Talk* I went back to my old stomping ground, Paramount, for a meeting with Hal Wallis. He was producing *Visit to a Small Planet* starring Jerry Lewis. This was to be Jerry's last picture for Mr. Wallis under their contractual agreement. Norman Taurog, who had directed many of Jerry and Dean's movies, was signed to direct. They hired me to choreograph a number for Jerry and Barbara Bostock, a Broadway dancer from New York who reminded us all of Shirley MacLaine.

Mr. Wallis told me he wanted a different look for Jerry. He handed me a script which said Jerry would be dressed "Beatnik-style." I worked out a dance routine that fit with the theme of the film. I made it kooky, yet a different kind of dancing than Jerry had done before. I showed up at Paramount to begin rehearsals. It felt great to be back on the lot and I popped into some of my favorite haunts, like the commissary and the Prop Department.

Jerry was shooting on the movie and wouldn't be available for a while, so I got a dancer to "dance-in" for him so I could start making up the routine.

I'd been working for about a week when I ran into Jerry. I had known him for years through SHARE, so we gave each other a nice hug and hello.

"I know you're rehearsing," Jerry said, "and it isn't fair not to have me there. As soon as I finish shooting today, I'll be over and show you what I can do."

Sure enough, he came over later that day with tap shoes in hand. It wasn't what Mr. Wallis had in mind, but I didn't say anything. He slipped into his shoes and started tapping. I think he showed me every tap routine he ever learned. It wasn't bad, but I thought, "What am I going to do? Mr. Wallis wants a Beatnik routine."

"See you tomorrow," Jerry said after he changed his shoes and was leaving. I sat there with my mouth open, wondering how I would ever please my producer without upsetting Jerry.

My interest in psychology had not waned after meeting with Dr. Barker, my own psychologist, a few years back. I continued reading book after book on psychology and human behavior. I knew there was something I could apply to this situation if only it would come to me. When I went home that night I got out all my books and started thumbing through, trying to find something I could apply. I filled my brain with several tips that might be helpful.

The next day I went to Paramount, fairly well-armed. I went to the stage where Jerry was shooting dialogue and asked if he had time to talk.

"I'll have lunch delivered to my dressing room," he said. "What would you like?" I arrived at Jerry's dressing room at the designated time, then sat down and started nibbling my lunch. I knew the first thing you always did when you had a suggestion was to pay a compliment.

"I really enjoyed your tap dancing, Jerry." And then I made small talk about the different steps and how he learned them.

"But I think it might be fun – since your character is from Outer Space – for you to do something entirely different."

Jerry sat there thinking on what I had just said. "You have such a strong following and your audience has already seen you tap dance. It might be nice to show them another side of your talent." Jerry didn't seem to mind this. He just sat there listening, which I took as a green light to proceed.

"What if I put a routine together and you come take a look?"

Jerry agreed to come and I felt tremendously relieved.

He arrived a couple days later and Barbara and Jerry's dance-in did the routine. It was goofy with all kinds of crazy rhythms, unlike anything Jerry had ever done. He liked it. Hallelujah!

At rehearsal during Visit to a Small Planet. *I'm standing next to the mirror with director, Norman Taurog, watching Jerry's antics.*

The next day I got a call asking me to see Jerry in his office. When I got there he was behind his desk. He talked seriously as a little airplane circled over my head. He evidently had a button under his desk that he would push to activate his toy. He pretended like the plane wasn't there, but it's pretty hard to have a serious conversation while an airplane circles a few feet above your head. It was wacky, typical Jerry Lewis kind of stuff.

"I want you to leave eight bars in the routine where I could do my own thing." I figured it was a good compromise — better than I'd hoped for — so I did it.

Jerry came to the rehearsal hall and began learning the routine with Barbara. He learned two steps then disappeared. All of a sudden he popped up from behind the piano, his face covered with bandages. It was so bizarre we had to laugh. Then he left.

"Is he always like that?" Barbara asked.

"I'm afraid so," I told her, wiping tears from my eyes.

Days went by when Jerry couldn't rehearse. By then, Barbara knew it well. She was supposed to wear a wrap-around skirt in the number. She had terrific legs so I thought of a gimmick where we attached a wire to the back of her skirt. At one point the prop man pulls the wire and the skirt goes flying off.

Jerry finally did come in and learned the entire number. He seemed happiest doing his thing. His "thing" consisted of jumping up and down and walking on his ankles and such.

The day of the shoot arrived. Everything went well on rehearsal. And then the cameras began rolling. Barbara and Jerry were doing a terrific job until just prior to the end of the routine. For some unknown reason, Jerry sat on the floor and pretended to row a boat. Poor Barbara just stood there with her mouth open, trying to ad lib.

"*Cut!*" Norman yelled. He looked at me as if to ask, "Was that all right?" If Jerry's rowing had improved the number I would have let it go. But it didn't really make sense. "I don't think the rowing is working," I told Norman. "And it isn't fair to Barbara." Norman told me he would keep shooting until I was happy.

"Okay, let's do another take," Norman yelled. After several more shots, Jerry did something that more closely resembled what I had taught him. I thought it was as good as we would get. That was the take Norman used for the movie.

Jerry is a most generous fellow. He gave me a cigarette lighter (I'm sorry to say I still smoked at this time) with a picture of him on the side. He was about eighteen at the time and the photo had been taken by Bruno of Hollywood. Jerry said my father had gotten him to pose for that picture so he thought I might get a kick out of the lighter.

When the picture finished filming and it came time to dub the footsteps, Barbara was no longer under contract and Jerry was off doing another movie. So, they called me in to dub the footwork for both of them. I took in a pair of high heels for Barbara and a pair of boots for Jerry. I got an opportunity to go back to one of my favorite places – the dubbing stage. Some of the same guys were still there. They were always so much fun.

"Hey, everybody," someone yelled, "look who's here! One Take Franklin." They had nicknamed me "One Take" because I was good at getting the sound right the first time through.

I slipped the headset over my ears so I could hear the music. I looked up at the film on a large screen. I dubbed Barbara's feet first with no problem. I changed into the boots to do Jerry's sounds.

The craziest thing to match, of course, was the jumping up and down and the ankle thing. I had to mimic what I saw Jerry do. I wish I had a picture of myself, holding the headset tightly, concentrating on the screen while jumping up and down. I know it was funny, because I noticed the guys in the sound booth cracking up. For the first time in my career, it took more than one take to get it right!

MY FIRST PARTY IN *THE APARTMENT*

Next, I finally got to work again with Billy Wilder on *The Apartment*, which he co-wrote and directed for United Artists. It was the first time I had seen Mr. Wilder since he directed me in *Double Indemnity*. *The Apartment* starred Jack Lemmon, Shirley MacLaine, Ray Walston, Edie Adams and Fred MacMurray, whom I also knew from *Double Indemnity*.

I was asked to create a mock striptease for Joan Shawlee for a "swinging" office party. Joan only takes off her necklace, but *Variety* said her striptease was "sexier than many in a strip joint."

Jack Lemmon had to weave through a crowd, carrying drinks as the camera followed him. I watched him trying to come up with a way to do it. I quietly went up to him and told him I had an idea. He was always ready to listen. I suggested he carry drinks above his head so the camera would always know where he was. He loved it and that's the way they shot it. Mr. Wilder never knew I had anything to do with that scene.

Me in the circle, dancing with my partner at Holly Golightly's party in Breakfast at Tiffany's.

MORE PARTIES: *BREAKFAST AT TIFFANY'S*

After *The Apartment* was released, I received a series of calls asking me to choreograph party scenes in movies. It might be difficult for some of the readers to understand what the "choreography" of a party is! Well, it is moving guests, people carrying drinks and trays of food, old friends seeing each other, rushing across the room and hugging, couples dancing and the variety of movement of which a "party" is actually composed. Oh, and making it all work for the camera without knocking it (and the director) over! Just for fun, at the next party you're around, look around at the complicated floor/traffic patterns, variety of tempos, rhythms and directions. And it all seems so "spontaneous." I "did" so many parties that friends started calling me "Hollywood's Party Girl."

I choreographed a complicated and fun party scene in Blake Edwards' *Breakfast at Tiffany's*. He asked me to get together so we could "woodshed" (meaning to go over repeatedly) a few crazy things we could do in the party. Blake said, "You should be in the party, too." So I appeared briefly on camera in the party I helped stage. Blake even gave me some lines.

AND MORE PARTIES: *THE INTERNS*

In 1962 I was asked to create a New Year's Eve party sequence for Columbia in *The Interns*. The picture starred a lot of fine, young actors and gave me the opportunity to help change the ethnic mix in American film. My friend, columnist Army Archerd, even wrote about it in *Variety*: "Bob Cohn, David Swift and Columbia Pictures defy a long-standing Hollywood film taboo – yesterday, in the wild, New Year's Eve 'interns' party sequence, they also incorporated integrated dancing — white and Negro, that is."

Columbia called me back to choreograph a sequel: *The New Interns* (1964). I was asked to stage several informal scenes and dances. There was a party scene with the doctors and nurses from the hospital. The bar had been set up with intravenous bags and hoses. You would fill a glass by releasing a lever on the hose. I thought it was an interesting touch.

I've never had a good memory for places or dates, but one day is etched in my memory as if it were yesterday. On November 22, 1963, we planned to rehearse all morning then shoot after lunch. We were in the midst of rehearsing the crazy, joyous party when someone rushed in hysterical. The party immediately came to a standstill and everyone turned to this person, who announced, "President Kennedy has been shot."

A hush came over the stage. We all stood there in shock. And then several people went to pieces. Many of the men broke down crying. That really surprised me. Like everyone in the country, I had tremendous respect and admiration for our charismatic and handsome leader. I had staged a number back in 1960 for a fundraiser for the then-Senator Kennedy when he was running for president. Sammy Cahn had written the song.

We waited on pins and needles until a few minutes later when we were told the President was dead. We were finally told to break for lunch and come back at 12:30. On the way I saw groups of people huddled together. Some people just stared into space.

We all reassembled at 12:30. After waiting a long while we expected to be told to go home. We were finally told that because of the cost of bringing back that many actors and extras we would proceed with shooting the party scene.

It's impossible to describe the despair and anxiety that afternoon. We were all devastated and yet we were filming a party scene. Everyone had to pretend to be having a good time. This was really a challenge to these young actors' abilities.

HONEYMOON HOTEL

MGM's *Honeymoon Hotel* (1964) was my next movie. It starred Nancy Kwan, Robert Goulet and Robert Morse — whom everyone called "Bobby." I staged a number for Bobby that took place on, of all places, a trash heap in a dump. After a

Honeymoon Hotel *with Henry Levin (left) and Robert Morse (right).*

long day, boy, did it smell! Once again, I was working with music that had been written by my friend, Sammy Cahn, and his writing partner, Jimmy Van Heusen.

In the film, Robert Goulet marries Jill St. John. Robert, his bride and his best man, Bobby, take a honeymoon to a West Indies isle where they meet Nancy.

I had to come up with a number for Nancy, but I was drawing blanks. Then an idea dropped out of the sky – literally! We had one of those rare Los Angeles storms. After it was over, I noticed palm leaves on the ground and picked one up. This became the inspiration for a number where Nancy used palms as fans.

It was during the making of *Honeymoon Hotel* that I had one of my greatest achievements. I quit smoking! A prop man brought me an article about the evils of smoking. I especially remember reading about nicotine and how it sticks to your lungs. I had wanted to quit anyway and this was the impetus I needed. I quit cold turkey.

TEACHING "THE WATUSI"

"I'd Rather Be Rich" (Universal, 1964) also starred Robert Goulet, along with Maurice Chevalier, Sandra Dee and Andy Williams. I taught Robert and Sandra the "Watusi" and helped Sandra create looks for one of her scenes. She had to shoot some publicity stills. She posed for a photographer's shot every split second. She would strike a pose, then there would be a flash from a camera. Pose. *Flash*. Pose. *Flash*. Pose. *Flash*. Sort of like an early Madonna "Vogue" music video.

On the set of I'll Take Sweden *with Rosemarie Frankland and Frankie Avalon.*

The "Watusi" was very popular at this time. I had to teach it again to Tuesday Weld in Lake Arrowhead for a Bob Hope picture called *I'll Take Sweden* (1965). Tuesday danced the number out on a dock with Frankie Avalon. At the end of the picture all the dancers had to jump into the icy waters of Lake Arrowhead. You can bet I didn't do it.

CAT BALLOU

I next got a call asking me to choreograph another picture for Columbia called *Cat Ballou* and would be working with another young actress. Although she had a famous father named Henry and had made other films, she was still not widely known. This film would make her a star. Her name, of course, was Jane Fonda.

Cat Ballou (1965) was a period picture set in Wyoming in 1894. It was a kind of western comedy. A woman named "Cat" (played by Jane) hires a famous gunman (played by Lee Marvin), to avenge her murdered father.

My big number was a hoedown that took place in a barn. Almost all the actors in the film, including Michael "Mickey" Callan and Dwayne Hickman, were in it. I was sorry Lee Marvin wasn't in the hoedown because I wanted to work with him. When I saw the finished picture I thought he was brilliant.

I didn't work with Lee Marvin, but I did get to work with that wonderful singer, Nat King Cole. He lived in Lake Tahoe, Nevada, during filming and was commuting back and forth to Los Angeles. He and Stubby Kaye made an appearance at one end of the barn singing throughout the hoedown.

Jane danced with several men during the hoedown and had dialogue with them as she danced. The number had to be staged so that she would finish the dialogue with one actor, then go to the next and have more dialogue. Elliot Silverstein, the director, had been a dancer so he had some ideas on what he wanted to see. He wanted the entire number to be shot without cuts. Everyone figured he'd want to periodically cut in for close ups and could not get it in one take.

Since the camera would be moving throughout filming, I had to stage its movement to follow Jane. I ended up with twenty different marks on the floor that I had to block with the cameraman.

Given these constraints, I couldn't do a legitimate square dance or a "Virginia Reel" because that wouldn't have given Jane the opportunity to dance with all of the men, nor would it have given her time to say her lines. I made up my own version of a country dance to accommodate Jane's movement and dialogue. (And to think, *Webster's Dictionary* defines choreography as "the art of creating and arranging dances." If only they knew what it *really* involves!)

The dance would be interrupted by a group of troublemaking cowboys who arrive unannounced and start a fight. These cowboys were not dancers; they were stuntmen. Some of the male dancers wanted to be part of the fight scene because they would make more money. They weren't allowed to because stunt work is too dangerous, not to mention there is a union for stunt men. I asked the stunt coordinator if I could watch as he blocked out the fight. Blocking fights is a form of choreography and I was interested to see it happen.

The fight starts because Jane's character dances with an Indian. Many of the girls in this scene were actually men in dresses who could take blows to the face. One of the stuntmen — the actor who played the Indian — did get his nose broken in real life during this fake fight.

The stunt coordinator held a rehearsal which seemed to go pretty well on the first run-through. But after that, subsequent run-throughs became a free-for-all. For instance, there were a couple of men who were supposed to catch a fellow who was falling backwards. As he got to the spot where the men were to catch him, they moved away. Instead of being caught, the man kept falling backwards, his arms flailing as he tried to right himself. I couldn't believe my eyes. Later, they were laughing about it. Even the poor guy who fell backwards was laughing.

I only had Jane for one day of rehearsal. Jane had trained in ballet and was very bright. I could show her what to do one time and she did it. Mickey Callan was the only other actor who also was a dancer and had been "discovered" playing Riff in *West Side Story* on Broadway. Jane's directional changes in this sequence were complicated. Professional dancers could have helped her by sending her off in the right direction to the next dancer, but since they were actors, not dancers, Jane ended up helping *them* to be in the right place at the right time.

We rehearsed with the cameraman on the day of shooting. The first time there was dialogue the camera crew marked the floor with a number one. Then we danced to the next partner and bit of dialogue. The camera crew marked the floor. We kept going through the entire number, painstakingly blocking for the camera and the actors.

After a few hours of this, Elliot came up to us, laughing. "They're calling from upstairs," he told us. "They don't know why we don't have a shot yet." Elliott told me not to worry. He wanted us to keep going as we were. By lunchtime we had it worked out. We came back after lunch and had one rehearsal. Then we shot this long and complicated sequence. We got it all in one take.

Elliot wrote me a letter after filming thanking me for how smoothly I had worked it all out. "And they said it couldn't be done," he wrote.

Shortly after filming, I was saddened to hear that Nat Cole had died. We all knew he was ill while we were shooting. He was such a lovely man.

COLUMBIA PICTURES CORPORATION
1438 NO. GOWER STREET
HOLLYWOOD 28, CALIFORNIA
TELEPHONE 462-3111

January 27, 1965

Dear Miriam:

    I have already expressed to you my deepest appreciation and great admiration for your work as choreographer on CAT BALLOU; but I wanted to drop you a note just the same and tell you again, because I can't say it too many times.

    The way you organized yourself and your dancers permitted me to photograph our square dance in half the time the producer thought it would take--so there, too, Charlie Brown!

                  Affectionately,

                  Elliot Silverstein

Miss Miriam Nelson
1506 Morningside Drive
Burbank, California

CHAPTER EIGHT

Meanwhile – Back in My Life

In the midst of all these wild parties, hoedowns, brawls and "Watusi" and "Twist" lessons, I received a call from Jack Meyers. I recognized his voice right away even though I hadn't heard from him in more than three years. I asked him how he was and about his marriage. He told me he and Joan had separated. I told him I was sorry to hear that, which I was.

"Miriam," Jack asked, "would you go to dinner with me?" I told him I didn't think it would be a good idea to be seen in public if he wasn't legally separated.

"Can I just come over and have a cup of coffee?" he asked. I didn't think that would hurt anything, so I said "yes" and he came over.

He shared some of the problems he was having in his marriage. I know every story has two sides, but I felt it was important for him to express his perspective. I mostly listened. "Are you seeing anyone?" he asked after a while. I was, and I told him so. I was dating a man my friends nicknamed "Mr. Flowers" because he was always sending me huge bouquets. Jack didn't press any further. I guess I didn't want to discourage him because I volunteered that I wasn't in love with Mr. Flowers.

After this cup of coffee, Jack would pop by the house once in a while. Pretty soon Jack and Joan divorced. Jack and I were going steady again. (Yes, I still believed in that outdated convention.) After awhile I realized Jack was the only man I wanted. This time, I knew in my heart that Jack was for me and at some point I would be ready to marry him.

I was still living in the house in Burbank, the same one I had bought with Gene, my former husband. I lived there with Chris and my mother (who helped care for Chris so I could work).

Jack and I had to get a house with enough bedrooms to accommodate the two of us, Chris, my mother, Jack's daughter Missy (Jack got custody) and a live-in housekeeper.

We looked at several houses but nothing was quite right. One day while driving over Benedict Canyon I saw a sign for new homes. I drove in and looked at one of the models. The house sat on a beautiful lot that overlooked the surrounding mountains. I liked it so much I had Jack come look. Jack was concerned there might not be enough room for all of us.

The real estate developer was so anxious to sell his houses he was willing to do almost anything. He found a way to put in an extra bedroom and bath in one of their four bedroom plans. Then they began building our new house.

Every day on my way to work I would stop to check the building progress. Before long, I could read plans upside down and backwards. I couldn't believe that almost daily the builders made some mistake. We'd work it out and I would go to work. On my way home I'd review the progress and see if the builders had corrected the errors.

At this time positive thinking was popularized by Norman Vincent Peale. I was studying this belief system with a Doctor Bitzer, and I was glad I did. I was able to see that each error in the process meant that the finished product would be better than the original plan.

For example, Jack and I decided to have a pool. The pool was supposed to be the same elevation as the house, but as digging began they discovered they had to build three steps down to the pool. I didn't want to step down to my pool. To appease me, they built a multi-layered deck around the pool with the first level at the same elevation as the house. The finished pool was more aesthetically pleasing than my original plan.

We were finally told the house had passed building inspections and we could move in within a week. Jack and I still hadn't gotten married and I wasn't about to cohabit without a wedding license, so I hurriedly arranged our wedding. I was going to put together a simple ceremony like I had with Gene. Odd, now that I think about it. Here I had staged huge extravaganzas like the opening of Disneyland, but for my own weddings I wanted it intimate and simple. I called my good friend Sheila MacRae, who was performing at the Desert Inn in Las Vegas, to ask her to be my maid of honor but Gordon and she had several shows to do in Vegas and couldn't get away.

"Why don't you fly here and get married?" she suggested. My first reaction was to think Vegas was "tainted" – gambling, seedy wedding chapels and all, and getting married there might be a hex on us.

"I'll arrange the entire wedding and reception," Sheila told me. "You won't have to lift a finger, except your ring finger. Gordon and I will even stand up for you, if you'll have us." She made it so inviting, I agreed.

I bought a pale beige silk wedding dress (I would never have worn white, since this was my second marriage) and a hat with a veil. Jack and I flew to Los Vegas.

A few friends from Los Angeles also came along, like Tom and Jan Sarnoff. Tom's father (David Sarnoff) owned NBC and Tom was the one responsible for getting us the wonderful stage scenery for all of the SHARE charity shows.

When we got to The Desert Inn, we couldn't believe how much effort Sheila had put into our wedding. She had reserved a banquet room and had created an altar with flowers on each side. It was lovely. She hired a minister and even told him what she thought I would like him to say. Of course, after this Jack loved to tell people that Sheila had hired an actor and we weren't really married!

But we were. Jack Meyers and I had finally tied the knot. The official date was September 25, 1965. I was now Miriam Nelson Meyers.

At the reception, they served hot and cold *hors d'oeuvres* and a lovely wedding cake. Sheila had arranged a musical group from the showroom orchestra and she had a female photographer, also from the showroom, take our wedding pictures. The only thing we had to do was to go to city hall to get a marriage license.

How's that for a good friend?

And you should know there is no such thing as a hex. Jack and I would go on to live together happily for twenty-four years until he developed a heart problem and I lost him.

Jack and I finally tied the knot in 1965.

Our wedding party with Gordon and Sheila MacRae.

Top: Young married couple (left), old married couple (right). Bottom: Jack, his daughter Missy and me.

CHAPTER NINE

Hawaii – The State and the Movie

No sooner had Jack and I married and settled in our new home, when it seemed that every time I turned around I was flying to Hawaii.

My first trip to Hawaii was to choreograph a sequence for an Otto Preminger picture, *In Harm's Way*, released in 1965. This epic film adaptation of a best-selling novel was about the bombing of Pearl Harbor. When the picture was released, *Playboy* magazine would describe the opening sequence as "an orgiastic dance scene," referring to a writhing dance I created for actress Barbara Bouchet.

The actual making of the picture was *anything* but sensual.

I arrived at Mr. Preminger's office in Paramount. Huge white paintings hung from the white walls of his spacious office. The legendary director sat behind a desk, eating a bowl of vichyssoise.

He looked up and addressed me as "Miss Nelson" in his German accent. I called him "Mr. Preminger." There was such an air of formality: I couldn't imagine anyone ever calling him "Otto," not even his own parents. He explained what he wanted me to do and I just sat there on the edge of my chair, listening politely.

Then he invited me to go down to the set and watch them shoot. I sat down behind the camera as he directed a scene with Paula Prentiss and Tom Tryon. They didn't do it the way he wanted so he made them do it over and over. He was especially rough on Paula. He finally made her cry.

He turned to me and said, "She needed that."

"No, she didn't," was going through my mind.

I had to audition several girls for a dance sequence with Hugh O'Brien. Mr. Preminger finally chose Barbara and I taught her the number and we rehearsed in Hollywood before going to Hawaii. The dance consisted of a lot of sexy moves and swinging around a pole. (Some friends have accused me of being the originator of "Pole Dancing.")

It was summertime and my son, Chris, the surfer, was out of school. "How can I go to Hawaii without Chris and his surfboard?" I wondered.

Then I got an idea.

"Mr. Preminger," I asked. "Would it be okay for me to bring my son to Hawaii if I paid his way?"

"Yes," he said. "Maybe he can play with my children. How old is your son?" I told him he was sixteen.

On the set of In Harm's Way *with Tom Tryon.*

"I guess my children are too young." He had married a young woman (she looked like a girl to me) and they had two children about four or five years old. I went home and told Chris about my idea. He was pretty excited. I called the freight airlines to find out how much it would be to ship his board. I was told the flight to Hawaii accommodates surfers with racks for their boards. Chris and I were on our way.

Paula boarded the plane carrying a big bag of cantaloupes. She was on some kind of a cantaloupe kick. Barbara sat down beside me. We talked about our mutual fear of Mr. Preminger. Then I remembered John Wayne was in the film. I knew John from my SHARE shows.

"John Wayne" I assured her, "won't let Mr. Preminger do anything bad to us."

We landed at the Honolulu airport and were shuttled to the hotel in Waikiki. We had a lovely room, but Chris barely got there when he grabbed his surfboard and headed for the ocean.

"Where is your son?" Mr. Preminger asked when I met him in the hotel lobby.

I told him Chris was already out surfing.

I rehearsed Hugh and Barbara in the hotel while the company shot other scenes.

Chris and I in Hawaii with the 'Jolly Jeep'. Preminger didn't believe I had a son.

Hugh played a Naval officer and Barbara, whose character was married to Kirk Douglas, had to be drunk and dance seductively for Hugh at the Officers' Club. Mr. Preminger came to see the number. He seemed happy.

"Where is your son?" Mr. Preminger asked.

I told him he was having a terrific time surfing.

We rode in a motor launch out to a little island where the Pearl Harbor Officers' Club was located. We were using actual wives and girlfriends of officers in the sequence. I explained the scene to them.

As the film was to open with this sequence, it was planned to be a long dolly (moving) shot of officer's hats on tables alongside a pool and finally coming to the dance floor where all the officers and their wives were dancing. That would be the beginning of Barbara and Hugh's dance.

"You'll all be on the dance floor dancing," I told the wives. "Barbara is going to enter and start acting up. One at a time I need you to stop dancing and watch the spectacle she is making of herself."

Mr. Preminger was ready to shoot the scene. "Miss Nelson," he said authoritatively, "does everyone know what they are supposed to do?"

I smiled and nodded and thought to myself, "I certainly hope so."

Everyone took their places at the tables around the swimming pool and the camera began rolling. I was pleased nobody made any mistakes. We got through the entire shoot without Mr. Preminger yelling at Barbara or me.

The shoot had stretched into the darkness of night and Mr. Preminger knew my son couldn't possibly be surfing. He asked why he didn't come watch us shoot. I told him he had wanted to go to bed early so he could catch one last wave in the morning before we had to leave.

Mr. Preminger said, "Miss Nelson, I don't believe you have a son. I think you have a lover in your room."

The next morning I rented a Jolly Jeep and drove Chris to the other side of the mountain (the "Pali," as the Hawaiians call it). We had been invited to spend a few days with Jack Regas and his wife, Kit, and their three daughters. Jack and I had been longtime friends and co-workers. He made the career transition to choreographer and then to director, and was currently directing the spectacular show at the Polynesian Cultural Center.

I had received a call to stage and direct the show myself a couple of years earlier. At that time I was doing a television show and they asked if I could recommend somebody. Knowing that the Polynesian Cultural Center cast would all be amateurs, I immediately thought of Jack. His enthusiastic and patient leadership would be a good fit.

We had only stepped into the door of the Regas home, when Jack made an announcement. "We're going to decorate a float tonight on the other side of the island." As it turned out, there was going to be a big parade to celebrate King Kamehameha.

We did manage to put away our clothes and have a bite of dinner before heading back over the mountain. We were up all night decorating the float with flowers. After we watched the parade, we went back over the mountain one last time.

That night we went to the Cultural Center to see the show Jack had staged. There were about 150 people in the cast; six islands were represented. It was held in an outdoor amphitheater with a lagoon between the audience and the stage. The background was a man-made mountain with waterfalls. It was beautiful and I was impressed. After the show I met most of the cast. Chris and I stayed with the Regas's the next couple of days and half the cast would be running in and out of the house.

Jack casually mentioned the Center wanted him for a new show, but he didn't want to stay on the island much longer. His daughters had "gone native," as he described it. They never wanted to put on shoes and the native boys were looking good to them.

Before Chris and I returned to the mainland, we passed a sign that said, *"Wiamea Beach — Enter at your own risk."* I slammed the brakes and had Chris get his surfboard and stand next to the sign as I snapped his picture. We got home and about a week later I picked up the developed pictures at the store. I'm not much of a letter writer, but I couldn't resist. I put the picture in the envelope and wrote, "Mr. Preminger, you see I *do* have a son."

HAWAII

My next Hawaiian job came shortly after for a movie that would be one of the most successful pictures of 1966. It was the epic *Hawaii*, based on the best-selling novel of the same name written by James A. Michener.

Portions of the film were shot at the Goldwyn Studio in Hollywood and I went there to work on those segments. One involved Julie Andrews and the girl who played her younger sister. They were playing the piano and singing and dancing around the living room when a righteous preacher, played by Max Von Sydow, walks in and is shocked!

I don't know how many people outside of the film business realize how frequently scenes are "choreographed," even simple dance movements that look spontaneous. I think the assumption is that the actors make up these movements. But a choreographer usually creates them.

This was the first time I worked with Julie Andrews. She would go on to marry my good friend, Blake Edwards, but I didn't know her before we made *Hawaii*. Another example of how lives can intersect: as my son, Chris, grew up, one of his first jobs was to deliver flowers. For days on end he delivered bouquets to Julie from Blake. Chris would ring the bell at Julie's house and leave the flowers with whoever answered the door. I'd always ask him, "Did you go in and say 'hello Julie'?"

He never did. He was a bit shy.

After Blake and Julie married, she became part of my circle. I remember I had them up to our house once. Jack's daughter, Missy, came home from school and walked by. All of a sudden she backed up. That was Mary Poppins sitting in her den! Missy asked Julie all kinds of questions about *Mary Poppins*: "How did you fly?" "How did you go down the banister?"

Julie was nice enough to describe it to her. Missy certainly had something to tell her schoolmates the following day!

Julie Andrews is about the most cooperative and professional of all the stars with whom I've worked. And she learns fast! I was always amazed by her aptitude. She also has a photographic memory. She'd learn a number one day and they'd shoot it the next and she'd perform it flawlessly. When they shot the parlor scene, George Roy Hill (the director) told Julie if she wasn't happy with the singing, they would re-record it and put it in after the shot. But she sang it perfectly the first time!

Filming moved to Hawaii and I was flown over to stage a ceremonial sequence. I had to do a lot of research on this one. I went to the library and read up on ceremonial dances. The studio connected me with an older Hawaiian man who knew traditional chanting. The rest came out of my head.

If you've seen *Hawaii*, you'll probably remember the sequence where the brother and sister are married to each other. I hired a few of the male dancers from the Polynesian Cultural Center, but, with producers trying to be authentic, the girls had to be bare-breasted and the Mormon Church wouldn't allow it — nor would the movie censors of the day. The girls I hired didn't want to dance topless, either. They wore huge leaf leis around their necks. As they danced or spun around the flowers would move and reveal all. I found out later the girls glued the flowers to their skin to keep them in place. When they took off the flowers after the shoot, they had a terrible time pulling the glue off. Some of their skin came with it. *Ouch.*

The second night we were to shoot, several of the male dancers didn't show. The company had given them paychecks at the end of the first day of shooting which was a big mistake because they spent it on a long — and wild — night on the town. We had to shuffle dancers and shoot from another angle so it looked like they were all there. After that experience, they didn't get paid until the entire sequence was finished.

Soon after I arrived back in Los Angeles I got a call from The Polynesian Cultural Center telling me what I already knew: Jack Regas was not going to do their new show. They wondered if I would be available. They needed me for six weeks. I talked with my family and we decided they could each come over for at least a week. I had seen the show, so I knew what I was getting into. Rather, I thought I knew. I accepted their offer and flew back to Hawaii.

Six groups of Pacific peoples were represented: Fijians, Tongans, Maoris, Tahitians, Samoans and Hawaiians. The dancers all had unusual names. I went back to my hotel at night and studied them.

The Polynesians also had different names for props and their dances had unusual names. Fairly soon I had memorized the words I needed like *oolie oolie*, which were like maracas covered with feathers and beads.

Each group had its own leader. The girl who became my best friend was the leader of the Tahitians named Arana Mapui. She lived with her family in a little house on the beach and invited me there many times for dinner. Her mother cooked an assortment of wonderful Tahitian dishes.

Everyone was wonderful to me. It was a great experience working with these people. The only person I felt a little uncomfortable with was the Fijian Chief. He always looked at me as if to say, "Who's this blonde *haole* girl telling *me* what to do?"

A few days before the opening my Hawaiian stage manager announced he was getting married. He could only get the church on they day we opened. The show was in good shape so I felt it was all right for the cast to take off for the wedding. I didn't get to go to the wedding because only Mormons are allowed inside their church. Afterward, I did attend a lovely reception and then we were all off to get ready for the show. Or so I thought.

I climbed the tall stairs to the light booth to look for my stage manager. He was to call the cues for the lights. He was nowhere to be found.

"He's not doing the show tonight," someone said. "Tonight is his wedding night." He never told me he wouldn't be there for the opening! It slowly dawned on me I was the only other person who knew the lighting cues. I wound up calling the light cues that night.

I was no longer relaxed, but the show was going well. When it came to the Hawaiian section, the girl I chose to do the beautiful hula didn't come out. Instead, her understudy did the number. I thought she was sick or had an accident. After the show I found out that Auntie Sally, the leader of the Hawaiian group, decided to put her favorite girl on. Of course, she was good, but not as pretty as the girl I chose. (Unlike working with the highly disciplined Broadway and Hollywood dancers of the time, the Polynesians *seemed* to do as they wanted.)

The fire dance always frightened me because if the hula skirts had dried out they could catch fire. The boys were in charge of making sure their hula skirts were made of fresh green leaves. Once in awhile they got lazy or were late and would put on an old skirt. As they twirled the fiery batons, if they got too close to their skirts, the leaves would catch fire and go up in flames. They would race to the lagoon and jump in to put out the fire!

The Samoans did a war dance with spears. In their culture, the more ferocious the face the more manly they were supposed to be. They could even pop their eyes partially out of their sockets! I asked one of them how he did that.

"You just open your eyes wide and push," he told me.

I tried it a couple of times but nothing happened. He told me I wasn't trying hard enough. I gave it a gung-ho and, by golly, I popped my eyes! I paid for it the next few days. The muscles around my eyes were so sore. I never tried it again.

Arana tried teaching me Tahitian dancing. I could get my hips going fast, but my shoulders wanted to go with them. You shouldn't move your shoulders at all. She had me put my hands on a wall to keep my shoulders still and said to just move my hips. I must confess I never did it very well.

I was a little better with the *poi* balls (which were about the size of a tennis ball and connected by a string). I held one in each hand and worked them up and down, trying not to have them strike each other. I also learned to play the ukulele. I learned something from each group. Their singing was especially beautiful.

I returned to Los Angeles to an empty nest. My son Chris had joined the Naval Air Corps in Florida. It was so much quieter at the house without him and his friends around. He did write regularly, thank goodness.

I didn't have too much time to mope around. Shortly after I got home, a scout for Sol Hurok, the impresario, went to Hawaii and saw the show. He liked it so much he booked it for the Hollywood Bowl. It was to be called *Festival Polynesia*. Since the Hollywood Bowl was much larger than the Polynesian Cultural Center, they imported at least twenty more Samoans from New Zealand. I went back to Hawaii to rehearse the show to fit it into the Bowl.

I began rehearsals to work the Samoans into the show. I was sitting up in the bleachers one night, holding a microphone and calling out directions. Incense was burning near my feet to keep the mosquitoes away. The Fijian leader, who had never been friendly, climbed the bleachers toward me. I wondered what it was all about. He sat down beside me.

"Are you Mormon?" he asked suddenly.

"No," I said.

"Good," he continued. "We come live with you."

It seems the Fijians were the only group of Polynesians that were not Mormon. They didn't feel comfortable living with Mormons in Hollywood because they liked their beer and Mormons wouldn't allow them to drink. I told the leader I didn't have enough bedrooms. He told me his group would stay in my garage. They wouldn't be any trouble at all. They would even serenade me every night. I told him I would have to think about it or some other polite excuse to put him off gently.

Before I had to tell him "No," I found out they had no choice. They had to stay with Mormon families so they could travel to and from the Bowl as a group. *Whew.*

This large group all flew to Los Angeles and moved in with their Mormon hosts. They had never been to the mainland before and we took them out to see the sights. They especially enjoyed a trip to Disneyland.

I had quite a few of them to my house for dinner on their night off. They were funny. If they felt like taking a nap they would fall asleep right in the middle of the floor. One girl told me I had so many pretty things. She had been in my bedroom looking through my dresser drawers!

They all flew back to Hawaii and that was the end of my Hawaiian adventures for awhile. It was a good introduction to working in other cultures.

METALECO

Periodically, an agent, Bob Vincent, would call me out of the blue. One such incident occurred in 1976.

"Miriam," he said, his voice brimming with enthusiasm, "I have a show for you in an exotic location. You'll never guess where!"

"It wouldn't be Hawaii, would it?" I asked.

I had guessed correctly. It was at the Honolulu Hilton.

They wanted the show to look part-Hawaiian and part-Las Vegas. It would feature a young Tongan man named Metaleco, who had a beautiful voice. I held an audition for pretty Hawaiian girls who could not only do the Hula, but dance Las Vegas-style (whatever that is). I chose eight.

The first half of the show was Hawaiian and girls wore traditional Hawaiian costumes. Then Metaleco sang a song that described his ambition of being a Las Vegas superstar. The second half of the show is a dream sequence. Metaleco appears as a Las Vegas star, dressed in a tuxedo and wearing a straw hat. I designed some flashy showgirl and dance costumes. Metaleco sang "Isn't She Lovely?" as these beautiful Hawaiian "showgirls" walked by.

We had a very successful opening and the show ran for six months. After it closed, the costumes and music were stored in Hawaii.

Several months later Bob Vincent called and said he heard the hotel was redoing our show. He wasn't seeing any money come in from it. He didn't know if they were doing our show or only a little piece. He asked me if I would fly over and see the show.

I checked into a hotel – not the Hilton. All afternoon I stayed cooped up in my room. I was afraid to go out for fear someone might see me. If they had, it would have given them time to change the show.

I felt like 007 that night as I went out in my sunglasses and wide-brimmed hat. I sat at the back of the room with my tape recorder. It was, indeed, the exact show I had done.

The next morning I flew back to Los Angeles and gave the tape to Bob. He had the headache of hiring lawyers and spending more money than he ever would have gotten back trying to settle this case. I don't think he ever got anything, but by then I was off and running on another job.

CHAPTER TEN

Putting the "Motion" in Motion Pictures

INGRID BERGMAN AND *CACTUS FLOWER*

I was a huge fan of Ingrid Bergman so I was excited when I got a call from Columbia Studios asking me to teach her how to dance for the movie *Cactus Flower*, based on the successful Broadway play. The movie was supposed to introduce Goldie Hawn to the world, although she was already well-known for her trademark laugh on *Rowan and Martin's Laugh-In*. Goldie would go on to win an Academy Award for Best Supporting Actress for her break-out role.

The people at Columbia told me Miss Bergman didn't want anyone to see her learn to dance. So, with my tape recorder and a cassette of "Proud Mary" under my arm I went to her bungalow at the Beverly Hills Hotel. My nervousness at meeting her was tempered by the knowledge that she was another Virgo.

I knocked on her door. There she stood, Ingrid Bergman, one of the goddesses of the silver screen, tastefully dressed but obviously ready to work. My anxiety instantly melted away. Ingrid couldn't have been more charming.

In her lovely accent she told me right away she was nervous. She even apologized that she didn't know how to dance. She went so far as to say she was sorry that she didn't want anyone to see her learn and that she made me come all the way to her bungalow. Little did she realize I would have gone to the moon to work with her.

The scene was to take place in a disco called The Slipped Disc. That gives you an idea of the kind of dancing that went on. Ingrid was to dance with a young man named Igor, played by Rick Lenz and then with a dentist, played by Walter Matthau. She had to talk to Walter while dancing with him.

The only mirror for us to watch ourselves was over the dresser. I set the cassette on top and started the tape rolling.

"Ingrid, just keep time with the music," I instructed. I had her bend her knees then straighten them. That was all. I wanted the accent to be on the straightening, but she kept emphasizing the squat.

I did the motion alongside her — putting the accent where I wanted it — and when she got the idea, I added head motions.

ING-RID-FINE-AL-LEE-SPOKE-AND-DANCED-AT-THE-SAME-TIME.

"While you're bending your knees," I offered, "let your head bob back and forth." Instead of letting her head move loosely, she pushed her chin up. It took some time with her imitating me and then, by golly, she got it! I figured that was good enough for a first lesson.

I met with her at her bungalow a couple of times after that initial visit. It wasn't long before she felt comfortable enough to move to the rehearsal hall at Columbia where we had the luxury of full-length mirrors.

A dance step called "The Temptation" was popular at the time so my assistant Toni Kaye and I taught it to her. In the movie she dances "The Uptight" and "The Boogaloo," and then teaches Walter "a new step" she named "The Dentist." Saying lines while dancing is one of the hardest things for an actor. It might sound simple, but try it some time. The first time Ingrid tried speaking her lines while dancing she spoke on the beat of the music. *She. Was. Speak. Ing. Like. This.* — It was funny! As Ingrid continued with her lines I put my hand over my mouth to keep from laughing out loud — I couldn't help myself. Ingrid caught me out of the corner of her eye. When she realized what she was doing, Ingrid started laughing, too.

"Let's go back to doing just the step," I suggested. "We'll add dialogue later." While we were dancing I said, "I'm getting hungry." She said she was hungry, too. I asked her what she wanted for lunch. As she rattled off suggestions I said, "Aha, you can dance and talk at the same time!"

She laughed. "You tricked me!" she said.

Off to lunch we went, feeling better about everything.

Our call-time for rehearsals was 9:00 a.m. One Monday morning I heard Ingrid running down the hall at about 9:05. She raced into the room out of breath, apologizing for being late. (I don't find many of the young actors and actresses today that conscientious.) Ingrid explained she had gone to San Francisco for the weekend to help Pia, her daughter, who had just moved. She had spent most of the weekend helping her line kitchen cabinets with paper. Imagine that!

Over the next several days Ingrid learned many more steps. By the day of the shoot, she was ready. The dance floor was crowded with professional dancers, including Goldie Hawn. Ingrid had to wear a mink stole in the scene. She twirls one end of it and wraps it around her waist while the young man holds the ends of it. Just before the call for "Action!" she looked to her chair and the stole was gone. She panicked and looked for it everywhere. Finally, Walter Matthau produced the stole. He had it stashed behind him. He loved to play tricks. I watched Ingrid perform and felt she deserved an A+. As the cameras rolled she came out with more wild abandonment than I had ever hoped for. What an actress!

Some years after that movie, I was invited to a ballet in New York. During intermission, my friend Howard Gilman of the Gilman Paper Mills introduced me to Ingrid's daughter, Isabella Rosellini. As we were heading backstage to meet the dancers, it occurred to me I had worked with Isabella's mother. I told her about our experience. Isabella said, "You're the lady she talked about. She showed us the steps you taught her. She had a really good time with you." (Let me tell you, that was really nice to hear!)

I also ran into Walter years after the film. He was cordial when I said "hello," but I could tell he didn't remember where we had met. A light bulb must have gone off, because a few minutes later he came up to me and said, "I have a story for you."

He said he was having dinner in Paris when Ingrid walked toward him. "She put out her hand and said, 'Hello, Walter, remember me? Ingrid Bergman.'"

JAN AND DEAN

William Jan Berry and Dean Ormsby Torrance were the popular 60's Surf Music group, Jan and Dean. They had such hits as "The Little Old Lady from Pasadena" when Paramount signed them to their first picture. The working title was "Easy Come, Easy Go," but we learned there would be nothing *easy* about this tragic filmmaking episode.

I was hired to stage Jan and Dean's numbers. I've never had a very good memory for names, but I had a particularly difficult time with Jan and Dean. My mind associates names with images. For some reason, Jan sounded like a good name for a blonde and Dean seemed like it should be for a brunette. However, the real Jan was a brunette and Dean was the blonde. I had to stop and think before I called either young man by name.

We began rehearsals at the studio. It was fun to work with Jan and Dean. They were so excited about being in their first movie. Jan was a real cutup. He would scare you to death by tripping on purpose at the top of a staircase and rolling down. He was so convincing he could have been a stunt man.

After we finished rehearsing our numbers, they began shooting the film on location. It wasn't a musical number, but for some reason I went along.

We were driven to a little railroad station in Chatsworth in the San Fernando Valley. We were going to shoot the last scene of the picture first. Why, I'll never know.

The cameras were mounted on a flatbed that was to be pushed by an engine. They began filming and I couldn't believe my eyes. They had Jan and Dean run down the tracks while this flatbed (pushed by a big engine) chased after them.

"Run faster!" the director kept yelling at Jan and Dean. They were jumping from tie to tie so they wouldn't twist an ankle. It seemed crazy to me, because if either fell he wouldn't have time to get out of the way of the oncoming train. I voiced my concern. I was told stunt men were running alongside and would help if Jan or Dean got into trouble.

"There's no way anyone could grab them off those rails in time," I thought to myself. The whole thing felt spooky. From my years in the film business I knew there were plenty of other tricks for getting this shot without actually having a train chase them. In spite of my concern, they got the shot they wanted. Then they went back to the starting point.

They had to shoot the reverse angle of an oncoming Super Chief train. When the film was cut together you would see the boys running down the tracks, then they'd look over their shoulders at this big train gaining speed from behind. The boys wanted to ride on the flatbed and watch the shoot because they weren't in it. The car was a little high for me to get up on.

"Come on, Miriam," Dean yelled. "We'll help you." Dean took one hand and Jan took the other. Up I went.

We rode backwards down the tracks as the camera filmed the approaching train, which was gaining on us.

"Can't it come any faster?" the director yelled into a walkie-talkie. The train already was bearing down fast enough to scare me. I was relieved when the director yelled "Cut! Let's do it again." I told Jan and Dean I thought it was dangerous. I suggested we get down. Of course, they didn't want to do that. A persistent fear kept gnawing at me.

"I want off," I said. Dean jumped off and helped me down. I told him again how dangerous I thought it was.

"As long as I'm off, I'll stay off," Dean said. The director, the first assistant, the script girl, the cameraman, his assistant and Jan all stayed on the flatbed.

Dean and I went to a shed so we would be out of the shot when the train went by. We sat on a bench and started talking. We heard the first train with the camera and crew start up and leave. Then we heard the Super Chief go by. After only about thirty seconds we heard a *CRASH!*

Some of the crew jumped into vehicles and went racing off. A few came back shortly and told us what happened: The Super Chief went racing up to the flatbed car. By the time the engineer realized he was gaining too fast it was too late for him to stop. The Super Chief hit the flatbed. The Super Chief was lower than the flatbed, so when it hit, it flipped up, over and off the tracks. Everyone on the flatbed went flying. I thought it would be a miracle if no one was killed.

"No sense in you trying to run all the way down the tracks," the crew told us. "They'll be on their way to the hospital before you get there."

Jan had cut his leg badly. He'd studied to be a doctor and knew by the way he was bleeding he would bleed to death. He ripped off his shirt and used it as a tourniquet on his leg. A Good Samaritan drove by and stopped to help. He drove Jan to the nearest hospital. Jan kept his foot elevated up on the dashboard.

It wasn't long after they left the scene that we heard sirens. We were driven back to Paramount. By now everyone at the studio had been informed about the accident. They didn't know who had been injured. When they saw us come in, there were lots of hugs and tears. I recognized one of the faces in the crowd. It was Gene, my ex-husband. He had heard about the accident on the news and stopped over to make sure I was all right.

The following day we learned the director was close to death. The first assistant had broken many bones. The script girl (I hesitate to say "girl" because she was a wonderful woman who had been a script girl for many years) was badly hurt and told she'd never walk again. The engineer of the Super Chief was thrown off the train and seriously hurt. Several other men on his train were also injured.

Before long, insurance companies were calling everyone involved to find out who was at fault. Was it the studio? The unit man? The director? I expected a call, but didn't get one, probably because my name wasn't on the call sheet.

The first day of shooting turned out to be the last day of shooting. The picture was never made.

Wasn't I lucky that I listened to that still, small voice inside my head that said, *"Get off"*?

ON *MURDERERS' ROW*
WITH DEAN MARTIN AND ANN-MARGRET

During that same time, I had the pleasure of working on *Murderer's Row* (1966). While putting this book together, I went to a video store in Santa Monica to rent the video to refresh my memory. I was a bit surprised when the sales clerk directed me to the "cult" section. It brought to mind scary images, like animal sacrifices. I was told that Matt Helm, the fictional lead character (a James Bond type), has a cult following.

Henry Levin directed two of the films in the Matt Helm series. I had worked with him before on *Honeymoon Hotel*. He was a nice, easygoing man, so I was delighted to work with him again.

Murderers' Row starred Dean Martin as Matt Helm, Karl Malden and Ann-Margret. I was told not to call her "Ann," as her actual name was Ann-Margret, two names hyphenated together, like my old friend Vera-Ellen. (We called her "Vera Dash Ellen.")

I had to devise a number where Dean and Ann-Margret play a scene in a discotheque. This was a bit tricky because the Matt Helm character was a detective, not a dancer. We wanted a lot of movement from Ann-Margret, because we didn't want the scene to feel static. I planned to incorporate such popular dances of the day as "The Swim," "The Monkey" and "The Pony." A reviewer referred to my creation as "chiropractic choreography."

I had three days to come up with an idea. I wracked my brain, but nothing was coming. Sometimes that happens. The day of the meeting arrived and still I had no idea what I'd do. As I was pulling into the parking lot at Columbia an idea started to form.

They say there are no original ideas, just fresh ways to present them. I remembered back to the "Liza" number in *The Jolson Story* where we sank a trampoline into one of the stairs. I figured I could steal from myself. What if we sink a small trampoline into the dance floor and we never see Ann-Margret's feet? Ann-Margret would be talking and going higher and higher and would force Dean to keep looking higher and higher. Finally, she would land on him, with her legs around his waist, while talking all the time. Dean only had to support her weight with one hand. Then she'd slide down his leg and he would pull her up. As I walked in to pitch my idea, I remember looking heavenward and asking, "What took so long?!"

Murderers' Row, *starring Ann-Margret (center), incorporated some of the popular dances of the day —* "The Swim," "The Monkey" and "The Pony."

The execs liked my idea, but they didn't think Dean would rehearse. He was busy, anyway, shooting for a few days. I started with a pianist, Ann-Margret and my assistant, Bob Street. Of course, Ann-Margret is a terrific dancer and so easy with whom to work.

When I was satisfied with what we'd done, I went to the stage where Dean was shooting. I asked him if he would come see if he liked what I had done. He agreed. When he came in, I actually introduced him to Ann-Margret: "Dean, meet your leading lady," I said. They got along right from the start. But then, Dean got along with everyone.

Ann-Margret showed the number to Dean with my assistant, Bob, as a "dance-in" in his place. Dean laughed and said it was "...the craziest thing he'd ever seen." He immediately wanted to learn it so I taught it to him. As he was leaving, he said, "Don't tell anyone I rehearsed. It will spoil my image. I'm only supposed to like booze and broads."

As I was leaving the lot, I saw Ann-Margret take Dean for a ride on her motorcycle around the lot.

When it came time to shoot the dance, I noticed Ann-Margret did something funny before every shot. I think she did it to get her energy up. She would scream, jump up and down and shake her hands.

She did her dance alongside Dean, her hips gyrating and with crazy hand movements like she was thumbing a ride. "It's like directing traffic," Dean said. "You're going to hurt yourself," he ad-libbed. Dean was just naturally funny, funnier than most comedians I knew. He kept the crew laughing all day. We all loved working with him.

In another disco scene, Ann-Margret wears a pin that contains an explosive device. Dean enters the club, sees the pin, rips it off Ann-Margret and throws it at the wall, where it explodes on impact. By the time they shot that scene, the dancers had been sent home. They wanted shadows of dancers on the wall when it blew up. I used myself and Bob Street to create the shadows.

I told Bob, "As soon as Dean throws the pin, duck down and cover your face."

The pyrotechnic crew connected an air hose to the wall and at the designated time they exploded a portion of it. It was made of drywall and I think they might have used a bit too much explosive. The wall blew up in a cloud of white dust.

The sound of the explosion reverberated throughout Columbia Studios. People came running to make sure everyone was okay. What they found were Bob and me and the whole crew, covered head to toe in white powder. The only way they could get it off was to use air hoses on us. (Note: this is another time that still, small voice paid off!)

Tony Bruno, my father's friend who owned the photography studio, called me after I completed *Murderers' Row*.

"Miriam," he told me, "your father is ill." I asked him how bad he was. He told me he wasn't expected to live.

I immediately flew to New York. Marge and Gower Champion were there and insisted I stay with them in their beautiful apartment overlooking Central Park.

I visited my father in the hospital. Daddy and I were talking and laughing. It was just like old times, until he motioned across the room.

"That man wants to give me a cigar," he said. I glanced over my shoulder to see a guy who was comatose. In spite of this momentary hallucination, my father's condition stabilized and I returned to Los Angeles.

I got a call a few months later. It was Tony again and he told me my father had died.

My father never lived in California, but he wanted to be buried there to be near my mother and me. We made arrangements to have his body shipped out to Los Angeles. The hearse met him at the airport and took him to a Jewish cemetery north of Los Angeles. We held a memorial service at the burial site. The Champions, always around to provide moral support, were by my side. My mother, however, was too upset to attend. I really think she always loved my father. It wasn't until months later she felt strong enough to go out to the graveside.

"You mean Danny's down there!" she gasped as she sunk to her knees. It struck me as an interesting reaction, something that would be good for a film. I would come to understand that reaction twenty-five years later, when I would go to Forest Lawn Memorial Park in Glendale to see Sammy Davis, Jr.'s grave. A carload of SHARE girls and I drove out to pay our respect. It was inconceivable to me that this huge talent could be gone and what was left was lying in a box, six feet under.

THE GREAT BANK ROBBERY
WITH GROOVY KIM AND CRAZY ZERO

I got to work with Kim Novak a second time on *The Great Bank Robbery* (1969). It had been thirteen years since *Picnic* and by now Kim had become a huge star. Her favorite word at this time was "grooooovy."

The picture also starred Zero Mostel. Kim and Zero played bank robbers disguised as evangelists. I was asked to come to the Music Department at Warner's to hear "The Rainbow Rider," a special number that my musical pals Sammy Cahn and Jimmy Van Heusen had written for the film. I stood at the baby grand piano with the director, Hal (called "Hy") Averback. Zero walked in and Hy introduced me. Much to my chagrin, Zero picked me up and sat me on top of the piano. He started kissing me all over my neck. I was screaming and everybody else was laughing. What a way to meet the star!

The Great Bank Robbery *publicity photo with Kim Novak and my protectors, the Mitchell Boys Choir.*

After that introduction I was careful not to get too close to Zero. I never knew when he might grab me; even his poor hairdresser stood as far away as possible while she combed his few hairs.

A scene was coming up where Kim would be trapped in a hot air balloon basket with Zero. When I asked Kim how she would deal with his horny teenaged boy behavior, she replied: "I guess, I'll just have to stand there and let him have a feel — then maybe it won't be fun for him."

Although the movie was a slapstick western, a big song and dance number took place in a church and involved Zero, Kim and twelve boys from the Mitchell Boys Choir. As we rehearsed, those dear little boys decided they would protect me when Zero would sneak up on me.

The idea of the number was to make a lot of noise in the church so no one could hear the tunneling under the bank. The boys banged pots and pans and Kim had a wonderful time beating a big bass drum — which she ended falling into at the "Finish." After the first take, Hy asked if I thought it was okay.

"No," I said. "Zero didn't do his cute little walk."

"We'll shoot it again," Hy said. "Go tell Zero what you want." So I did.

"Why should I make you look good?" Zero asked.

It was the most off-the-wall-thing I'd ever heard. He did have a crazy streak in him, but on the next take he did it right.

During rehearsals, the first assistant asked me to come to the back lot. Kim was shooting there and needed help. I went into her dressing room trailer. She wore this long evangelical "Sister Sarah" dress. She said they were going to shoot a scene for foreign release and she wanted me to help her with it. I had no idea what she was going to do. She turned away and when she turned back, she ripped open her dress which was a break-away. She was totally nude on top.

"What should I do now?" Kim asked, referring to her naked breasts. I was quite taken aback.

"You ought to put tassels on them," I offered facetiously.

"Groooovy!" Kim whooped. "I knew you'd come up with something." Cut to the next day. I get another call. Kim wants to talk to me so, again, I go out to her trailer. I find Kim there with her dresser. She did the same startling turn and, lo and behold, there were tassels!

"*Now* what shall I do?" Kim asked.

Having never twirled tassels myself, I told her about a woman named Carrie Finnell who was well-known for tassel twirling. She could just stand there and make the tassels twirl, so I figured it had something to do with muscle control.

I wondered if they would be set in motion if Kim made a body movement. I asked Kim to make a body movement that might cause them to go around in circles. Kim followed my instructions and, by golly, those tassels started to twirl. We all started laughing. Kim kept practicing. She got real good and some kind of centrifugal force took over because one of the tassels reversed. Now they were twirling in opposite directions. We were laughing, bordering on hysterics.

"You've come a long way, baby," I managed to get out between peels of laughter, remembering how shy she had been on *Picnic*. We were laughing so hard her dressing trailer began rocking.

"What in God's name were you doing in there?" everyone asked when we came out.

I couldn't wait to update my resume: Tassel Twirling!

MY THIRD TIME WITH KIM IN *THIRD GIRL FROM THE LEFT*

I was reunited with Kim for the third-and-last time in 1973 when I got a call from my director friend, Dick Quine. He was doing *Third Girl from the Left*, a made-for-television movie which was to star Kim and Tony Curtis. Kim's character was the "third girl from the left" in a nightclub chorus. Because Kim is a tall, leggy girl I had to hire other tall, leggy girls to dance alongside her.

She had done some dancing since the last time we worked together and had developed rhythm. As we rehearsed I was surprised by how well Kim danced and how high she kicked.

Several days into rehearsal, I got a call from Dick. "I'm quitting the picture," he told me. "Creative differences." But he assured me it wouldn't affect my job.

The "creative differences" had to do with Andre Previn's ex-wife, Dory, who had written some of the music for the movie. They postponed the shooting for a few days. All of a sudden we had a new director, Peter Medak. He was terribly British. He did a lovely job and we finished that film. But, I missed Dick.

Coincidentally, this TV film was produced by Hugh Hefner and Playboy Productions. Little did I know that my future would include a closer look at Mr. Hefner!

IT AIN'T OVER TILL THE FAT MAN DANCES

I got the opportunity to work with Luciano Pavarotti, the opera singer, on his first (and only) picture, *Yes, Giorgio* (1982). In the movie, his character asks the musicians in a restaurant to play romantic music as he dances with Kathryn Harrold, his leading lady. Everyone was concerned about the romantic dancing because of his weight. They thought he might not be able to dance cheek-to-cheek.

The director wanted to see how the dancing would work, so he asked me to come to the set to work with Mr. Pavarotti. When I got to the studio I ran into a hairdresser I had worked with in the past. She

On the set of Yes, Giorgio *with Luciano Pavarotti.*

was working on this picture, too. "Don't be surprised," she said laughingly, "when Pavarotti says 'in my opinion'." Apparently it was an expression he used a lot.

The hairdresser and I walked together to the sound stage where everyone had gathered. Most men are a bit inhibited when a girl has to teach him to dance, so to break the ice I thought we'd have a little conversation first. Mr. Pavarotti was charming. We talked for ten or fifteen minutes and when I felt he was relaxed I said, "Why don't we put on the music and we'll just dance. You lead me."

I was curious to see what came naturally. So was the director, who stood nearby. When the music started, Mr. Pavarotti pulled me into him. I couldn't believe it. It was like being pulled into a giant feather-down pillow. He was very nimble and danced me all across the floor. And there we were, dancing cheek-to-cheek. I glanced at the director and could almost hear a sigh of relief. We spent another hour together. I taught him a few ballroom steps and he dipped me into a back bend.

The director said, "We'd better start running the dialogue simultaneously." As soon as Mr. Pavarotti started the dialogue he swayed back and forth, but the director wanted it to be a bit fancier. We made two or three attempts then Mr. Pavarotti stopped cold.

"In my opinion," he began, "my character would not be dancing all over the place while speaking this romantic dialogue." I caught the eye of the hairdresser and had to bite my tongue to keep from laughing.

When it was time to shoot the scene, he still swayed during his dialogue, but the director made him keep doing the scene until he got the shot he wanted. In truth, I felt a bit sorry for Mr. Pavarotti. English didn't come easily and it must have been hard for him to think of all those words and remember his feet at the same time.

ZIEGFELD: THE MAN AND HIS WOMEN

Although fewer movie musicals were being made by the major studios because of poor box office results, one of the highlights of my career came in a made-for-television musical film for NBC called *Ziegfeld: The Man and His Women*, produced by Mike Frankovitch. I staged twelve numbers and also played the role of "The Choreographer."

I met with Buzz Kulik, the director, in November of 1977. Since this was a television production, we didn't have a large budget, but they wanted it to *look* like a major movie. I was told the emphasis of the movie was not on dancing: it was on the story. I didn't have to stage full numbers and I shouldn't be disappointed if, in the middle of a number, they cut away to a dramatic scene.

Marilyn Miller was one of the biggest stars in The Ziegfeld Follies. She was known as "The Darling of Broadway" and was primarily a toe dancer. Her part hadn't been cast yet. Alyson Reed, a young dancer, came and auditioned and I thought she was terrific. Based on my recommendations, Mike and Buzz considered her, but also auditioned other girls.

They selected Pamela Peadon, a girl who was appearing in *A Chorus Line* and had more acting experience. They felt because the role included dialogue, they couldn't spend as much time perfecting scenes. I cast Alyson in the dance ensemble, hired her to be in Donald O'Connor's nightclub act and eventually cast her in a "Dream Ballet" in Blake Edwards' smash hit, *10*. She "played" Bo Derek, dancing with Dudley Moore on the beach in Acapulco. Alyson went on to play the role of "Cassie" on Broadway and in the film version of *A Chorus Line*, and was cast by Blake Edwards as one of the female leads in his comedy, *Skin Deep*. She eventually played the role of Marilyn Monroe on Broadway. Coincidentally, Norma Jean Baker was renamed "*Marilyn* Monroe" after Marilyn Miller, that "Darling of Broadway." Alyson currently is the flamboyant Drama Teacher in the successful *High School Musical* Disney film series. It is reaffirming to know that my "hunches" were right.

I was given a list of song titles from Ziegfeld shows and decided to use Irving Berlin's "A Pretty Girl is Like a Melody." I wanted to do it with only "Marilyn," instead of the usual way with many showgirls. The number started in a rehearsal hall and I wanted "Marilyn" surrounded by a semicircle of mirrors.

"You can't shoot into mirrors because the camera will show," I was told at the initial meeting. I talked to Gerald "Jerry" Finnerman, the cinematographer. Jerry thought he could do it, but the stage, camera and anyone onstage would have to be draped in black, which meant more money.

I'm standing in white on the far left, during auditions. Seated at the table, 3rd from left is Ziegfeld's daughter Patricia Stephenson, Mike Frankovitch the producer and, standing behind him, director Buzz Kulik.

As the number opens, a ballet teacher is coaching one of his pupils. This becomes a dream sequence where he sings "A Pretty Girl is Like a Melody" and all the mirrors start moving. We did this by putting them on casters and having male dancers move them into place from behind. "Marilyn" dances in and out of the mirrors as they move, then she disappears.

As the mirrors move offstage she reappears at the top of the stairs in a tutu. When she gets down to stage level she goes into a big dance routine. At the end, the mirrors close in on her, she disappears again, and when the mirrors open up she's in her practice clothes at the barre. The final words to the song are:

> *"She may leave you and then, come back again,*
> *A pretty girl is just like a pretty tune."*

In another number I needed to create for "Marilyn" in the story, she had just been told that her husband was killed in an automobile accident. Ziegfeld makes her go on stage to do her number, a dramatic moment. I tried coming up with ideas for the music for this number, but I was really stumped.

One day as I was sitting alone in my office, I looked up at a picture that had been hanging there all the time. I had never really looked at it before. It was a picture of a girl standing with her arms out and huge butterfly wings. She wore a tiny, wispy chiffon dress. Lo and behold, I found a song called "Poor Butterfly" in the catalogue

Valerie Perrine, as Lillian Lorraine, in the film's biggest dance number.

of songs from Ziegfeld productions. Wasn't that the perfect number for this spot?!

Pamela Peadon danced it beautifully. On the close-ups you could see tears stream down her cheeks. I stole the ending from *Swan Lake*. In that, the dying swan goes to one knee, sits on that leg and her wings slowly flutter to cover her face and her body.

Valerie Perrine was cast as Lillian Lorraine, one of the leading female roles who ended up having the film's biggest dance number. Valerie told me she had been a Vegas showgirl and could walk down stairs without looking, but even so, she wasn't a dancer.

In the film, the show's director asks Ziegfeld, "What should we do with her, she can't sing, can't dance, can't even act!"

Ziegfeld's answer, "Make her a *star!*"

Valerie is a very big girl. What came out of her the first time we heard her sing was a tiny voice. She kind of "talk/sang." There was discussion about using someone else's voice, but they decided it would be funnier if they used Valerie's real voice.

I had to dream up a lot of ways to camouflage the fact that Valerie was not a trained dancer. Have I mentioned yet that I love balloons? They're colorful, festive and cheap, and they cover up a lot of sins. I wanted pillars of balloons that would start as a clump on the floor and rise up to become a pillar. During one of our weekly meetings I asked if I could have hundreds of balloons. Buzz agreed. But once I started thinking about balloons I couldn't stop.

I wanted a clear plastic cube, about ten feet by ten, at the top of a huge staircase. It would be filled with balloons. The front had a sliding panel that would slide open and out would pop Valerie. She would descend the stairs with balloons spilling out around her. I also had Valerie dance with a huge balloon. It was actually a weather balloon painted silver. As she threw it up in the air it was pulled off camera by an invisible wire.

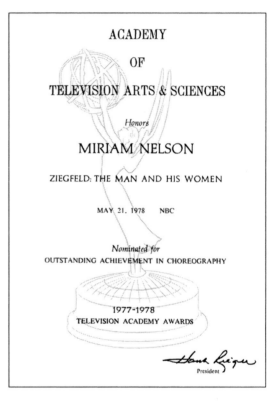

ACADEMY

OF

TELEVISION ARTS & SCIENCES

Honors

MIRIAM NELSON

ZIEGFELD: THE MAN AND HIS WOMEN

MAY 21, 1978   NBC

Nominated for
OUTSTANDING ACHIEVEMENT IN CHOREOGRAPHY

1977-1978
TELEVISION ACADEMY AWARDS

President

I kept coming up with new ways to use balloons. It seemed as though at each subsequent meeting I was pleading for more balloons. The balloons became a running joke during the making of this movie.

"You and your damn balloons," Buzz would say.

I experimented by tying balloons to a ribbon to make a balloon boa. It worked. At one point I had all the girls — twelve in all — wear balloon boas. At the end of the number, Valerie stood at the bottom of the stairs while the girls attach their balloon boas to her back. It became a balloon train. (We actually had a cut where we attached more balloon boas than you saw the girls attach. We used a total of 3,000 balloons on Valerie's gown!) When Valerie walked up to the top of the staircase, she stepped onto a platform that lifted her even higher. The camera pulled back to a long shot of the staircase covered in a train of balloons.

The last shot of the picture was a close-up. After the music ended, Buzz yelled "*Cut!*" Valerie, standing atop the platform surrounded by balloons, was so excited about the number she let out a squeal. "I feel like a fucking star!" she yelled.

My cheap little balloon trick turned out to be the most expensive in the show. But it made for terrific still shots. A picture of Valerie and all her balloons was chosen for the cover of *TV Guide* the week the movie was telecast. Each of my twelve numbers made it into the final movie in their entirety.

It was a big day for me when I got the call that I had been nominated for an Emmy for "Outstanding Achievement in Choreography." I was nominated along with George Balanchine and Alexandra Danilova, who had done *New York City Ballet: Coppelia Live from Lincoln Center.* But we all lost to Ron Field, for *Ben Vereen — His Roots.* Oh, well, at least I was in good company!

CHAPTER ELEVEN

Commercials = Residuals

As I mentioned earlier, the career of an actor/dancer/choreographer/director/producer is made up of bits and pieces. One thing I did in between TV and film commitments was to make commercials. I started making commercials in the late 1950s, primarily as a choreographer, but, once in a while, I went to casting calls as an actress. If a commercial is successful and goes national, it pays high residuals.

I remember making a commercial for Joy soap. Three girls looked up at a bottle of Joy with adoring faces. One girl looked so blissful I wanted the other two to match her attitude.

"What are you thinking about?" I asked the girl.

"The beachfront property I'm going to buy with the money I'm making from this commercial," she said.

I sometimes got an acting part even when I wasn't trying. I remember spending the good part of a day auditioning girls for a cereal commercial. I taught them to dance down the aisle of a supermarket, pushing a cart. I did this with several different girls as the sponsors watched. At the end of the day they pulled me aside with their decision.

"We've all agreed on the girl we want," they said.

"Who?" I asked.

"*You!*"

I appeared in commercials for Gino's Pizza, McDonald's, Puffs, Buster Brown shoes, Doublemint gum, Chevron and so many more that I've lost track. Oddly enough, I have never received residual for my choreography and staging in films or television, but I have (and continue to) receive them as an "Actress."

Go figure!

There were times that I worked with unknown actors who were just beginning their careers and went on to become successful. Once I was called in to stage a hand cream commercial for a girl who had to do a little dance around a big bed. We spent a day rehearsing her swinging around the bedpost. In 1975, I worked with this same girl. By then she had her own series called *Police Woman.* The unknown girl, of course, was Angie Dickinson.

Before Ted Danson did *Cheers* and became a movie star he was "The Aramis Man." We shot one of the commercials at a mansion in Pasadena. Aramis gave away an umbrella with every purchase so they wanted to put an umbrella in the commercial.

Ted and a pretty girl danced on the patio and, as he bent her backward, it started to rain. The rain was created by men on the roof who sprayed them with water. A man under the camera handed Ted an umbrella and he continued dancing under it with his partner.

Since Ted was not a dancer I made up things he could do such as step up on a bench and jump off. The sponsor wasn't happy with the girl's hair so she was sent inside to have it fixed. In the meantime, I was asked to take her place so the cameraman could keep rehearsing the shot. All of a sudden I felt raindrops on my head even though the umbrella was up. Of course, it was leaking. At the end of the rehearsal I was given a replacement umbrella to use in the actual shoot. You can bet it was tested first.

David Nelson, one of the sons of Ozzie and Harriet, directed many commercials. His wife, Yvonne, was a member of SHARE. David asked me if I would audition as a tap dancer for a commercial for The Great American Bank. When I arrived at the audition about fifteen people were waiting. I knew a few of them. They were all good tap dancers. When I finally got inside, six or seven people sat at a long table, including the choreographer who had already been hired. I didn't know her, but she was in the Broadway company of *A Chorus Line,* so I assumed she could tap.

"Who can do double wings?" the choreographer asked. Double wings are both feet flying out to the sides at the same time. Only a couple of us raised our hands. It struck me funny to be doing double wings on an audition for a bank commercial. A time-step, yes, but *not* double wings. They played music and I stepped out to do the double wings.

"Do you want it to look easy?" I asked facetiously and did the feet. "Or do you want it to look hard?" and I added my flailing arms. It was pretty silly. The people who were auditioning us began to laugh. Four were chosen, including me. We started rehearsals the following day. Once our group gathered, our choreographer admitted she didn't tap well. We dancers started making up our own routines. We did our own solos and the choreographer kind of put them together.

We started rehearsing the commercial. Unlike most films, where you record the sounds of taps after filming, we were putting them in before. Later in the day the choreographer started putting her hair in curlers. She sat in front of the mirror putting on her eye makeup. It got close to the time to record the tap sounds and she kept checking her watch. She wasn't nervous about our commercial; she told us she was auditioning for another commercial and was afraid she might be late.

"Have you ever had to record taps?" she asked me. I wanted to laugh. She was clueless. I told her I had recorded, at least a time or two. Even with my sarcastic tone she didn't get it.

"If I have to leave before they get here for the recording, would you supervise it?" I guess it didn't occur to her David would show up, too. I agreed. She left and shortly thereafter the recording crew arrived.

"Where's the choreographer?" David asked when he showed up a while later. We said she had an appointment. When he saw the way we dancers were working together, he told me, "If I need a choreographer again, you can be sure you'll get it."

CHAPTER TWELVE

A TV Potpourri

BOB HOPE CHRYSLER THEATER
WITH ELKE SOMMER

Seated at a table in a fancy restaurant, I was scanning each woman who arrived, wondering if she might be Kate Drain Lawson, whom I had agreed to meet for lunch. Kate was the costume designer for *Bob Hope Chrysler Theater* at NBC and we were going to discuss Elke Sommer's upcoming appearance.

One would think of a costume designer as looking very chic. Several well-dressed women came and were seated, without paying any attention to me. A woman walked in dressed in a turban and cotton muumuu that flowed to the floor. It was the late Sixties and women wore pretty wild outfits, but even so, this was out there. I totally dismissed her as my lunch date, but she worked her way toward me.

"Are you Miriam Nelson?" she asked.

"Yes, I am."

"Nice to meet you," she continued as she sat down across from me. "I'm Kate Drain Lawson."

I couldn't believe it. *This* was the costume designer? We looked over the menus, ordered lunch and began to talk about the show. Kate turned out to be very sweet.

I had already met with Elke and the producers. Elke could sing in many languages so we did "Willkommen" from *Cabaret*. Elke asked me to come to her house to look at some things she had in her closet. She had a beautiful, white satin evening slip cut on the bias that caught my eye. I asked her what she thought about wearing something like that. To my surprise she stripped bare revealing, I must say, a terrific body. She put on the slip and I thought it worked well because she could use a feathered boa or a fur jacket, etc. over it. Kate liked the idea of the satin slip for Elke, but not in white. It wouldn't be good for television. So she had a copy made in mauve.

The show was performed at the Pauley Pavilion, a basketball court at UCLA that was brand, spanking new. NBC built a stage in the middle of the court. Five cameras were situated around the stage. They hung all the lights on pipes above the stage so it could be lit well from all angles. The day before we were to shoot we went in for a rehearsal. The rehearsal went well and we all left feeling good about the show.

We came in the next morning and, to our chagrin, one of the pipes holding the lights had broken. All the lights had crashed onto the floor. That brand new floor of the UCLA basketball court was ruined. There was a wild race to get new lights and have them hung before show time. After the show, NBC put down a new floor. God knows what it must have cost.

MORE *HOPE* — WITH BARBARA EDEN

The show was so successful Hope decided to do his next show from Madison Square Garden, which was opening on February 11, 1968. This time I was going to stage a number for Barbara Eden.

I researched the original Madison Square Garden because I thought I might be able to use its history in the number. I learned many things happened there, including tennis matches, dog shows, circuses and political rallies. I thought it would be fun for Barbara to sing about how she would like to have been involved in all these fun happenings. I was given permission to ask Billy Barnes to write special material. As always, Billy did a terrific job.

I had Barbara (in dance form) play tennis opposite twelve guys. Barbara was the ringmaster and the fellows were prancing horses, like in a circus. During the dog show segment, Barbara wore a fur jacket and she had an Afghan on a leash to match. The number climaxed in a scene where Barbara is the center of a political rally. She was being elected President of the United States!

We all flew to New York in the middle of winter for this exciting event. As we rehearsed in a hotel ballroom secured for us by NBC, a blizzard raged outside. When we finished we stepped outside for a taxi to take us to our hotel but there were no taxis in sight.

Our hotel was several blocks away, but we started walking, figuring we'd see a taxi along the way. We carried our tape recorders and rehearsal clothes. We didn't have hats or gloves so we were freezing! There wasn't a single taxi on the streets and when we realized we wouldn't be getting one, we ducked into a little store and bought hats and gloves. We walked the entire way to the hotel.

Madison Square Garden was barely finished by show time. Mayor Lindsay and every other notable New Yorker came out in their best "bib and tucker" to see Bob Hope and Bing Crosby do one of their "road songs." The "road songs" came out of Bob and Bing's series of "Road" movies, such as *Road to Morocco, Singapore, Zanzibar, Bali, Hong Kong*, etc.

Lucky guests also were treated to Jack Jones, Phyllis Diller, Pearl Bailey and a host of other singers and dancers. There was a glamorous party after the show. I was glad to see Bing again. He told me he remembered having a good time at my party years before, when I was a chorus girl at Paramount.

When I got back to Los Angeles, my son, Chris, and his girlfriend, Denise, were planning their marriage. (I can't remember if Chris and Denise had "gone steady" as

I had with my beaus. Maybe the tradition had died by this time but I do know they dated for quite a few years.) I adored Denise and was thrilled that she and Chris were getting married. The ceremony was held at a big Catholic Church in the Valley on May 18, 1968. They would give me my first grandchild, Christian, born one year later. Two more boys, Joshua and Matthew, would follow.

Chris with his three sons, Christian, Matthew and Josh.

Bob Hope did another show with Barbara Eden at the NBC studio in Hollywood and I had to come up with a concept for a musical number for Barbara. I kept hearing "Don't Tell Mama" from "Cabaret." I thought, "What if Barbara becomes a stripper and tells the story of what led up to it?"

First, we showed her as a teenager. The dancers showed Barbara their favorite record albums and she picked them up and used them as fans. Then we showed her graduating in cap and gown. While the dancers threw their caps in the air, Barbara held hers in front of her bosom and swung the cap's tassel around. We dissolved through to a feather boa with a tassel on it. Barbara started down the runway as a stripper. She was handed fans as she headed down the runway, then would begin singing, "Don't Tell Mama." I asked Billy Barnes to write the special material lyrics. As always, he did a fantastic job.

THE *REAL* LANA TURNER

At a break during rehearsals for Bob's show, we started playing "If you could be anybody, who would you want to be?" I said "Lana Turner." I thought she was so beautiful. Larry Billman, who was assisting me and dancing with Barbara, never forgot I said that. Once he made me a funny book with pictures cut out of old movie

Which one is the real *Lana Turner?*

magazines. One picture was the famous pose from *The Postman Always Rings Twice* with Lana in white shirt, white shorts and a white turban on her head. His caption read, "Miriam in rehearsal togs." Sometimes he would call me "Lana."

Well, years later, Lana was being honored at The Thalians Ball (another wonderful Hollywood group) and I choreographed the opening number for them. A photographer was there taking pictures of all the celebrities. I told him I would love to have my picture taken with Lana Turner. He said there would be time after the show. He waited for the right moment when Lana was free to take me over and introduce me to her.

"Lana, this is Miriam Nelson, the girl who choreographed the opening of the show for you." She was very sweet and thanked me. My friend said, "Let me get a picture of the two of you together." Well, when he gave me the picture, I sent a copy of it to my friend Larry with the caption, "Which one is the *real* Lana Turner?"

Larry has also nicknamed me "Toots"…which makes me giggle.

DANCING WITH OSCAR

In 1970, Mike Frankovich called and asked me to choreograph one of the nominated songs for the 42nd Annual Academy Awards. I had worked for Mike on several movies he produced at Columbia, the most recent being *Cactus Flower*.

I met Mike and his creative staff and we listened to the five nominated songs so I could pick one for which to create a dance. I chose "Raindrops Keep Falling on My Head" from *Butch Cassidy and the Sundance Kid.* Someone suggested we use Gene Kelly, Debbie Reynolds and Donald O'Connor and dress them in yellow slickers, à la *Singin' in the Rain*. We made phone calls, but Gene and Donald weren't available, so we scrubbed that idea.

I hadn't seen *Butch Cassidy and the Sundance Kid*, so I figured I had better go watch it. I liked the sound of B.J. Thomas's voice and, as I sat there watching, I searched for ideas. As soon as I saw Paul Newman showing off on a bicycle as B.J. sang the nominated song, I knew what I wanted.

"*That's it!*" I thought. I envisioned several Butch Cassidys on bicycles riding around with girls.

I called Mike's office to see if the secretary could get me a picture of B.J. and she did. B.J. was very good-looking, which made me want to use him. This turned out to be a big break in his career. He was still relatively unknown and I knew I wouldn't have to feature him in the number as I would if he were an established star. I called Mike. "Don't hire anyone or come up with any ideas until you hear about mine."

Mike and I met and I told him what I envisioned.

"How many bicycles do you want?" Mike asked.

"How many can you afford?" I answered.

"Will twelve be enough?" Mike wanted to know. The prop man gave me the name of a man who owned vintage bicycles, which I wanted because *Butch Cassidy* was a period picture. I called him and he said to come over. I drove to his home in Hollywood and he opened a garage filled with bicycles of all styles and ages. Bicycles were even hanging from the ceiling.

He showed me a few funny bikes like a high-wheeler, a bicycle built-for-two and one with a back wheel that was higher than the front so it went up and down when you rode it. Of course, I had to find a way to use all these wonderful bikes. He also had a unicycle. I asked him if he could show me how it worked. He got on it in front of his house and rode a few yards and fell over! Then he got back on and fell again.

"I'm a little out of practice," he told me. "But I'll work on it." Then he showed me something I'd never seen.

"How would you like to go for a ride on a bicycle built-for-three?" I got in the middle seat between his son and him and we pedaled up and down several streets in Hollywood. I must say we did get a lot of attention!

I wanted young, energetic dancers who were also daredevils because I envisioned them doing crazy stunts on those bicycles. I had seen a fabulous new ballet company called The Burch Mann Dancers and, for some reason, images of their youthful and athletic "Americana" dancing stuck in my brain. I hired twelve couples from the dance troupe. I wanted one girl to stand on the back of a bike in an arabesque, put her hands on the boy's shoulders and sail across the stage. The Prop Department anchored little stands to the bikes. I wanted some girls to be in a back bend across the center of the bicycles and some to ride the handlebars. We experimented with all kinds of craziness until I could see the variations that were possible.

Columbia opened a wall so I could have two full sound stages on which to rehearse and they constructed ramps for the bikes. The bicycle man delivered the bikes and stayed with us, practicing the unicycle behind a partition. Every once in a while we heard a *crash!* They marked the floor off to the exact dimensions of the stage at The Dorothy Chandler Pavilion. The orchestra would be in a pit and a ramp would go out over the orchestra. I had visions of the unicycle riding out on that ramp, turning around and going back up on the stage. And then I heard a *kerplunk* and decided I didn't want him falling over into the orchestra pit for fear of endangering the musicians. So I pushed the thought aside.

My usual rehearsal pianist wasn't available, so Elmer Bernstein, the conductor, suggested a kid visiting from New York who he thought had a lot of talent. If I didn't like him he would get me another. The pianist was terrific! His name was Marvin Hamlisch.

Marvin asked if he could see the entire score from the movie. Marvin found some wonderful musical moments that were in the movie but not in the song. He wanted to incorporate them in our number. Until then, to my knowledge, no one had ever played anything other than the song exactly as written.

"I wonder if we'll get in trouble if we use them?" I asked. It wasn't so much a question as it was a caution. He was a young, likeable pianist with a rosy future and I didn't want him to damage it.

"Let's do it anyway," Marvin said. I'm glad we did because what he created was wonderful. Curiously, no one ever mentioned it.

B.J. would open the number. He'd enter wearing Western garb and shoot a gun. The first time we tried it, the gun made so much noise it blew out his microphone so the prop man put in half the amount of powder and then had a few other microphones positioned so he could replace it, if needed. B.J. sang the first chorus alone and I had him walk out on the ramp and sit on some stairs close to the audience. Toward the end of the first chorus he would go back up on the stage.

At the conclusion of B.J.'s song, I had bicycles come across the stage from different directions. The bicycles, after they crossed offstage, would have to whip around so they could go back on. As you can imagine there was a lot of activity offstage. Some bicycles would go up the ramp and come sailing down and across onstage. I kept telling the male dancers not to come too close to the edge of the stage because they could end up in the orchestra pit, scaring the girls.

At one point I had all the bikes come on at the same time and crash in the middle of the stage. The girls got up and went into a dance and the boys took the bikes upstage, left them there and came down to the join the girls. At the end, the girls do a big step while the boys got the bikes, came down through the girls and reared them up like horses. The girls jump on the boy's backs and — *TA-DA* — that was the end of the routine.

I had Marvin over to dinner many times. He was new in California and didn't know many people. Already at this tender age he had an ulcer. I poached chicken for him, made mashed potatoes, and served Jell-O® pudding.

One night my step-daughter Missy had a girlfriend over. They wanted to do a show for us. They went into the den with Marvin and closed the door. We could hear him playing the piano and Missy and her friend singing. Marvin was great with the girls. He had been a social director in the Catskills where he had organized many shows. They finally came out and did their show for Jack and me.

The day of the Academy Awards show was fast approaching so we moved rehearsals to The Dorothy Chandler Pavilion in downtown Los Angeles. It excited me to hear the music played for the first time by that wonderful orchestra. The boys did come dangerously close to the pit many times, scaring us all.

One of the dancers, Gary Morgan, had worked for me before. He was a good acrobat. By now I had decided to try him out on that unicycle (you just *knew* I had

Top: On stage at the Academy Awards, 1970. Bottom: Finale of the number "Raindrops Keep Falling on My Head."

to do it!) Gary learned to ride the unicycle immediately but I didn't have him ride out onto the ramp over the pit. There are limits, after all.

The show was being broadcast live, just like my early days in television. I got that funny feeling in the pit of my stomach when I heard the music start. B.J. went out shooting his gun and nothing disastrous happened. The dancers performed the number and it all went flawlessly.

After the applause, B.J. came back out and started singing the end of the song. I had a little boy come across on a tricycle. He was also wearing a Butch Cassidy outfit and derby hat. He pretended to have a gun and went *"Bang, Bang, Bang,"* at B.J. The boy was to make his exit by going up a ramp and off into the distance. He had done it perfectly in rehearsals until the last time. He made it up halfway then slid back down. His father came up apologizing and said he would rehearse him. But the boy got such a laugh from the dancers I decided to leave it in. At show time he did get a laugh. I let him have a second shot at it. This time he made it up and over.

In 1974, Jack, Missy and I were watching the Academy Awards. The phone rang. It was Missy's friend. "Missy, are you watching the Academy Awards?" she asked. "Our piano player just won the award!" Actually Marvin won *three* Oscars that year, one for *The Sting* and two for *The Way We Were*.

That would be just the beginning of Marvin's multi-award-winning career.

The second time I worked on an Academy Awards show was 1978, the year *The Deer Hunter* won for best picture. I was hired to stage a special number called "Oscar's Only Human," featuring songs that became standards but hadn't been nominated, like "New York, New York," "Singin' in the Rain" and "On the Good Ship Lollipop."

Steve Lawrence and Sammy Davis, Jr. were going to sing the number. For my money, Steve and Sammy had such terrific voices they could have sung without moving, but I went in and did my thing. When the music cried for some movement, I would have them sway or walk them across the stage. The movements they did were minimal.

The day of the show we were given an early call to rehearse on stage with the cameras. They weren't ready for us when we got to the Dorothy Chandler Pavilion, so a girl took us to a room upstairs with rolls and coffee. She said she'd be back to get us when it was our time. Then she disappeared.

Steve, Sammy and I sat there talking. Steve was his usual funny self, maybe even more so. After a while the girl popped back and let us know it wouldn't be much longer. We sat there for well over an hour before the girl came back and took us down. Sammy said if Steve hadn't been so funny he might have gone downstairs and stamped his feet a bit. I was very proud of Steve and Sammy who, of course, did top-drawer performances. The audience loved the number.

The crew, who can be seen by the audience like the cameramen, the stage managers and spotlight men, had to wear tuxedos, which I think is very classy. To this day, I have never done a show where a stagehand wasn't dressed properly if he came on stage. I hate seeing him come out in a T-shirt, especially if he has a big stomach!

The general public would get a kick out of seeing what goes on before the Academy Awards show, because they have stand-ins for the presenters. They come out holding the Oscar, then announce a fake winner. They have pictures of different stars on the seats so the cameras can cut to the picture of the person. After rehearsals a lot of us had fun having our pictures taken with that Oscar. And yes, Oscar is heavy!

Come show time, I'm glad I'm backstage. I don't relish sitting all those hours in a formal. It's much more fun mingling backstage with the stars.

Fred Astaire did a number on this show. We had a nice visit which pleased me. Fred was shy. I guess he felt easier talking "one dancer to another."

"How's Gene?" Fred asked.

"Fine," I said.

"What's he doing?" he wanted to know. I told Fred that Gene was working on a movie and that was the end of that. Fred came over later that night. He acted embarrassed.

"Why didn't you tell me you and Gene divorced years ago?" he asked.

"I thought the entire world knew," I told him.

FRED ASTAIRE AND THE FUTURE OF DANCE

Every time I got a call to do *Battlestar Galactica* I would think, "Oh, Lordy, what will I do this time?" It's one thing to do a dance that has already been done, but its another to come up with something from the future. It takes a little doing.

I wracked my brain to come up with something that looked futuristic. It got so everything I saw made me think, "Would that be an idea for a number?" I saw a garden hose and thought that if it had lights, I could use it for a number. I snaked the hose over the floor. As the couple danced, the guy would pick up part of it and put it over the girl's head or around her waist. Or they could lean into it or away from it. You get the idea. Another time I found pillars on the back lot that were about three feet tall. I used them in a number called "Energizer Dance." If someone touched a pillar, they would become energized and do a spastic movement.

On this episode in 1979, I got a pleasant, if not intimidating, surprise. Fred Astaire was going to play a villain on the show! His grandchildren, John and Johanna, had asked, "Grandpa, if you're a movie star, why aren't you on *Battlestar Galactica*? It was their favorite TV show, so he asked his agent to phone and see if he could get a guest-star spot on the show. You can imagine how surprised the producers were!

In the scene I was to stage, Fred had some dialogue with my dear friend Anne Jeffreys while dancing in a spaceship disco. Fred was concerned that if he was on a dance floor, people would expect him to perform a musical number and felt it would diminish his villainous character. We decided to film him from the waist up and surround him with other dancers. I made up a crazy hand dance, a variation of patty-cake that included a few turns. It was pretty simple stuff. The morning we shot the director asked me to demonstrate the routine for Mr. Astaire. I've done plenty of dancing in my life but this was mostly hand movements, so I held my breath. Fred Astaire was a legend. I don't think I breathed the entire time I showed him the routine.

"That's fine," Fred said. "Would you teach it to me?"

Between shots I had the wonderful opportunity to sit and talk with him. "You never know what you can do until you try it," I remember him telling me. We talked about his choreographers, including Hermes Pan, and how he created some of his wonderful numbers.

What a memorable day that was for me — I finally got to work with Fred Astaire and I got his *hands*, not his wonderful *feet*.

LYNDA CARTER

It never hurts to have at least one friend who is a Superhero. I became friends with *Wonder Woman* before she landed the role. Lynda Carter had been booked to "open" for Buddy Hackett in Las Vegas and needed to have a nightclub act created. She was a singer and dancer and I liked her immediately.

I took Lynda to meet my dressmaker, to have a costume made. She didn't have a place to stay, so I invited her to stay with us while we rehearsed. Lynda is a big, beautiful girl who always makes quite an impression. Jack was talking on the phone the first day I brought Lynda home. After I showed her to her room I walked back by the den and overheard Jack tell his friend, "You won't believe what just walked through here!"

The Korean Children's Choir with Julie Andrews, me and comedy writer Buzz Kohan, 1975.

JULIE ANDREWS

I got another chance to work with Julie Andrews on her one-hour ABC television special, *One to One*, in 1975.

The experience reinforced for me how truly amazing Julie is. The Korean Children's Choir performed on her show and Julie learned and remembered every one of those children's names. I think there were about thirty-five of them. I fell in love with one of those Korean children, an orphan named Oh-Me-Soon who had the loveliest disposition. I even talked with Jack about adopting her. It didn't happen. To this day I feel a little ache in my heart when I think about what might have happened if we'd brought that girl into our lives.

TWIGGY

Twiggy had learned tap dancing in London (before she made her film debut in *The Boyfriend*) and danced kind of heavy, more like a man. She wanted to be more feminine. She liked my style and wanted to copy it. Twiggy wanted me to choreograph her British television show, but we found out I wasn't able to since I wasn't a British citizen. She was in Los Angeles and met with me over several months. I taught her everything I could in the time we had together. She later wrote to tell me that she was using everything I had taught her and was sorry I couldn't be there to work with her more. I must say, I was a bit resentful that we open our arms to all artists to work here, but we're not allowed to work in many other countries.

COLUMBO AND MRS. COLUMBO

I had been hired to stage some musical numbers for Janet Leigh and her male co-stars for a 1975 episode of *Columbo*. They needed someone to play the part of a choreographer. Guess who got the job? *Moi!* I was supposed to teach the "Leading Lady" (Janet) and a "Dancer" (Scott Salmon) in a rehearsal hall. I had to act like a choreographer, saying my "5, 6, 7, 8." That was easy.

John Payne, playing the part of the producer, asked me, the *real* choreographer playing the *role* of the choreographer, to demonstrate the step. Curiously, after trying to come up with a good name for my character, they decided upon "Miriam." So I was Miriam the choreographer playing "Miriam the choreographer." Talk about life imitating art. Or is it the other way around?

I had one line, "We're ready for you now." I never thought Janet and I sounded alike until we had to dub the dialogue. They gave me a line to say I didn't remember saying. They realized they had given me Janet's line. I told Janet and she said they had given her my line to re-record. That episode seems to be running more than any other because my residuals are down to about eight dollars a check.

A few years later in 1979, I did an episode of *Mrs. Columbo*, the spin-off of the original series, with Kate Mulgrew. Kate is the actress who went on to become the Captain on *Star Trek: Voyager*. As Mrs. Columbo, Kate and a girl playing her daughter did a dance for a PTA show. They wore straw hats and carried canes. I was surprised that Kate moved as well as she did. I figured she must have had dancing lessons.

In another episode I played against type. I was the mean "Ballet Instructor." As we rehearsed I walked down the line of the girls doing their work at the *barre*. I made comments as I passed each one.

"Be angrier," the director kept saying. "Be mean!"

Each time we rehearsed I tried being meaner. It was not my nature, but I guess I did a good job because shortly afterward I started rehearsals for a SHARE show where, after a few days of rehearsal, a few new girls confessed they had been scared to death of me.

"For goodness sakes, why?" I wanted to know.

"Because you were so mean on *Columbo*," they told me.

WORKING WITH MALE STRIPPERS

In an episode of *Sheriff Lobo* (which starred Claude Akins), Gloria DeHaven played an old flame of the sheriff's who tried to get his permission to put on a strip show in a nightclub. He envisions all these dancing ladies and grants her permission. Little does he know, it will be an all-male strip show!

I was given the enviable job of finding male strippers. I didn't know where I was going to find them until someone suggested Gold's Gym. I went to Gold's and posted a notice.

Someone else told me I had to see the Chippendales, real life male strippers, to see how they do it. The studio arranged it. I didn't know what I was getting into. The audience consisted of gals between the ages of twenty and thirty-five. Each fellow that came out was a muscle man dressed in a costume. As he danced, he stripped.

"Take it off! Take it off!" the girls screamed.

The men stripped down to the tiniest trunks and kept dancing. Some of the girls put money in their g-strings. I watched the audience as much as I did the dancers. They screamed and carried on. I hadn't seen anything like it since the Beatles. It was amazing!

I held auditions and found a big fellow who danced quite well. We wanted him in a suit, but I don't think he'd ever owned one. His muscles were so big the studio had a suit of white tails made for him. It was constructed so it would break away.

We rehearsed at Universal Studios. It was interesting to talk to these fellows. I found out they could go to a bar and no one would bother them. Some were bouncers. Some of the shorter fellows said they developed their muscles to attract girls. They sure did attract attention! One day while rehearsing about six of these fellows walked with me to the commissary for lunch. James Garner walked by.

"Hi, Miriam," he said. "What are you doing with these guys?" Then he flexed his bicep for me.

HILL STREET BLUES

Hill Street Blues was the first time I was called to choreograph a show in which my son Chris was the editor. The day I went to the studio for my first meeting, I went up to his editing room and surprised him — he couldn't imagine what I was doing there. I was so pleased to know he would be editing my sequence because it would be done well. He's the best! He's worked on *West Wing, Scarecrow and Mrs. King, China Beach, Six Feet Under* and *Lost* — receiving (as of this writing) four Emmy and two Ace nominations. I am one proud momma!

The first day on any series begins with most everyone involved sitting around a table. The script is read by the actors. The assistant reads the parts of those who are not there. It's amazing how much detail goes into these shows.

The first sequence I would stage took place in the police station. A rock group was to get in the way of everyone. We only had a couple of days to rehearse before shooting. I devised a musical bit where two fellows pick up a girl just as Daniel J. Travanti walks into the room. Daniel doesn't realize the girl is hanging above his head.

Life *Magazine's tribute to Hal Roach comedies. I staged the sequence. Here I am between photo sessions, with James Garner, trying to see water 'roll off a duck's back.'*

Another sequence was shot in a dangerous part of downtown Los Angeles. As I got close to the location, I drove through a makeshift village created by the homeless. I spotted a studio policeman and pulled up to him. He told me where to park. I started walking down the hill to the location. I wasn't nervous until a ragged, unshaven man came toward me.

"I'll just look straight ahead and walk fast as we pass," I thought. He kept walking until he got alongside. I worried he might try to shake me down for money, or worse. As he got close he said, "You want to get married?"

I cracked up and laughed the rest of the way down the hill.

I found the company shooting the scene. The director asked me to check out an alley with the assistant director. The rock group would dance and sing on a truck. I started down the alley to find the best location. Three derelicts, two men and one woman, sat on the dirtiest mattress I ever saw. The woman had a rubber tourniquet around her arm and a needle stuck in a vein. I had heard about such things but never dreamed I would see it. My stomach turned over.

"Can't anybody get any privacy around here?" she yelled. They jumped up and ran down the alley yelling, "This is our own private alley!" We finally did shoot the sequence. I was glad to get out of there.

MURDER, SHE WROTE

I find that most British actors know more about movement than Americans as their theater training is very thorough. I got to work with another British actress who knew how to dance. Her name is Angela Lansbury. The show was the delightful and long-running series, *Murder, She Wrote*.

In one episode Angela and a young actor were going to do the "Texas Two-Step." As research, I rented *Urban Cowboy* to watch John Travolta and Debra Winger perform the dance. In a Texas Two-Step the man places his right hand behind the girl's neck and his left arm holds the girl's hand straight down.

I arrived at the ranch with my tape recorder and music. I taught the actor the dance, but there was a slight problem. Although he had good footwork, he could not keep his left arm straight, holding Angela's down while saying his dialogue. Knowing what a pro Angela is, I finally took her aside and asked if she would hold his hand down and said he wouldn't know the difference. She did it and we got the shot a lot faster that way.

Angela always stopped around 4:00 for afternoon tea. One day she invited me into her trailer to join her. We had a nice visit over tea and cookies.

SISTERS

My work on the series *Sisters* usually involved dream sequences. In one of them, Swoosie Kurtz's character would get her mink coat out of storage, put it on, and dance down the street. I choreographed her to swing around a light pole, dance with a boy, then poke fun at a banker. Then the dream would go "bad." An animal rights protest group runs toward her and throws red paint on her coat.

We began filming at the studio one morning. The paint, of course, was not thrown by a protester. It was thrown by the prop man. The first time he threw the paint some of it hit Swoosie in the face. They had to fix Swoosie's face and clean the coat. This happened three more times. Each time the coat had to be cleaned.

"We're losing the light!" the cameraman yelled. Everyone was getting nervous because the sun was going down. The cameraman knew if we didn't get the shot soon, it would be too dark. They did another take and got it right just in the nick of time.

I choreographed another sequence where Julianne Phillips' character dreams she is pregnant. Dressed in top hat, she danced down a flight of stairs singing, "Me and My Baby." One thing's for sure, the characters on *Sisters* surely had funny dreams!

DESIGNING WOMEN

Another funny show I did was *Designing Women*. In this episode we learn that Meshach Taylor's character had been in prison years ago. He's asked to come back to entertain the prisoners. He agrees and gets Dixie Carter to sing a song. Then one of the big, rough prisoners asks Julia Duffy if she can jitterbug. She tries to refuse, but he pulls her up and off they go.

I took Julia and the male dancer behind the set to learn the steps. I was amazed that this big actor could dance so well. While I was teaching them, Julia tried to take over. She kept saying she knew how to jitterbug. But she kept doing the same step over. Step. Touch step. Touch step. Touch step. It wasn't very exciting. I took the actor aside and told him to lead Julia through the steps I taught him. He did it and *voila* — jitterbug!

THE JOHN RITTER SHOW

The John Ritter Show needed a comical musical number. The three leading males would perform a song in drag with feather boas and I would teach them the dance number. They had no problem doing the routine as long as I was doing it in front of them. The director decided I should perform the dance on a platform behind the camera while they were shooting so the boys could remember the routine. This technique has been used many times in movies.

The show was shot before a live audience. Later someone told me the audience was watching me more than the guys. Nonetheless, the guys looked great.

A few years after this show I watched an interview with Billy Bob Thornton. I couldn't believe how different he was from his *Sling Blade* character. His speech, his facial expressions and his rounded shoulders were all perfectly normal and after a moment I realized I knew him. But from where? Then it hit me. He was one of the fellows from the drag number. Then I also understood why John Ritter was in *Sling Blade*.

ALICE IN WONDERLAND

I hope that by now you realize that a career in show business involves working in all types of entertainment with all kinds of talent. I've worked with difficult directors, temperamental actors and even gone up against Mother Nature. But throughout my career, I only had one job I would describe as "A Total Disaster"!

Alice in Wonderland was a star-studded, made-for-television movie produced by Irwin Allen, husband of one of my SHARE sisters. Irwin had directed a string of disaster pictures like *The Poseidon Adventure* and *The Towering Inferno*, which should have been a forewarning, but it wasn't.

I looked forward to rehearsals because many of my friends were in the movie. Steve Lawrence and Eydie Gorme were "Tweedle Dee and Tweedle Dum" and I rehearsed them. Martha Raye and Imogene Coco did a number together that I choreographed.

Quickly the film started going bad for me. I learned early on that my hands were going to be tied. Mr. Allen told me not to change the music. I had never been told this before. He wouldn't even let me talk to the director, unless he was there. It was difficult, if not impossible, to have any communication with Mr. Allen. He made himself unavailable to me.

And then, as they say, the "you-know-what" hit the fan. I got a call from one of Mr. Allen's secretaries. Robert Morley, playing the "King of Hearts," was coming to town earlier than was originally thought. Could I use him? I booked time with the actor and we began working on his number. As we rehearsed another assistant came up to me.

"Mr. Allen would like to see you," she told me nervously. I went to his trailer and didn't even sit down before he started in on me.

"How dare you have a rehearsal without me knowing it?" he demanded.

"I got a call from your office," I told him. It was obvious the mistake had come from his people. "Nonetheless, you should have checked it out," he told me. After that, something shifted. The next disagreement was over the "Cheshire Cat." I had Telly Savalas, playing the Cat, sit on a log and lick his paw and rub his face. Irwin said the cat should stand and, if anything, put his hand up on the tree. We just couldn't see eye-to-eye. He bawled me out a couple more times and I thought about leaving, but it really wasn't my nature to quit. Remember, I'm a Virgo, the peacemaker. I like a happy ending. Alas, it was not to be.

One day another choreographer showed up on the set. It was all handled politely. I don't even know who told me. It went something like: "Your services are no longer needed." I put my tape recorder in my bag and headed for the door. It was the first — and only time — anything like this ever happened in my career.

CHAPTER THIRTEEN

My Dancing Life with Disney

As I am writing this, it is hard to realize that Mickey Mouse and I go back more than a half century. In 1954, in the midst of my other film and TV work, there was a job opportunity which offered me a long and fulfilling association. Sherman Marks, a producer at ABC, called and asked me to meet him at his office. He was putting together — in the words of Ed Sullivan — a "really big show." Sherman told me he was in charge of the televised Grand Opening of Disneyland on July 15, 1955. The show (which was going to be live) would be narrated by Art Linkletter, Ronald Reagan, Bob Cummings and other stars.

I would be responsible for choreographing numbers using a couple hundred people. It was a big challenge. I sat down with Sherman and he reviewed my resume. He told me he wanted me as choreographer, but he noticed I had never done a job on this scale.

"Miriam," he asked, "if you get this job, how will you communicate with so many people?"

"I guess I'll just yell louder," I told him. He must have liked my attitude, because I got the job. I immediately hired Jack Regas to assist me.

The opening number would be a parade with all the Disney Characters. They would dance their way through each of the five different "Lands" of Disneyland, including Tomorrowland and Adventureland.

I held auditions and selected thirty-two dancers who could play Mickey Mouse, Alice in Wonderland, Snow White, and on and on. Some of these dancers would go on to become choreographers on their own, like Bobby Banas and Ward Ellis.

A different director was assigned to each of the five "lands." Each director had his own booth. Sherman Marks, the producer, had his own central booth. From his booth he could talk to each of the directors. He had monitors so he could see what they had on camera.

After several weeks of rehearsal in a hall in Hollywood, we moved to Disneyland in Orange County. While we rehearsed, they were still constructing the buildings and finishing the landscaping by planting grass and trees around us. None of the restaurants had opened yet, so we brought our own lunches.

It was so hot I allowed my dancers to wear shorts, T-shirts and some of the girls wore halter-tops. Almost immediately, I received a personal note from Mr. Disney. He asked me to have my dancers cover up because they were distracting the workmen. He wanted to be sure to open on time.

The day before the show we had a full rehearsal. One of the first numbers took place in Frontierland. A man dressed in Western clothing asked me where I wanted the cowboys and horses. I didn't know *I* was in charge of cowboys and horses, but I guessed I was so I told him. As I talked to him and the other cowboys, I discovered one of them had show business experience. So I put *him* in charge of the cowboys.

When the gates to Frontierland opened the horses would gallop through and peel off on either side of a flagpole island. I positioned two of my assistants to direct the cowboys on their horses to the left or right. I did this without realizing both assistants were scared to death of horses!

After all the horses had arrived, Fess Parker as Davy Crockett and Buddy Ebsen as his sidekick George Russell would come galloping over a hill. Fess would break into a number about his rifle called "Old Betsy." At that point, my dancers would go into a big number. They hadn't paved the streets yet, so when they went into the number the dancers were kicking up a lot of dust. The boys all carried rifles. The girls were supposed to step on the rifles and the guys would flip them over. The rifles hadn't arrived, so we practiced with wooden dowels.

At this eleventh hour, Sherman kept trying to change shots. He was so tired I thought he was going to lose it. The directors accommodated him for a while, then became disturbed. In Sherman's defense, he had planned the show for months. He had a vision. But there comes a point when you have to let the director do his thing. Sherman had gone one step too far. By the end of the run-through the directors were ready to mutiny. They called a meeting. I sat in and listened. They discussed the problem and how best to deal with it.

Mr. Disney got wind of what was going on so he called a meeting. Anyone who wanted to do the show must be in his office in a half hour. Those who didn't could leave. The directors kicked this back and forth. They decided the only way they could do a good show was to *disregard* Sherman's directions. Come "Show Time" they would take off their earphones and do the show as they wanted.

The directors and I traipsed up to Mr. Disney's office and the directors told him they had resolved their problems.

By this time it was nearly 11:00 at night. Someone decided that because it was so late and we had to be back early in the morning, they would get us motel rooms. Drivers took us to our motels. When I entered my room I learned I was sharing it. One of the secretaries was lying on the bed. She obviously had just drifted off because the cigarette in her fingers was still burning. I carefully removed it and threw it away. I didn't have extra clothing since I didn't think I'd be spending the night. So I washed out my underclothes and fell into bed, exhausted.

The next morning we were back at Disneyland bright and early. We began rehearsing one of the numbers. The director yelled for the camera to back up to the spot where it had been the day before. Since he was watching from the booth he didn't realize a tree had been planted overnight in that spot.

The first shot when we aired was on Mr. Disney sitting on a rock in front of the Castle.

"Are we on the air yet?" Mr. Disney asked.

It was an old cliché. Of course we were.

He warmly welcomed everyone — which included the television audience and the invited guests who were mostly Disney employees and their families. The audience was in the hundreds, perhaps thousands.

Goodwin Knight, the Governor of California, gave an opening speech. Hundreds of pigeons with red-and-white streamers on their legs were released. Balloons flew, trumpets blared and the Disneyland Band started marching down Main Street U.S.A. The dancers, dressed in Disney character costumes, were skipping and hopping behind the band. It's a wonder they didn't keel over from the heat. They had been in those costumes so long waiting for the show to start and the sun was so hot that day.

Art Linkletter, the first narrator, was positioned on a balcony overlooking Main Street. Watching the monitor, he would make comments like, "Here comes Snow White." We had never rehearsed the show at the same time of day that we actually were going to perform the show. The sun was shining directly into the monitor and Art couldn't see a thing. When he talked about "Snow White" you'd actually see "Davy Crockett." When "Cinderella" rode by in her carriage, Art was grasping at straws and called her "Mickey."

The rehearsal in Frontierland – done with wooden dowels – had gone well. For the performance, the Prop Department handed out imitation rifles which were not sturdy. When the girls stepped on them, many broke. We got lucky because during this routine the director cut to one couple whose rifle did not break. None of the television viewers saw the catastrophe that actually occurred.

Little roads weave their way through the back parts of Disney. We were given a truck to transport the dancers to Frontierland. Our driver kept getting lost. Everyone was frantically directing him. "Go here!" "Turn there!" The dancers were going to have difficulty making the change even though they had dressers to help.

When we got there, we jumped off the truck. I helped the girls with the quick change and Jack helped the boys. The number was to start with girls on balconies, then the male dancers were to slide down poles like firemen. I was told just before we went on the air, "Your dancers can't slide down those poles because the paint is still wet." I ran around like a crazy woman, making changes. Then I realized the whole area where the dancers were to dance was filled with guests.

"Where's the crowd coordinator?" I yelled. He asked the people to clear the dance area. The crowd coordinator asked if they could sit at the tables and chairs that surrounded the area. I yelled "yes" then ran back to the booth to work with the director.

The number started with a little African-American boy doing a tap dance. It would be up to Jack to make certain the boy was in his proper position. The boy was nowhere to be found!

"I think I saw him walk down toward the Mark Twain riverboat," someone suggested to Jack. He dashed off and, sure enough, the boy was sitting with his hand in the water, staring up at the big boat. Jack picked him up, raced back, put him on his mark and jumped out of the "Shot" just as the camera went "on." To my recollection, the number went off just fine in spite of all the behind-the-scenes madness.

On to the Disneyland Castle! I chose the best-looking cowboy to be the "White Knight" and a grimacing one to be the "Black Knight." The whole sequence started with the two of them rearing their horses.

"Open the drawbridge," an actor yelled.

The castle gates opened and my dancers came hopping toward the camera, beckoning the children behind the camera to follow them into the castle. We had never rehearsed with children. Each character was given a specific direction to lead children. For example, "The White Rabbit" was to take a few children to the merry-go-round. "Alice in Wonderland" would put some of them in teacups. The characters couldn't believe their eyes when the gate opened and, instead of a few children, saw *hundreds* of screaming children. So instead of beckoning the children into the castle, the children *chased* the Disney characters inside! They scrambled to grab a kid here or there and would set them on various rides. Whenever I run into one of those dancers today we always talk about that first show. Indeed, we were making Disney history!

THE GOLDEN HORSESHOE REVUE

I hadn't heard from "Mickey" in awhile when I got a call from "one of his people" in the late Sixties. I headed off to Disneyland and Mickey and I resumed our relationship without skipping a beat.

Robert "Bob" Jani was now the Disneyland Director of Entertainment. He asked me to create a brand new Christmas Parade, a new show in Tomorrowland and make a new version of *The Golden Horseshoe Revue*, which had been running in Frontierland since "Opening Day." I put on my Can-Can hat and started creating.

In addition to three principals, there were eight girl dancers. The first four shows were danced by one "shift" of four girls and the last four shows were danced by a second "shift." Toni Kaye, my favorite girl, did a solo of "spotters," which is like a cartwheel but instead of going sideways you go forward. She once volunteered to substitute for a girl who didn't come in for her "shift," and by the time Toni did all eight shows, we figured she must have done at least one hundred "spotters." She was one of those girls who could do anything and eventually became one of my most valuable assistants.

We rehearsed at night when the park was closed after the "guests" had left. (Everybody goes through training to learn to say "guests." I wasn't required to go through school, but I did learn to say "guests" and a lot of things unique to Disneyland.)

One night I was the last person to leave rehearsal. I walked along a path in the pitch dark in the direction of my car. All of a sudden I heard war whoops. It scared the daylights out of me! I started running, jumped in my car and was out of there! The following morning I found out that I had heard a tape recording that played periodically at the Indian Village.

I guess Mickey liked *The Golden Horseshoe Revue*, because it ran virtually unchanged for the next thirty-one years.

Top: Rehearsing the Golden Horseshoe Revue. Bottom: Backstage during Fantasy on Parade. Dancers dressed as butterflies emerged from the sides of the caterpillar to perform along the parade route.

FANTASY ON PARADE

I created and staged a completely new *Fantasy on Parade* in 1968 on which Disneyland spent a million dollars on the costumes. Most of the performers in the parade were high school kids and could only work a full day on weekends or during their Christmas "break" from school. What grueling weekends they would be! I would start at 8:00 in the morning with a group (or "unit"). We worked in a large open blacktopped "backstage" area behind Disneyland, next to "The Ranch." I would have each unit for two hours and teach them as much as they could absorb. Their leader would then take them to another area to keep practicing while I worked with another unit.

This went on all day. It's hard to be heard when you're outdoors in a large space. I had a megaphone and a whistle, but I hated using them. I remember the Native American performers on their way to the "Indian Village" looking at me like, "Who is this girl telling us what to do?"

One day we started with "The Jungle Book's" Colonel Hathi's unit, which consisted of a big elephant that swayed as he walked. As we marched by the corral at The Ranch that housed the working horses at Disneyland, the horses ran to the fence to get a closer look at this strange animal. First they just stared. Then, as the great elephant marched alongside, they began to whinny. We all had a good laugh.

The dancers were wonderful and were thrilled to be working at Disneyland. When the big day came, I was very proud of them. They used that parade every Christmas for many, many years to come.

ON STAGE U.S.A.

On Stage U.S.A. opened in June of 1969. There was an "Opening" and a "Closing" production number with guest celebrities appearing in between. *On Stage U.S.A.* ran for months while the stars changed almost weekly. I remember Pat Boone was one of the guest stars.

On Stage U.S.A. took place in an open air theater in Tomorrowland. The Monorail ran just behind the stage. Jack Carter, a well-known comedian, got a lot of jokes from the fact that the Monorail ran practically over his head. I'll never forget one night when I saw two boys running down the tracks. As soon as they went past, the Monorail appeared. My heart was in my mouth. I missed most of the show worrying that those boys got hit. I never heard a word so I guess they were all right. You'd be surprised how crazy kids get when they get into the park.

One show had a circus theme. I hired eight girl dancers to do the numbers. I kept waiting for them to hang four trapezes in the rehearsal hall. I didn't know why it took so long, but I started the routine without them. We pretended to go forward and backward and do all the tricks. It was getting close to show time and trapezes still had not arrived. I worried if we didn't get them the girls would not be able to do it. I kept calling the Prop Department.

"That's Disney," they would say when I'd get upset. To me, Disney epitomized perfection so I couldn't accept it. The trapezes finally arrived a couple of days before the opening. I couldn't believe it. Those girls went right up and did the routine they had done in make-believe. I've heard of visualizations and found it does work!

After *On Stage U.S.A.* had finished its summer run, I took my grandson, Chris, to Disneyland. By then he had two younger brothers, Josh and Matthew, and I took them along, too. "Brer Bear" was dancing on a corner and I took my boys over to watch. When "Brer Bear" finished his number, he shook hands with my boys.

"Hi, Miriam," he said to me. Those boys were flabbergasted. They couldn't figure out how "Brer Bear" knew their grandmother and I never told them. I don't know if they'd even remember, but it sure made an impression at the time.

When performers are in costume they *become* the character. They were trained so that no matter what happened – and there were times little boys would pull their tails or hit them – they were never to get back at them. Once, a little boy harassed a character so badly he did give the kid a little swat. He was fired immediately! I felt sorry for him, because I knew what he went through.

DISNEY ON PARADE

While doing *On Stage U.S.A.*, I was also involved on a huge project for Disney — even bigger than the opening of Disneyland. It was to be a touring arena show that would open in Chicago in December of '69 and subsequently go to all the major cities in the U.S., and then worldwide. The show was called *Disney on Parade* and I thought the title was misleading. People would think they were going to see a parade, not a full-blown show.

Still, I was excited until I found out the show was opening in Chicago on Christmas Day because I had always spent Christmas with my family. I had the nerve to say I didn't want to do this show unless my family could be flown back there to be with me. No one ever accused me of being a prima donna, but this one time I requested something above and beyond the usual amenities. I wanted a decorated tree for my hotel room. Disney agreed.

One hundred and thirty-five performers were in the two-and-a-half hour show. The mechanical stage, 170 feet by 70 feet with a proscenium and revolving center, was the largest ever to travel up until that time. It would take fifteen 40-foot trucks to haul the stage and the rest of the equipment around the country.

I was asked to lead a creative team of set, costume, prop and lighting designers, animators, composers and arrangers to devise eleven Production Numbers that used more than 500 costumes. I hired three choreographic assistants, Larry Billman, Leslie Bouchet and Phil Phillips to help me create and perfect the miles-worth of dance steps. Our challenge was to create live stage adaptations of the classic animated Disney films.

Until then, arenas had been used for presenting ice shows, rodeos, dog shows, sporting events, and political rallies, but not a show based on dance.

Disney gave me an office at their studio in Burbank. They built me a miniature stage model that sat on a six foot-long table, with little people about two inches tall, intricately detailed as only Disney can do. I sat there at my model stage with my drawing pads and my pencils.

The show opened with a "rock" version of a Disney song ("How Do You Do and Shake Hands") performed by all the Disney characters. In an ice show, you can get anywhere you want to in seconds. It takes a lot longer to make an entrance when you're on foot, especially in costume. I had to calculate how long it took to walk, skip, hop and run. I marked off every ten feet in the hallway outside my office with the tiniest pencil marks. (I sometimes wonder if they're still there.)

With stopwatch in hand, I walked off ten feet and marked down how long it took. Then I timed myself skipping and hopping. When I started running the length of the hall, one of the songwriters saw me whiz by his office, jumped to his piano and sang:

> *She's late. She's late for a very important date.*
> *No time to say hello, goodbye,*
> *She's late, she's late, she's late, she's late.*

I designed a tea party table that was about twenty feet across for the "Alice in Wonderland" segment. It came apart in sections like pieces of a pie. The teacup on each section spun around and the spoons in the cups would spin. At the end of the Mad Tea Party the table flew apart into all directions. All these motions were controlled by people under the table.

The "Three Little Pigs" and the "Big Bad Wolf" would do a comic number to "Who's Afraid of the Big, Bad Wolf?" And the wolf would blow the house down!

We had a "Cinderella Ball" which was quite beautiful. Near the end of the number the lights went down. Elaborate gowns worn by the girls lit up with battery-operated twinkle lights. It looked gorgeous to see these dancers waltzing around and it became the prototype of the classic "Main Street Electrical Parades" at Disney theme parks around the world.

When we put out a "call" for dancers, we received hundreds of applications.

In 1969, Disney was a very conservative company and had no idea that *their* world would soon drastically change. In 1970, the "Yippies" invaded Disneyland because of the theme park's policy of not admitting men with long hair and/or beards. Although the Disney Company is now one of the corporate leaders in embracing religious, ethnic and lifestyle diversity, nearly forty years ago they were naive and narrow-minded.

Since the popular show choirs of the time, "The Young Americans" and "The Kids Next Door," were the role models for the "look" of the performers at Disneyland: young, fresh, and "apple pie," Bob Jani had a notion that male dancers had to be virile. He equated "virile" with "straight" and made it clear to me that Disney didn't want homosexuals in the show. Of course, it made no difference to me. I have had gay men friends since my early days on Broadway. I tried coming up with a reason he should hire gay men.

"There aren't a lot of straight men who are dancers, anymore," I told him. But he told me to hire straight guys, even if they couldn't dance well, and teach them how to dance enough to get by. The girls could do most of the most difficult dancing.

Of course, when I auditioned dancers, I couldn't very well ask them if they were gay. I guess I was supposed to go by their looks and how they acted. I narrowed down the dancers and got Bob involved in the final selection because I didn't want to be blamed if any of them were gay. We hired all the dancers. I don't need to tell you that we found out later that several of them were gay.

We hired several circus performers for "The Dumbo Circus," which was the first act Finale. It began with the cast carrying in sections of rings and placing them on the floor. The audience didn't know until they were almost finished they were building a three-ring circus. Once it was done, I created a parade, typical of all circuses, to open this section.

We had jugglers, aerialists, acrobats and a terrific clown act. The clown drove out in a car which broke down. The clown then climbed out to try to fix the car and it would drive away by itself, beeping its horn. For the thrilling climax of the Circus, we had Mickey Mouse on a high wire riding a motorcycle.

We needed rehearsal space for the high wire, flying apparatus and other stage equipment, so we went to the Long Beach Arena, where we would eventually preview the show. That also allowed parking space for the circus performers who traveled in their own RV's and motor homes.

I soon learned that circus performers have a strict "class" system. One of the acts was a married couple who invited me into their RV for a drink. Their RV was comfortable; nothing fancy. They asked me if I wanted beer or wine.

Shortly after, another couple invited me over for a drink. They owned a motor home and it was really beautiful. They had lovely drapes, carpeting and throw pillows. They served martinis and *hors d'oeuvres*. We had fun. I found out later they didn't fraternize with the other couple.

After spending nearly a year developing this show, we were finally settled in Long Beach to preview the show in a full-size arena. We got to see our stage for the first time: it was about the size of a football field and painted a beautiful shade of blue. Bob was so anxious about the stage he asked us to rehearse in socks.

Bob knew I was friends with Gower Champion and asked me if I could get him to come see our first run-through. Gower had heard me talk about it so much he wanted to see it anyway. There were still a lot of rough edges. We used Toy Soldier costumes for the first time and the dancers couldn't see well so they weren't walking in straight lines. The girls climbed onto the flying apparatus for the first time. We tried out the carousel for the first time. We had a lot to do before opening, with no time to waste.

All of a sudden, Bob got everyone's attention. He gave a lengthy talk about putting on makeup. There was a lot left to finish, but I sat there listening. By now, Gower was getting upset. Afterward, I introduced Gower to Bob. Bob wanted to know what he thought of the show.

"I think it's going to be great if you let Miriam get on with her job," Gower told Bob. I was a little embarrassed for Bob, because I dearly loved him. But he had a lot of respect for Gower, so he did let me get on with it.

After the preview in Long Beach, the trucks were loaded and the show headed to Chicago. They flew Jack and our daughter Missy on a small Disney jet called *Mickey Mouse*. My husband laughed when he heard the pilot talk to the landing tower: "This is *Mickey Mouse* requesting landing instructions."

Bob Jani wanted *Disney on Parade* to hit Chicago with all the excitement of the Olympics. Performers would wear sweaters with a big "D" on the front. He wanted them to come off the plane and have photographers and reporters greet them. This would make for great publicity for the papers.

Bob was really concerned about the image we projected. It had to be wholesome, clean-cut and All-American. He got the shock of his life one night in Chicago while he was sitting in a coffee shop in the hotel lobby. Something caught his eye so he looked up. Who should come flouncing down the hotel's grand staircase all dolled up in a beautiful gown but one of the male dancers!

The stage and equipment arrived from Long Beach a few days before us and the crew went to work to get it all assembled. Bob couldn't wait for them to finish so we went out the day it arrived. It had been snowing all day and when we got to the arena we noticed the doors were open so they could carry in the scenery and heavy equipment. Snow had blown all over that new floor, but that wasn't the worst of it. Lights were being hung. It looked like total chaos. What should be driving across that lovely blue floor but a tractor, with chains around its wheels. I thought Bob was going to faint. The stage had to be repainted before we opened.

Thank goodness the Disney Executives didn't come to see the show in Chicago. That gave us a chance to break it in. For most of the Chicago run we had many problems. For one number, the dancers were dressed like playing cards. They were to march in order: fifty-two in all, plus two jokers. The stage hands hadn't put the cards in the correct order. Girls tried finding their costumes and bumped into each other. By the time they found their costumes and got in line they were all mixed up. It looked as though the number had been dealt a "bad hand."

Two round carousels descended from the ceiling during the circus number. They had T-bars suspended from them. When they came down to the stage floor, the aerialists would grab the T-bar and then, as it was going up, would flip themselves into a sitting position. They would perform a beautiful aerial number while the circus continued below.

One time, as the apparatus started going up one girl wasn't making it. She tried flipping herself up but try as she might, she couldn't do it. I held my breath. The man controlling the carousels recognized she wasn't going to make it so he let the carousel she was hanging from come down. But another potential crisis was about to happen. As he lowered the carousel down, the parade of Disney characters started marching toward it.

The characters could not see above them because of their headpieces. They marched around the suspended girls. How they missed bumping into them I'll never know. About that time the girl was able to get back on the bar, they pulled the carousel up and the show continued.

Another routine on the apparatus was called "The Iron Jaw" and when I describe it, you'll know why. The girls were butterflies. Each girl hooked a mouthpiece – especially made to the shape of her mouth – to the apparatus and then slipped it in her mouth. The contraption was raised so the girls hung by those mouthpieces. Barbette, a legendary expert in aerial work, looked at the girls' teeth like you would look into a horse's mouth to determine if they were qualified for the job. The lights went out when the routine started. All you saw were these beautiful hand-painted china silk wings, about a ten-foot wingspan, that showed under ultraviolet light. Then the carousel

Top: Cartoon drawn by a Disney artist during presentation to production staff (left). Publicity photo (right). Bottom: Disney On Parade — *Phil Phillips, Leslie Bouchet, Larry Billman, and me hamming it up backstage.*

would go up and around so it looked like they were flying. At the end of the number the girls dropped their wings. Because the girls were in black, you didn't realize they were still up there. The audience gasped because it looked like the girls had all fallen. My rehearsal pianist, Paul Suter, composed a beautiful piece of music for this.

The next stop after Chicago was Detroit and the Disney echelon finally arrived. By now, the show was running smoothly; the full deck of 52 cards in the "March of the Cards" was all neatly in order. The Executives were very happy with what they saw and told me so. They said after seeing the show that they knew it would go on to run for a long time.

The show did, in fact, travel for several years and in several editions after that — but without me. I left my assistant in charge to keep that first show "clean," as they say. I used to get postcards from the dancers from places like Philadelphia and Cleveland and around the country. Its success encouraged the Disney Company to eventually go into partnership with Irvin and Kenneth Feld to produce "Disney on Ice." Some of the dancers had called the original "Holiday on *Wood*" so it was a natural progression.

About fifteen years after the show I was shopping in a supermarket in Los Angeles when a young man approached me.

"Remember me?" he asked. He looked familiar but I couldn't place him. He said, "I was your Prince Charming."

It was while I was working for Disney that I got a frightening call from Jack. My mother had complained of pain in her heart. Jack called the ambulance and they took her to the hospital. She had a heart problem that we knew about, so I feared it might be serious. I was pretty shaken so Jack wouldn't let me drive home alone. Chris and he drove out to Disneyland to get me. My mother died on December 10th, 1968. It was so painful losing her. She'd always been there for me. She was my Rock of Gibraltar. She was an inspiration, too. My mother could do anything. She painted, sewed, cooked and even made lovely lamp shades out of silk. She wasn't afraid to try anything.

One thing that helped me through this difficult time was the memory of a wonderful trip my mother and I shared shortly before she died. She always wanted to see the majestic Sequoia trees in Northern California so she and I got in the car and took a trip up there. By then my mother could only see peripherally. She walked up to a tree and put her arms around it.

I buried my mother in a tiny cemetery in Westwood, not too far from where Marilyn Monroe is entombed. I'm comforted to know that people are coming and going every day, there are always fresh flowers and it is right beside a movie star. I like that.

CARNIVAL DE CARNIVAL

I had just returned from doing a big show in Hawaii, when my old friend, Bob Jani, called one afternoon. "What are you doing Monday?" he asked. I knew from experience that when Bob Jani called it was something big.

"It doesn't matter," I told him, "I'll be sure to be available." And I'm glad I was. He needed someone to go to Paris. Once a year, the French celebrated the carnivals from different countries with decorated barges that floated down the River Seine. The parade was called the *Carnival de Carnival*. Finally, as much as I loved Hawaii, I was being asked to go across the other ocean. I had never been to France.

Several countries that had carnivals would decorate a barge that they would float down the River Seine. Our barge would be decorated as the Magic Castle and we would have Mickey and Minnie, Mary Poppins and about twelve other Disney characters. Three young people met me at the airport. One of them picked up parts of the costume for Mickey that was checked in on my baggage ticket. All of the other costumes had been shipped. I carried the music with me that had been recorded at Disney studio. They put me up in a hotel that was so close to the River Seine I could walk right down the hill to the boat, anchored next to the other boats. I had about five days to rehearse.

The ship was divided in half by the castle. You could see the castle from both sides of the river. The number would start with the characters running on one side then around to the other. They would perform a two-minute dance. Whether it was "Mary Poppins and Bert" or "Mickey and Minnie," they would do a dance and run around the boat like crazy people. Then they would go below deck. When the music started again, they would come up and do it over.

Some of the dancers were handpicked because they had to do little solos. The ones that ran around and acted crazy in character costumes were really young firemen. You need young, energetic people to get into these outfits and wear the heads. Because the barge was traveling, every two minutes we had a new audience. We kept repeating this dance over and over.

I remember the boy who worked opposite Mary Poppins. He couldn't speak English and I couldn't speak French. He kept pointing at himself and then at his feet. I kept looking at him not understanding. All of a sudden he broke into a wild tap step. I did a wild step back. We broke into hysterical laughter and became fast friends. Dance truly *is* the universal language!

One of the secretaries who worked in the Disney office in Paris offered to take me sightseeing when I had time. (I didn't even know Disney had an office in France until I worked there.) One day we dashed into the Louvre. We had time to see the Mona Lisa and a few statues before dashing back to rehearsal. It wasn't until several years later that I went back to Paris and was able to take my time enjoying the Louvre.

We took a test-run late the night before the show. Most of the local residents wouldn't know what we were doing. It was dark, the lights were lit and it was quite an experience.

The following day, people started coming from all directions for the parade. They were lined against the banks of the River Seine. By the time it was over they figured they had over a million people watching the parade that day. I have some wonderful pictures of the Disney characters talking to the girls from the Brazilian ship.

After I finished the job, I called Sandra Moss, a SHARE sister who was spending her summer in Nice, France. Sandra was married to Jerry Moss, who was the "M" of A&M Recording Studio. I flew from Paris to Nice and Sandra met me at the airport and took me to her beautiful villa, which she leased from Gregory Peck.

The next day she took me sightseeing. We drove to Monte Carlo. I expected Monte Carlo to be chic – with men in tuxedos and women in formals – but it wasn't like that. I was disappointed to see people gambling and dressed in cutoff jeans.

Another afternoon we went to lunch in this little village overlooking the water. We ran into another Virgo, Jackie Cooper, and his wife, who joined us for lunch.

It was an unusual lunch. Everything was served in baskets. We got whole loaves of bread in baskets, cold meats in baskets and chunks of cheese in baskets. I decided I wanted to serve a meal in baskets sometime. Of course, we had wonderful wine. In fact, everywhere we went we had wine. I discovered I do like French wine!

During rehearsals for Carnival de Carnival.

Before I left for France, Jack and I had decided to sell our home in Benedict Canyon. I had a lot of good memories there, but Chris had left home years ago, Missy had moved out and my mother had died. It was just the two of us and we didn't need all that space. Besides, we had purchased some properties in Palm Springs and were spending a lot of time out there, especially on the weekends.

Jack called me while I was in France to tell me a penthouse apartment had become available in the building that Lawrence Welk owned. Mr. Welk lived there with his wife. The movie actress, Joan Blondell (who had been married to Dick Powell before my friend, June Allyson, married him) had also lived there.

Jack described the apartment to me, although I knew the building. It had a wonderful view from the full-length balcony on the 17th floor. You could see the Ferris wheel on the Santa Monica Pier to the south and Malibu was visible up the coast to the north.

Jack was reluctant to move while I was in France. But he was bolstered by encouragement from my son. "Be glad she isn't here," Chris told him. "That way you can move faster." I suppose he did have a point. I would have wanted to go through every little bit of paper. Instead, I came home to a spacious penthouse on the ocean, filled to overflowing with cardboard boxes.

CHAPTER FOURTEEN

Politics and Pyrotechnics

PRESIDENT NIXON

In 1969, Bob Jani had offered me an unusual opportunity. He wanted to take *The Golden Horseshoe Revue* to Washington for a Foreign Correspondence Dinner with President Nixon. So the cast and crew of the Disneyland show boarded a plane and we flew to our nation's capital.

The dinner was a formal sit-down. I was surprised to find out I was the only female at my table. It struck me as odd, in fact, at how few women were there at all. I feared our little Disneyland show might be a bit tame for the group of mostly men. I sat beside a once-famous actor named Conrad Nagel, who was the current President of the Screen Actors Guild.

We put on our show and it was warmly received. Afterward, we were ushered into a private room to have an audience with President Nixon. He shook hands with everyone in the cast.

"Where are you from?" the President asked me.

"Chicago," I said.

He had something interesting to say about Chicago. He then proceeded down the line. As I listened, I realized he did the same with each person. It was a good way to open a conversation. He was very cordial to our group. He told us how much he liked Louis Armstrong.

"Mr. President," one of his aides said, "it's time to leave."

"Just a few more minutes," he told him. The President seemed to enjoy talking with us. He wanted the photographer to take a group picture. He put his arm out for me and I took hold — someone snapped the picture! It now hangs on my wall. When friends see it they think I'm Pat Nixon.

"Mr. President," his aide said again, tapping his watch, "it's time to leave."

"I'll be with you in a minute," the President said.

The thought crossed my mind that this show of interest might be an act. I found

Standing next to President Nixon along with the cast from The Golden Horseshoe Revue.

out later from people who were close to Nixon that he was a sincere person. He probably was having a good time.

Near the close of Nixon's first term as President, Bob Jani called and asked if Jack and I would like to produce and direct his reelection campaign in New Hampshire. Art Linkletter would be the emcee. Nelson Rockefeller, the governor of New York, would be the main speaker. Of course, many senators and congressmen would be coming. I thought it was a neat idea.

We flew to Washington one afternoon in February. The following morning we were told to meet a small group of men at a little airport. We were going to fly to New Hampshire to look at the armory where the campaign would be staged.

When we arrived at the airport I got a bit nervous because all I saw on the airfield and runway were little planes. I couldn't see myself flying to New Hampshire in one of those, especially in winter. All of a sudden a little plane circled the field and landed. It taxied to the gate. Two nice-looking young fellows got out. Jack told me it was a Lear jet.

The jet held six passengers in addition to the pilot and the copilot: four men from Washington and Jack and me. What a feeling it was to take off in a Lear jet. It felt as though we were going straight up, which, I guess, we were. As soon as we leveled off, the co-pilot got out some sweet rolls and a jug of coffee.

"Wait until they see us arrive in this," one of the Washington fellows said. I was surprised, because I expected him to be blasé. But he was as excited as I was. Because of snow and icy conditions in New Hampshire, the runway had to be sanded before we could land. We were met by top government officials who whisked us off to the armory.

For security reasons, the stage had to be placed so our dignitaries could enter and exit without going through a crowd. We decided where to put it. We told the decorators where the bunting would go and how to place the chairs. We discussed the lighting and sound. Then we went back to the airport.

Again, we went straight up! When we leveled off the pilot whipped out sandwiches and cold drinks for lunch. We landed back in Washington, made a connection to our regular flight and flew back to Los Angeles. One week later we were back in New Hampshire. The armory had been transformed exactly as we had envisioned.

Lionel Hampton was one of the performers. He had written a song about Nixon that a group of cheerleaders from local schools were going to sing. The cheerleaders arrived late because of the icy roads. In spite of the freezing weather they were dressed in their short skirts, sweaters and sneakers. Of course, they carried pompoms. I taught them a quick routine.

I thought Rockefeller, being our biggest star, should have an entrance with a lot of hoop de doo. That afternoon, I asked Rockefeller's aide if he thought Rockefeller would mind if he entered down the middle aisle with the cheerleaders behind him.

"Rockefeller will do whatever you want him to do," he told me.

Rockefeller would do anything I wanted him to do? Wow! Talk about being on a power trip! Rockefeller also was a little late arriving because of the weather.

Art Linkletter was late, too, but we got a call he was on his way so we didn't worry. Jack had written all of Art's cues and introductions on "3 x 5" cards. The minute he arrived we sat down and let him quickly run through the cards. He calmly and quickly got it. In between, he worked in jokes. He was funny and perfect. The show went off without a hitch. Art is such a pro!

When it was over cars and buses were lined up to take us all to the airport. It had a small waiting area and it was now close to midnight. Nobody thought to have coffee for us. The incoming flight, a DC-3, couldn't land because the runway hadn't been de-iced. The pilot circled around as if coming down, then he took off again.

One of the guest speakers at the convention was John A. Volpe, then Secretary of Transportation. He went up to the tower and was trying to get the pilot to land. We all let out a "Whoop" when we finally saw those lights coming down. We boarded the plane. The stewardesses (this was way before we called them "flight attendants") didn't look too happy.

"How was your flight?" I asked one of them.

"Terrible!" she said. You can imagine I wasn't too thrilled to get on that plane.

Once we were airborne Jack reminded me I often talked about "the best summer of my life"... referring to that time back in Glenn, Michigan, a spot no one else had ever heard about.

"I'll bet the gentleman behind us can talk about Glenn," he said "because he's the Michigan Congressman." I turned around to the Congressman and told him what fun I had in his State. I asked if he knew Glenn.

"Of course," he said, "I've been through there many times." We had a good ole talk and it took my mind off the flight.

When we got back to Los Angeles we had a phone call asking us if we would do the primaries in Florida. So off we went to the beautiful Dade County Auditorium. The theater came equipped with a stage, a light booth and a good sound system.

Do you remember what I said about balloons? *I love balloons!* A group of Nixon volunteers came in and I had them blow up red, white and blue balloons. We made clusters of them and decorated the theater.

Red Skelton was the Master of Ceremonies. When he arrived, he pulled out a star with his name on it and hung it on his dressing room door. The political guest star would be the Governor of California, Ronald Reagan.

There is never any true rehearsal for this kind of show. The speakers and celebrities fly in at the last minute, do their thing and fly out. Jack was positioned backstage to cue the people on and off stage. He knew a lot about theater productions because he had acted and sung in college. I was up in the light booth cueing the lights. Jack and I wore headsets so we could communicate with each other.

Reagan was supposed to come in on a small plane, but something happened and they flew him in on a big one. The plane was going home totally empty except for him. They asked us if we would mind flying back that night instead of the next day as scheduled. They sent someone to our hotel to pack our suitcases and bring them to the theater.

"As soon as Reagan goes on," Jack said, "come on down. I'll meet you backstage." When Reagan finished his speech, we were ushered out to the stretch limo which drove us right up to our plane. Jack and I took our seats up front and Red Skelton sat across from us. Reagan boarded, carrying a briefcase. He was going in back to get a little work done. The only other person was the pilot who had flown the plane in. He was asleep. A new pilot was taking us back.

We had two stewardesses to take care of the four of us. As soon as we were airborne they brought us wine. They laughingly set a bottle on each of our trays and then they served us a meal. Red was still high from his performance. He kept telling us funny stories and jokes. Pretty soon he was standing in the aisle telling his funny stories for Jack and me. We were laughing so hard and so loud that Reagan came up and sat beside us. "I can't stand it," he said. "You guys are having such fun up here."

Reagan was also a good storyteller. He did a great imitation of Truman Capote. He told us about Capote's experiences in jail, interviewing prisoners to gather material for his book, *In Cold Blood.* As Reagan told the story of Truman, imitating his high-pitched, nasally voice, I couldn't help but wonder what the prisoners must have thought.

What a rare treat this evening turned out to be. Red Skelton and Ronald Reagan stood in the aisle giving Jack and me our own private show, lasting at least a couple of hours. Finally Reagan said, "I *have got* to get some work done," and retreated to the back of the plane. Then Red pulled out his satchel. He asked if I wanted to listen to some tapes of music he had written for ballets and symphonies. I think someone had translated his music into orchestrations. One song was even recorded by The London Symphony Orchestra. I learned later that Red wrote music every day. He sang into a tape recorder. When he didn't write music, he wrote poems. His mind was forever creating. He also was quite a fine painter of clowns.

We landed in Los Angeles in the middle of the night. A car whisked Reagan off to his home. Another took Red to a little plane that was going to fly him home to Palm Springs. A third car took Jack and me home.

Some time after our political adventures, I was awakened one morning by a ringing phone. Jack had already left for work and I was getting caught up on my sleep. I fumbled for the phone.

"Hello," I said.

An officious-sounding man said, "I'm looking for Miriam Nelson."

"That's me," I told him.

"This is the FBI."

That woke me up in a hurry. I don't remember what I said, but I guess I sounded skeptical. He told me his name.

"Hang up," the man instructed me, "look up the FBI in the phone book and call me back."

I still thought it was all a big joke, but I looked up the number, called the FBI and asked for the name he gave me. I was put right through.

"I'd like to talk to you," he said.

"What about?" I asked.

"We have to speak privately."

I told him I was headed to work and wouldn't be available until after 5:00.

"Fine. I'll be there."

My mind went racing. What would the FBI want with me? It was a difficult day for me. I could hardly work because of the mental contortions I put myself through. We paid our income tax. Maybe one of our friends was in trouble.

The appointed hour finally arrived. A car pulled up in front of our house and two nice-looking young men, dressed in dark suits with shirts and ties, rang our bell. I ushered them into the den and we all sat down.

"Why would The White House have called your phone number?" one of them asked.

"My husband and I just produced a show for Nixon." I must say they perked up after I told them I was in show business.

They showed me some pictures. They wanted to know if I could identify any of the people. They laid the photos on my coffee table. Some looked like candid shots taken with a telephoto lens. Others looked like something out of a police lineup.

I didn't recognize anyone. I told them I was not good at remembering faces, but my husband might. They asked when he would be home. I told them in about an hour. They gave me the number of the phone in their car, then left.

I could hardly wait for Jack to come home so I could tell him this crazy story. When the FBI said they wanted to "speak privately," I thought it might be something no one should know, not even my own husband, so I hadn't told him. (Now you see why friends trust me with their deepest, darkest secrets.) Jack came home and after updating him I called the number the FBI agents gave me. They must have been sitting in our neighborhood because they were at the front door in five minutes.

Jack didn't recognize any of the people in the pictures, either. He did remember the names of a few people with whom we had dealings. The FBI agents never told us what it was all about.

It wasn't until the Watergate scandal broke that we realized who we were with in the Lear jet on our way to New Hampshire. The men who had been so excited about the Lear jet were Ehrlichman, Halderman and Dean.

This was the beginning of serious trouble for President Nixon. I tied a black ribbon over the picture I had of him that was hanging in our home.

It wasn't too long after that when I awoke to find Jack reading the paper at the kitchen table.

"Remember that man you talked to about Glenn on the plane ride home from the New Hampshire primaries?" he asked.

"Sure," I said. How could I forget? I had such a good time talking with him.

"He's just been appointed President."

That Congressman was Gerald Ford.

"HONOR AMERICA DAY"

The following summer Jack had a reunion of his Military Academy in Missouri. We decided I'd go along and make it a vacation. We flew to St. Louis for the reunion and rented a car for the return trip to Los Angeles.

We headed out from Missouri and on to Kansas. We drove for hours. I hadn't been in Kansas since *Picnic*. Corn must not have been in season when we made *Picnic* because I had never seen so much of it in my life! It stretched as far as the eye could see and was, like the song lyric says, "as high as an elephant's eye." I started craving corn on the cob.

Jack and I with Willard "Bill" Marriott and his wife, Allie.

We finally stopped and checked into our hotel. I couldn't wait to get into the dining room. "I'd like corn on the cob, please," I told our waitress and sat there anticipating the sweet delicacy I would soon be enjoying. Our waitress brought out my dinner and laid it in front of me. I couldn't believe my eyes. It wasn't fresh corn. It had been frozen! Our waitress told us the corn we had seen was for cows. What a disappointment.

We continued on our trip the next morning. We had planned to spend a night in Las Vegas but I had a message on my answering service to call Bob Jani immediately. I got through to Bob and he told me about a 4th of July rally Bob Hope was helping to coordinate. The rally was called "Honor America Day," intended to "show Americans can have a good time together despite their differences." (This was during the contentious period of U.S. history when there were political demonstrations over our involvement in Vietnam.) The rally would take place in Washington, D.C. Bob wanted me to help organize the celebrities.

"I'd love to help," I told Bob, "but Jack and I are on vacation."

"Bring Jack, too," he said. "We can use lots of help." We turned the car in at a rental office in Las Vegas, got on a plane, flew home, repacked, and boarded a chartered plane the next morning. It's amazing what you can do if you have to.

The plane was filled with celebrities. They included Bob Hope, Red Skelton, Miss America, Kate Smith, Dinah Shore, Les Brown and his Band of Renown and Fred Waring and his entire Glee Club. Dinah asked if I had rollers or bobby pins so she could put up a few curls.

We landed and were shuttled to the Marriott Hotel where we stayed. After we checked in Jack and I went out to see the location. The rally would take place on a big stage at one end of the reflecting pool under the Washington Monument. They had pitched white tents behind the stage for the stars.

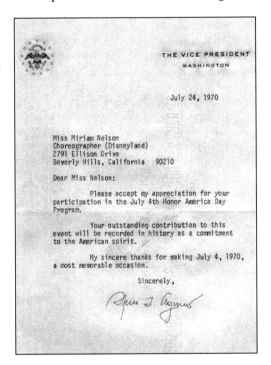

THE VICE PRESIDENT
WASHINGTON

July 24, 1970

Miss Miriam Nelson
Choreographer (Disneyland)
2791 Ellison Drive
Beverly Hills, California 90210

Dear Miss Nelson:

Please accept my appreciation for your participation in the July 4th Honor America Day Program.

Your outstanding contribution to this event will be recorded in history as a commitment to the American spirit.

My sincere thanks for making July 4, 1970, a most memorable occasion.

Sincerely,

During rehearsals the stars waited at Constitution Hall. Just before they had to rehearse on stage, our stage manager called the limo driver on his walkie-talkie and had him bring over our first star. That way they didn't have to be there waiting to rehearse.

Three towers had been built for the narrators and television cameras from ABC, NBC and CBS. The networks had tossed a coin to see who would get the tower with the best view. Joe Garagiola, Sr. and Barbara Walters would be on one of the towers.

The day of the rally we were driven to the stage to begin rehearsals. It was a really hot day with high humidity. The event was intended to be non-partisan to "honor America" as the name implied, but some interpreted it as a pro-war rally. Hippies had gathered on the other side of the reflecting pool. Their anti-war demonstrations had grown violent; they had recently knocked a klieg light into the reflecting pool.

Then a group of them started coming toward the stage. I was afraid they would storm the stage and knock over the towers. Police on horseback held them back. Just then the sky grew dark. I hoped for rain so we didn't have to do the show. My prayer was answered. Rain came down in buckets.

The stars were sent back to the hotel to wait it out. As we were on our way to a limo, I passed by Les Brown sitting with a handkerchief tied at four corners on his head to keep cool. He was writing out an orchestration for someone whose music hadn't arrived.

Our driver kept saying, "This rain will pass" as he drove us to our hotel, but I secretly prayed it wouldn't. Those hippies had me concerned. But my prayer wasn't answered. The rain did stop and we went to finish rehearsals. The rain must have cooled off the hippies because they were gone.

My work consisted of telling one star to enter from stage left, the next from stage right, and so on.

"I think Kate Smith should have a center entrance," I suggested.

"What are you going to do?" Red Skelton asked, "Tilt the stage and roll her out?" referring to her rather large girth. Red was a naughty boy!

After rehearsals we started the show. We only had one hitch. Bob Hope was performing when Jack Benny came out from behind the curtain. He almost got to center stage before he realized he interrupted Bob. He couldn't have been more apologetic. He told the audience he thought he heard his name. Then he backed off.

After the show, Willard "Bill" Marriott, founder and owner of the Marriott chain, hosted a lovely sit-down dinner for the entire cast at his hotel. The meal was served around midnight. Over glasses of champagne, Bill, his wife Allie, Jack and I hit it off immediately. This was a really classy affair: no sooner would you take a sip of champagne when a waiter would fill it back up to the brim. I guess I kind of lost track of how much champagne I was drinking. Bill showed a tape of the show for anyone who wanted to see it. Before going back to the room, a group of us had a nightcap. I didn't realize until I got back to the room that I was drunk.

I've been drunk only about five times in my life. Each time I vow I'll never do it again. I always feel terrible.

When I got into bed, the room was spinning. I turned on television. As long as I focused my eyes on the television the room didn't spin. But I couldn't look straight at it. I had to turn my head and look out the corners of my eyes.

On the airplane ride home the next day Jack burst into hysterical laughter.

"What's so funny?" I asked, trying to muffle my voice.

He said he had a vision of me sitting in bed trying to watch television while facing the wall. I was so mad at him. I didn't think it was funny at all.

"LET FREEDOM RING AGAIN"

When the time came to celebrate our nation's bicentennial, Bob Jani asked if Jack and I would jointly produce and direct a show called "Let Freedom Ring Again" at the Kennedy Center in our nation's capital in 1976. Our friend, Bill Marriott, was chairman of the Historic and Cultural Society, Inc. and figured prominently in the big show.

The script for the show consisted of four sections: The Spirit, The Government, The Land and The People. A Native American Princess, dressed in her beautiful native regalia including a gorgeous feathered headdress, opened the show with an Indian prayer. It seemed fitting for the nation's birthday. Art Linkletter would follow with an introduction. Dr. Billy Graham would offer another prayer. Telly Savalas was the central character in a narrative titled "The Land of America."

Mr. Marriott flew in three-hundred-and-fifty singers from the Mormon Tabernacle Choir from Salt Lake City, Utah. We had risers on the stage for the choir.

Believe it or not, it takes about fifteen minutes for that many singers to file in and take their places. I worked with the choral master so he could mark his music to fit the dialogue. I was up all night working on it.

Telly Savalas arrived wearing a shirt opened practically to his navel. He wore lots of gold chains hanging around his neck. It didn't seem appropriate to me, but to each his own, I suppose. So many people had gathered around him it was difficult to get his attention. I finally had to take him by the hand and lead him away so we could get to work.

Telly listened to every word I had to say. It is always interesting to me that no matter how big the star may be, they always pay attention to what I have to say because they realize I'm the only one who knows what they're supposed to do. Telly was very nice and professional in spite of his appearance.

O.J. Simpson was the next star with whom I worked. He seemed to get a kick out of the fact that he was doing a dramatic reading. When we did the show he wore a tuxedo and carried a leatherbound script. He looked elegant and did his reading very first-class. He walked off stage with great dignity to the wings where I was standing.

"How was it?" O.J. asked.

"Great!" I told him. He went into a wild couple of dance steps as if he had just scored a touchdown.

During rehearsals I admired a lovely silver and turquoise ring the Native American Princess was wearing. She took it off immediately and insisted I take it. She said it is their custom when something is admired to give it away. Too bad I hadn't admired her gorgeous silver and turquoise necklace. I guess First Lady Mrs. Betty Ford had — she wound up wearing it.

When Bob Hope took the stage the choir began singing "Thanks for the Memory." Bob didn't rehearse with us, so when the choir began singing he was so startled he turned and looked up at all of them. He said he'd never been introduced in such a grandiose fashion.

There was discussion about who should close the show. Mr. Marriott was going to receive a beautifully sculpted porcelain bird by the artist Beam. His grandson, dressed in his Boy Scout uniform, would carry it on stage and present it. Should that close the show? Or should we have President Ford close it? Or should Bob Hope close it? Hope said he was going to play a round of golf with the President that afternoon and they would talk about it and he'd let me know.

After rehearsal we had just enough time to dash back to our hotel — the Marriott, of course — and change into our formal clothes before returning to the Kennedy Center.

A few minutes before the show started a security guard came up to me and said, "There's a man outside asking for you. But he's not wearing his button so we can't let him in." He was referring to a colored button that was required for admission. When I raced to see who it was I saw our lighting director standing there, looking helpless.

"Let him in!" I screeched. The guard told me he couldn't unless someone above him authorized it. "Do you want lights on the stage for this show?" I shouted hysterically. He said he did. "Then let him in." He must have believed me because he let him in.

President and Mrs. Ford, who were attending a cocktail party just prior to going on, still hadn't arrived. Jack and I kept checking our watches but felt comforted because we were told everything goes off like clockwork when it has to do with the President.

Sure enough, at exactly the right moment at least a dozen trumpeters around a mezzanine played a beautiful fanfare I'd never heard. The President and Mrs. Ford entered and were seated front row center of the mezzanine. We cued the Indian Princess and I tapped the light man sitting next to me and said, "Light her!" Our show was off and running.

Secret Service men suddenly appeared in the wings. One was holding the Presidential Seal. It was his job before the President spoke to place it in front of him on the podium. I tried making a joke, but he was dead serious. He told me he had to check the podium just before it was taken onstage because speaking into the microphone could activate a bomb.

Bob Hope said the President would say a few words and Bob would close the show. That's the way it went.

Bill and Allie Marriott invited us to dinner the following night. Their chauffeur picked us up at the hotel. We drove a short distance to a big, old, rambling house that was certainly not fancy, but it *was* comfortable. Allie told me they had lived in that house for forty years.

Before dinner, Bill Marriott brought out the family album. On the first page were Bill and Allie in front of a root beer stand. That was how they started their empire. It was a fascinating American success story. There's a coffee shop called Allie's kitchen at each Marriott Hotel, named after Allie Marriott. Bill also told us he would never build a hotel that you couldn't see from the highway.

When we went in for dinner, I recognized the butler as the same man who had been our chauffeur. He served a lovely dinner on pretty china and crystal. I was amused that the butter was served in a plastic carton sitting in a silver bowl.

"Let's go see the fireworks," Bill said after dinner. We all loaded into the car and were driven to one of his hotels. Bill hadn't called to tell the staff we were coming. They scurried around to find us a good room. As we stood there waiting, a girl in cut-offs and T-shirt studied a picture of Bill that hung behind the counter. She looked at the man in front of her. Then back at the picture.

She finally asked, "Are you him?"

He nodded.

"Neato!" she said.

Our room was just large enough for a bed, a dresser and one chair. But it did have a floor-to-ceiling window for viewing the fireworks. A table arrived with cold drinks and a few bowls of peanuts and pretzels. Every time Bill reached for the bowl Allie slapped his hand and reminded him they were too salty. He had a heart problem.

The fireworks were spectacular. They went on for the longest time. We had an incredible view of them bursting out over the Potomac River.

After the fireworks were over, they drove us back to our hotel. The next day Jack and I were going to New York to see the Tall Ships and some Broadway shows. I love Broadway and go there every chance I get. When Bill heard we were going to New York, he invited us to stay at his hotel overlooking Central Park. Bill said he would call his manager in New York and we could stay as long as we wanted.

When we arrived in New York we were given the royal treatment. We were put up in a suite on the 23rd floor with a view of Central Park. Flowers, fruit and wine had been placed in our room. We stayed for three days of fun.

Jack had a kind of devilish sense of humor. He got one of the Marriott postcards and wrote a funny note to Bill. It read:

> *"When we checked in, they hadn't even made up our beds yet!"*

We received a card a few days later from Bill:

> *"Now you see how busy we are. We call them 'hot beds' because there isn't enough time between guests."*

Bill Marriott had a terrific sense of humor, too.

We had a standing invitation to go to the Marriott ranch in Arizona. I'm sorry we never had the chance to go. Mr. Marriott passed away before we got there.

Maybe he snuck a salty pretzel.

CHAPTER SIXTEEN

Cabarets, Casinos and Centerfolds

One afternoon in the late Fifties Marge and Gower called and said they were leaving for Las Vegas in the morning. I should pack my duds and they'd pick me up on their way. It would be my first trip to the desert gambling town, so I was very excited, but hardly knew what to expect.

"The Champs" had just bought a new car. When you bought a car in those days, you were instructed to drive it slowly to break it in. So, we headed for Vegas at no more than forty miles per hour. It wouldn't have been bad, but "The Champs" brought their cat, "Clara Bow," along for the ride. Clara Bow yowled during the entire trip. There wasn't anything we could do to get her to stop.

When we were about halfway to Las Vegas we stopped for lunch. As we left the restaurant we bought a big bag of malted milk balls. We started eating them the minute we got in the car. So, we decided to limit ourselves to one milk ball per mile. We'd watch the speedometer. As soon as we hit the mile mark we'd eat another. By the time we got to Vegas we all were pretty queasy.

I would make that trip to-and-from Las Vegas many times over the years. I staged acts for Donald O'Connor, Janet Blair, Dennis Day, Demond Wilson (from TV's *Sanford and Son*), Shirley Jones and her husband Jack Cassidy, Barbara Eden, Anthony "Tony" Newley and many, many more. "Staging" is different from choreography, as it does not necessarily involve dance steps but rather *moves*: an arm gesture on a certain word in a lyric, a "sway," the timing of an "entrance" or "transition" to a musical cue and other "broad brush strokes" of making a performance look seamless.

Tony Newley and Alan King were on the same bill at Caesar's Palace and I staged an opening number for them to do together. It was a special material song about hats.

255

With talented Donald O'Connor in Las Vegas. Donald was president of the Professional Dancers Society before he passed away.

Anthony Newley, I don't remember her name, Alan King and me.

Tony asked me if I could come up with anything new for him to do. He performed his whole act as if there were a hundred people there, but it was only for me. He liked gimmicks. I came up with a couple of ideas, mainly having to do with his microphone. He was so pleased with them he incorporated them into his act.

JANE RUSSELL

I staged an act for Jane Russell which was scheduled to tour many countries. "Traveling" was the theme of the show and her brother had built her a wonderful prop. It was a wooden box, about three feet square. Jane would lift the lid, which had a battery operated propeller on top, and the light would go to the propeller. You couldn't see Jane behind the lid. She pressed a button and the propeller started going around. While it revolved, she pulled a costume change out of the box. When the propeller stopped and she lowered the lid, the light hit her in a new costume. She walked out from behind and went into another number. I remember one change, in particular, was a raincoat that set up "A Foggy Day in London Town."

I liked working with Jane; she was a nice gal. I was reunited with her in 1992 when I was hired to produce and direct the opening of a mall in Las Vegas. Jane and other celebrities, including my friends Ann Miller and Cyd Charisse, were there to cut the ribbon.

We all went to dinner after the show. Cyd was a quiet girl and I wasn't having much luck engaging her in conversation. Then someone at the table brought up traveling. I mentioned my favorite trip was Africa and seeing all those animals. All of a sudden Cyd lit up. "I love animals," she told me. For as long as I have known Cyd, the best and longest conversation we ever had was about those African animals.

GORDON AND SHEILA MACRAE

Probably the biggest chunk of time in Vegas was spent with my friends Gordon and Sheila MacRae. I started staging Gordon's solo act before Sheila joined to make it a "duo."

I remember when my son Chris was about ten, Gordon and I were getting an act ready for Vegas. Sheila told me she would be joining us and bringing their kids. "Why don't you bring Chris?" she asked, so I did. Sheila got us a room at the motel behind the hotel where Gordon was appearing. There was a big pool right in the middle and you didn't have to look far if you wanted to know where everyone was. The MacRaes' kids and my son were "water babies."

When we arrived in Vegas, Gordon and I rehearsed the entire day. Afterward, we took the kids out for dinner. Most of the MacRae kids ordered filet mignon. At home Chris was in a hamburger phase, so it amazed me to hear him order filet mignon, too. He had his fill that night. The girls only ate half of theirs and gave Chris the rest.

After dinner, we put the MacRae housekeeper, Mamie, in charge of overseeing the kids. I left money for Chris to buy cereal and milk from the store that was on the premises. Gordon and Sheila wanted to see the closing show of the act they were replacing, so off we went. We got back late.

I was awakened around 6:00 a.m. by the smell of bacon and eggs. Chris was proud of himself because he had made this beautiful breakfast. I was exhausted, but of course I got up and ate. After he went out with the kids I went back to sleep.

We had a rehearsal later that day with the orchestra and lights. Gordon opened and put on a terrific show!

"Put on your bathing suit and let's take the kids to Lake Mead," Sheila said the next day. We all piled into the station wagon and off we went. It was a hot, *hot* day and we didn't have air conditioning. When we got to Lake Mead we noticed a boat ramp leading down to the water. We couldn't believe it! Sheila drove right down it into the water. The water rose above the hubcaps. We opened the doors and fell into the Lake. The kids thought that was really neat.

One night Gordon asked Sheila to come out on stage with him. She did her "Southern Belle" impression (which she used to do at our "Mouse Pack" parties) and sang a duet with Gordon. Sheila also did terrific impressions of Barbra Streisand, Jackie Kennedy, Tallulah Bankhead, Zsa Zsa Gabor, Dinah Shore, Katharine Hepburn and Lena Horne.

It wasn't long until Sheila officially joined the act. Gordon did impressions, too. He did Perry Como, Dean Martin, Elvis Presley and Frank "Crazy Guggenheim" Fontaine from *The Jackie Gleason Show*.

As the MacRae's act grew more complex, so did my job. Harry Crane wrote most of the comedy and several writers, like Sammy Cahn and Shirley Henry, did special material songs. Sometimes Sheila and I wound up writing special material. We stayed up well into the night doing it. Before I knew it I was in charge of lighting, too. I designed the lighting then told the crew what I wanted.

Gordon and Sheila never went somewhere remote to break in new material as some other performers did. They headed straight for The Riviera in Las Vegas. They also played at the Coconut Grove in the Ambassador Hotel in Los Angeles and the Waldorf in New York. I went with them wherever they played. I'd stay several days after the opening to be sure everything was working, then I'd come home.

Vegas probably wasn't the best place for Gordon because of all the gambling and the drinking. After Gordon played a round of golf, he stayed at the club to play cards with the guys. It became obvious he was drinking too much. He started missing rehearsals. When he was absent, I would play his part so we could continue with the rehearsal.

I think Gordon's voice was the most beautiful of all the male singers I'd ever heard, so it hurt to see what he was doing to himself. I tried to piece together things he said or did to understand what caused this self-destructive behavior. Once he told me his mother didn't think much of his career. She thought he should have studied opera. Another time he told me was thinking of taking a year off to study opera in Europe. That never happened.

After years of fun and work it broke my heart when Sheila told me she and Gordon decided to separate. I think it broke both their hearts, too. I saw it coming, so it wasn't as much of a surprise as it was to their other friends.

After the divorce, Sheila found success when Jackie Gleason selected her to play his wife in the "Honeymooners" sketches on *The Jackie Gleason Show*. The show also had musical numbers and The June Taylor Dancers were featured. You'll remember June was the lovely dancer from The Chez Paree nightclub in Chicago who used to arrive late at night with my mother to make fudge.

Sheila went to Miami, Florida, where they filmed the show. Jackie, also known as "The Great One," wanted to rehearse near his home there. Sheila told me on the first rehearsal it felt right to take Jackie's arm during a scene.

"Don't touch me," Jackie said to her. "Don't *ever* touch me!"

Sheila had to stand still as Jackie paced back and forth. That's the way they played each and every scene. If you ever watch reruns of his shows with Audrey Meadows, you'll see the same formula. Jackie thought Sheila's hair should be red so they dyed it. Sheila eventually got some red wigs because it wasn't doing her hair any good.

After Sheila gained recognition from the *Gleason* show, she began doing many guest-spots on other television shows. She eventually decided to put together her own show and called me to help. Meanwhile, Gordon called me to stage a special number for him. So I was working with both of the MacRaes at the same time. When a friend heard what I was doing she said, "It's like having stock that split."

Gordon was famous for his appearances in the film versions of *Oklahoma, Carousel, The Desert Song* and his many Warner Bros. musicals with Doris Day. It was once said, "Gordon could do a whole act of 'closers.'" I worked on "Walking Happy," which was perfect for Gordon to do his impressions. "It's the kind of walk you walk when you're Dennis Weaver," the lyrics began. Gordon did a perfect impression of Dennis, the actor in *Gunsmoke* who limped. Then he did John Wayne.

Gordon went to Broadway to appear in *I Do, I Do* with Carol Lawrence. I was in New York at that time, too, working on another job. I called Gordon to say hello and he invited me to dinner to meet his new wife, Liz. Even though Liz knew I was one of Sheila's oldest and closest friends, she seemed pleased to meet me. I knew Gordon and Liz had a baby, but it was still a shock to see the baby in the playpen. All of Gordon's other children were grown.

Sheila's new act was a song-dance-and-comedy revue in which she did many of her wonderful impersonations. We got three big, good-looking guys (Garrett Lewis, John Frayer and Larry Billman) who were wonderful singers and dancers. Sheila got the Gleason rehearsal hall in the morning because they were off for the summer. When we walked in June Taylor had her circles drawn on the floor. June was known for overhead, Busby Berkeley-style shots. Being the nuts we were, we ran in, flung ourselves on the circles and began doing those overhead-shot moves.

On our way to rehearsal in the morning we used to stop at a bakery to pick up donuts. The man behind the counter kept staring at Sheila. We figured we knew what he was thinking, but we played it nonchalant. One day he finally worked up his nerve.

"Did anybody ever tell you that you look like the girl who plays Jackie Gleason's wife?" he asked Sheila.

"Why, *no!*" she said.

"You even *sound* like her." He called his wife out to take a look. We played it straight and never told them who Sheila really was. We took our bag of donuts and left, giggling.

One of Sheila's numbers was based on her part as Jackie's wife. The fellows played three of the characters Jackie played on his show. They wore rubber masks to look like Reggie Van Gleason, Joe the Bartender and the Poor Soul (the meek little guy in knickers). The costumes had padded stomachs because Jackie was much larger than any of them.

Sheila's point of view was that she couldn't get away from Jackie Gleason. She always had nightmares. One involved the elegant Reggie. Then he disappeared and another appeared until all three characters entered her nightmares. Each had his own theme song. It came off really well.

Another number consisted of the three fellows assembling pieces of wood. It turned out to be a stool, five feet tall, on wheels. They picked Sheila up and put her on it, then wheeled her around as she sang a pretty song. With her feathered skirt she looked like she was floating in space.

In just about every girl's act, the guys have to do a number on their own to make time for the star to change her costume. I wracked my brain to do something different. I got a crazy idea. I remember seeing the Navy throw a glowing liquid on the water to spell out "S.O.S." I had seen "black light" effect on stage, but this was different. You can't "paint" in black light.

I made many calls to the Navy before I found a man who knew what I was talking about. He told me the liquid I wanted was expensive because it faded after an hour. I talked the man into coming to my house with a small vial to show me and some dancers what it could do.

I invited the male dancers to my house for the meeting. The man from the Navy arrived with his vial. The first thing he did was paint the liquid on a plant. I clicked off the light and — by God — that plant was *glowing*! We all went crazy. I clicked the light back on. Garrett dipped the brush into the liquid and painted a skeleton on his clothing. We turned off the light and, sure enough, he was a glowing skeleton. He danced like a skeleton. We all laughed hysterically. I turned the light back on. John bravely painted crazy markings on his face and his mustache. Larry painted a picture on a handkerchief. There was no end to our creativity.

I slowly began to devise a number. Sheila pre-recorded "The Joker," which would allow her time to change and the orchestra didn't need to have their lights on. This way the theater could be pitch black.

The number began while the stage was still blacked out. All the audience could see was a bit of that glowing liquid, being painted in the shape of a joker face (similar to a jester, with a pointy beard). What they couldn't see was that Garrett, dressed in black, had thrown a tablecloth over an easel. He dipped a brush in this liquid then painted a joker face on the tablecloth.

A second dancer, in black, pulled the tablecloth off the easel. He crumpled it up and carried it off stage, a glowing mass. At the same time, Garrett painted another face. The third dancer removed that face, crumpled it and carried it off stage while Garrett painted a third. At that moment Sheila came on in the dark. She held a folded handkerchief that had been painted with a joker's face. Sheila opened it on the line "The joker is me." As she crumpled the handkerchief the light hit her so the audience didn't see the handkerchief. The illusion made it appear as though Sheila had been gliding around the stage with a glowing, joker face.

No one ever knew, until now, how we did that.

One night some of the liquid flew off the brush and landed on a woman's fur coat.

"My fur's glowing," she yelled. Luckily, the liquid did not stain so the hotel couldn't be sued.

GARY CROSBY

Gary Crosby, one of Bing's sons from his first marriage, was putting together a nightclub act of his own in the early Sixties. His agent hired Harry Crane to write his dialogue and Sammy Cahn to write special material songs. I was hired to direct and stage the act.

Gary projected a clean-cut, All-American look, not unlike Pat Boone. Gary had never danced, but I gave him some movements that fit a few of the songs. By that time, he had proven that he had talent and the potential to be a star. His high-powered agent and manager were there opening night. Gary came out in a white tuxedo and went into his opening song which he did very well. Then he spoke. What came out was not the nice, likeable kid we had rehearsed. He turned into Don Rickles! We all sat there aghast. He played that character, a kind of smart-aleck, throughout the act.

After the show we descended on Gary. I didn't really need to say anything because his manager and agents were angrily giving him a what-for. The second night he toned it down and did a wonderful show.

The next day Gary showed me a letter from Bing. Gary seemed angry because his father was treating him like a two-year-old. He'd written things like, "Be a good boy."

We all had hopes for Gary's career. But it was a challenge to match his father's incredible fame and success. Although he did have some good roles in films and on television, Gary's career never came close to his father's.

CAROL CHANNING

We SHARE girls have been putting out a daily calendar for over forty years. When I open my 1969 calendar I see a tidy little inscription that reads: "XXXO, Carol Channing."

I began that year by staging a few numbers for Carol's act. I had an idea for the lighting on one number. If you know Carol, you know she always wears a white beaded dress. I wanted to light her face with a pink light and change the color of the dress by changing the color of the light. Carol didn't understand what I was describing. She wanted to see it. The cues for the lights were musical so I went up on stage, held the dress in front of me and as the orchestra played I moved my lips along. Carol sat in the audience with her microphone and sang the lyrics.

My husband Jack happened to walk into the showroom just in time to see me on stage. He didn't realize Carol was singing from the audience. After I finished he came up to me. "That was a *fantastic* impression of Carol," he said.

Years later, when I told stories about Carol on my cruise ship talks, people would come up afterwards and ask if she has the same persona that she projects. They often want to know: "Is she wide-eyed and naïve in real life?"

I say, for the most part, yes. One cute example: to this day Carol introduces me as "Miriam Franklin." She met me as Miriam Franklin over half a century ago when she was the understudy for Eve Arden in *Let's Face It*. She knows I went on and mar-

Me with Carol Channing and Marge Champion during our 'girly' lunch in Palm Springs, one afternoon.

ried Gene and then Jack. However, when Carol meets someone, the name she hears sticks in her head no matter what happens afterward.

The times when Carol is different from her persona are in her hotel room late at night after a show. I spent many a night hanging out with her. She kicked off her shoes, removed her crazy wig and put on an old bathrobe. We would talk over our order of Chinese food about many serious subjects, things you wouldn't expect from the wide-eyed, dizzy blonde she plays.

LORNA LUFT

Remember Lorna Luft, Judy Garland's little girl, the one my assistant was afraid of flushing down the toilet during "Ford Star Jubilee?" Well, she grew up just fine. She started singing, too, just like her mother.

In 1973 Lorna's father, Sid Luft, asked me if I was available to stage an act for Lorna. I went to his home in West Los Angeles and met with him and Lorna.

Lorna is fun-loving and likes to laugh, just like her sister, Liza Minnelli. Lorna tells great stories. Those two girls are very close. I remember being in Jack Haley, Jr.'s house, when he and Liza were married. Liza, Lorna and I sat in the kitchen and had coffee and girl talk. One of them started singing one of Judy's songs and it was a perfect imitation. Then the other sang another. It might have seemed sacrilegious to anyone who didn't know how much these girls adored their mother. After all, imitation is the sincerest form of flattery. We three girls were practically falling down with laughter.

Lorna wanted to sing rock and roll, but Sid thought she should sing familiar songs, including some of Judy's. Lorna didn't want to do her mother's songs. I imagine it was hard enough being sister to Liza, let alone the daughter of one of the most famous and well-loved singers of the twentieth century. Lorna has a nice, soft quality to her voice. I think she sings better than Liza, which Liza admits.

I came up with an idea that Lorna liked. I suggested she might tell the audience that she wishes she had been born earlier so she could have been in vaudeville. That way, she could do some familiar songs and new ones, too.

After the special material was written for her, we got with pianist Lew Brown and started trying out the numbers. One number was a song and dance to both parts of a German comedy act. Milton Berle put me in touch with a comic that hung out at the Friars Club in Beverly Hills. The comic recorded the act so Lorna could study the accent.

Another song was an old, fast tune called "I Know That You Know." We had a blowup doll that looked like Fred Astaire. "Fred's" leg was connected to a piece of metal that we attached to Lorna's ankle. Lorna wore a long feathered skirt that covered the metal. When she went spinning it looked like she and Fred were a dance team.

We opened the show in the Regency Hyatt Hotel, on Peach Tree Lane, in Atlanta. The entire act was well received. One night after the show we were hungry and tired. We ordered room service then Lorna rested on the king size bed. Fred, the blowup doll, was beside her. I got on the other side. I can still visualize the room service waiter's face when he brought us our food. He didn't know quite what to make of it.

Every night I sat in the audience with my notebook and made notes. One night Lorna introduced me to the audience. "How many notes have you made tonight?" she asked. I held up the notebook. We got a good laugh.

From there we went to the St. Regis Hotel in New York. The act went over very well, so I could return to Los Angeles knowing she would be comfortable. Before I left, Lorna gave me a gift. It was a little gold bear pin I had admired in the hotel jewelry store one day. Lorna had gone back and bought it for me.

Another of her engagements was to be the opening act for Sammy Davis, Jr. in Lake Tahoe. After the show one night, Sammy invited us to his suite. I had heard that Sammy liked to cook and because he spent so much time at the hotel they put in a full kitchen for him. I *assumed* he was going to fix us a wonderful meal.

By the time I arrived with Lorna, Sammy's agent and his girlfriend were there. Everyone has heard wild stories about Hollywood parties. I had never seen one that matched the stereotype until now. They were doing coke. I felt uncomfortable immediately, but tried to act like nothing was out of the ordinary. Sammy asked, "Miriam, do you want a line?" Honestly, I would've sooner shoved bamboo under my fingernails but didn't want to look like a prude. Instead, I came out with the wildest thing I could think of. I said, "I'll have a scotch."

The next time I saw Lorna was when she put together a new act for The Factory in Los Angeles. She finally got to sing the rock songs she always wanted to sing. I thought Lorna was trying to model herself after Bette Midler, but she has a softer look and a much prettier voice. When she tried to go in that direction she came off a little tough, which I didn't find attractive for her.

Flash forward twenty years. We're at the Roosevelt Hotel in Hollywood and we're here to see Lorna's latest act. She sings great songs that let her sweet quality come through. It's an all-around terrific performance. I'm pleased to see it because I always had a soft spot for Lorna and wanted her career to soar.

EYDIE GORME & STEVE LAWRENCE

Two of my favorite people to work with are the talented Eydie Gorme and Steve Lawrence. Steve is so funny he could hold his own with any comedian. They called me to stage a Gershwin medley that was about twenty minutes long and was the finale for their act at Caesar's Palace.

Eydie and Steve are not known as dancers, although they both move well. Eydie studied tap so I put a little soft shoe in one song. But the staging I did was quite simple. Steve and Eydie are married so we worked on their act at their house in Beverly Hills. Weather permitting, we worked poolside. This was back in the day before wireless microphones (1974, to be exact), and I had to be careful to not get the cords to their mikes tangled. I got two dowels the length of a microphone, drilled a hole through one end and threaded clothesline through them. I anchored the clothesline to simulate microphones and cords.

We worked every day for weeks. Many times their two sons, Michael and David, got home from school before I left. They always gave their mom and dad a big hug and kiss. They're a very loving family. Many times, as I was leaving, the boys were shooting baskets in the driveway. They taught me how to shoot. I was never very good at it, but I had fun.

When we went to Vegas the boys came along. I used to meet them in the hotel coffee shop for breakfast. Steve and Eydie had taught Michael and David how to sign the check and write "plus 15%." I never had much of a head for mathematics so that got my attention and I started doing it myself.

The showroom at Caesar's had two grand pianos and a forty-piece orchestra. Nick Perito was their conductor. At our rehearsal it was exciting to hear the music that, until now, we had only heard on piano.

Sammy Davis Jr. closed his act the night before Eydie and Steve opened. We all watched his show from the wings. He did a lot of crazy things, knowing we were there. After the show we all went out to eat. A man I had not met sat at our table. He stared out the other way and never looked at any of us. I learned later that he was Sammy's bodyguard. I never knew why Sammy felt he had to have a bodyguard.

Steve and Eydie's lives would be shattered a few years later when, tragically, their son Michael would die from a heart condition. As any parent understands, his death was devastating, especially to Eydie. She couldn't work for the longest time. I believe it was David, their other son, who convinced Eydie that work would be the best cure for her sorrow. David traveled with them and conducted the orchestra. Eydie could never sing "If He Walked Into My Life" after Michael's death. It was such a pity because she sang that song better than anybody.

The Singing Playmates publicity still. Michele Drake, Heidi Sorenson, Sonie Theodore and Nicki Thomas.

THE SINGING PLAYMATES

Did you ever wonder what *Playboy* centerfolds were *really* like? I got a call from an agent asking if I'd be interested in staging one of the most unusual acts I ever worked on, called "The Singing Playmates." I wasn't sure what a *Playmate* Centerfold *did* — except be beautiful and expose a lot more flesh than I would ever have the guts to expose!

"What kind of act?" I asked nervously. It was to be a Vegas-style act they could use to "open" for name performers like Don Rickles, Alan King or Buddy Hackett. I thought that before I agreed I'd better meet the girls to see what I was getting into.

I went to the rehearsal hall on Sepulveda Boulevard one evening to watch them perform. Hugh Hefner had converted a store into a rehearsal hall with a new dance floor, mirrors on the wall, a ballet *barre* and couches, chairs and a well-stocked refrigerator. It goes without saying these young women were beautiful and had gorgeous bodies but their singing was fair and their dancing was fairer. I had my doubts about their abilities, but Mr. Hefner was paying terrific money.

The girls could only rehearse at night, which was fine by me. I had already been asked work on *Sesame Street Live* during the day. Talk about contrasts. For the next several months my days would be filled with "Bert and Ernie," "Kermit" and

"Miss Piggy" from *Sesame Street* (more about that later) and my nights were spent rehearsing four *Playboy* centerfolds.

The playmate who dreamed up the concept was Ms. July 1977, Sondra "Sonie" Theodore — who was Hugh Hefner's girlfriend. The other four were Heidi Sorenson, Miss July '81, Michele Drake, Miss May '79, Nicki Thomas, Miss March '77 and a playmate named Kelli, who quit the act pretty quickly.

Sonie was the best singer of the group and had a crazy sense of humor. Even so, I knew it was going to be a big job to mold them into a professional group. For the

Hugh Hefner dropped in to see how rehearsals were going.

most part, they were small-town girls with no professional experience. We'd only been rehearsing a day or two when it became clear the lack of experience was not the only challenge I had to overcome.

These girls had so many personal problems – mostly related to boyfriends – you wouldn't believe it. I decided to keep a journal. One girl was tired one day. The other had a stomach ache. "Michelle off." "Heidi's head on Mars." "Michelle upset." "Sonie cried." One day the girls had a big fight and none of them came to rehearsal. "Heidi mad." "Nicki can't talk." "Heidi threw up." "Nicki cried." "Michelle cried." "Nicki mad." "Heidi out." "Heidi back." "Heidi mad." It was so rare when a day passed without incident that it was noteworthy: "Everyone good!" The exclamation point was in the original entry.

I listened to all the songs the girls knew and decided a good opening song would be "I'm So Glad I'm a Woman." They wore flats, boots or sneakers as they rehearsed. I asked them to bring in a pair of high heels. Would you believe it, none of these playmates had a pair! I gave them a shopping assignment. I laughed to myself at that first rehearsal watching them try to walk around in heels. They looked as if they were little girls in their mother's high heels.

The piano player never seemed to play a song the same way twice, so I brought in Richard "Dick" Priborsky who had been the conductor for Marge and Gower. I had worked with him many times over the years. Dick is great at creating "dance arrangements" and I knew he could also help the girls vocally.

I was often invited to the Playboy mansion, but I always declined because I had heard wild stories and I didn't want to be embarrassed. One day Mr. Hefner made me an offer I couldn't refuse. I was invited to a lunch meeting at the mansion for a progress report and to present my ideas for the act. I lunched with the girls, their

Rehearsing with the Playmates.

agent and Marjorie Throne, who was in charge of handling the money for the act. Marj has become one of my best friends. After we were served a delicious meal on the patio, we were asked into a formal dining room. Mr. Hefner entered, dressed in his trademark satin pajamas, and we were introduced. He took his seat at the head of the table and then we all sat.

"So, Miriam," Mr. Hefner asked, "how's the act coming along?" I told him all of my ideas. Some of them were going to cost a bit of money and I fully expected he might not go along with them. But he went along with each and every one of them. *Whew!* He was very cordial to us. And that was the end of the meeting.

After the meeting, Mr. Hefner left and the girls took me on a tour of the mansion. Mr. Hefner had a large collection of wild animals that were caged. It was like going through a zoo. He had monkeys and an assortment of cats. He even had an aviary. I got to see the infamous grotto, which was part of the pool. You could swim from one side of the grotto to the other.

The girls were especially listless one night during rehearsal. Of course, who should walk in but Mr. Hefner. The girls called him "Hef," but I could never bring myself to being that familiar. I never saw the girls shape up so fast in all my life. He asked to see some numbers. The girls really put on a show for him. They had such energy that for the first time, I could see this act was going to work just fine.

The girls needed to get used to performing in front of an audience. I asked the manager if we could do the act someplace where no one important would see it. As it turned out, the first time the girls performed was on New Year's Eve, 1981, on *The Tonight Show with Johnny Carson*! The girls were scared spitless, but got through it. They got a booking shortly after that show in Atlantic City. I was able to work the booking around my commitment to *Sesame Street*, so I went along.

We were surprised when we got to Atlantic City, because the girls were the starring act. They got a booking in Manila and then Japan. The bookers in Manila sent me a letter telling me my ticket would be forthcoming in a few days. The girls went ahead to do some publicity layouts. Day after day I looked for my ticket. It never arrived. Finally, the day came I had to leave. I asked Jack to take me to the airport.

"How are you going to get to Manila with no ticket?" my husband asked as he was driving me to LAX.

Being the Pollyanna I am, I said it would work—and it did! They didn't have a ticket for me at the airport, but they had me on record. I was met at the airport in Manila and driven to the hotel where the girls would be performing. I went into the ballroom to see the stage before I went up to my room. It had been built especially for The Singing Playmates. I couldn't believe the expense that had gone into this special stage. It had a dressing room on either side. The curtains would go up. Risers were on one side for our twelve-piece orchestra.

The girls were real cute. They had prearranged to have a woman come to my room and give me a massage after my long trip. The massage was terrific! The next day we met for rehearsal. The musicians were already rehearsing when we got there. The girls told me I should be glad I didn't arrive in Manila as early as they had. They were wined and dined by some pretty lecherous Filipino men.

The music sounded fine and the rehearsal went off just great. We were invited to a big dinner the night before the show, but who could eat? We pretended to, so as not to offend our host. Just prior to the show, I was told the man who was going to introduce the Singing Playmates had not arrived and I was going to have to do it. I always thought a male announcer sounded better on a microphone than a woman but there didn't seem to be anyone else to do it. It was a strange experience. I made the introduction off stage. The room was so big each word I said echoed back. I kept thinking I had to stop talking until the echo stopped. I found the trick is to keep talking and not listen to yourself. Everybody seemed happy, so I guess it was all right.

The next day the girls had been scheduled to be in a commercial. They wanted me to come to be sure it went well. The man directing was doing so many bits and pieces it would have taken days to shoot. I couldn't stand it any longer.

"Might I offer a suggestion?" I finally asked. I showed him how he could move his camera and make a longer, continuous shot. I don't know what he thought of me, but he was courteous and followed my suggestion. We got out of there and rushed back to the hotel so the girls could get dressed and made up for another show. They played a few days then we boarded a plane to do the same thing in Japan.

Dick and I went to the Playboy Club in Tokyo to check it out. The stage was much smaller than the one in Manila and there was no room for an orchestra. Dick was pretty upset. He had been promised twelve musicians and it looked as though it wasn't going to happen. I met with the Japanese crew who were working the lights and sound. I tried telling them there wasn't room for the orchestra but they didn't seem to understand much of what I was saying.

Dick got the bright idea to use the tapes we had recorded in Manila. The girls would mouth the words. We brought in some curtains for the girls to make changes since there were no dressing rooms. The show wasn't like Manila, but the audience sure loved The Singing Playmates, so I guess it didn't matter.

The girls were finally booked into The Playboy Club in Century City and I was asked to make certain that the act was "clean." On opening day—much to our surprise — Mr. Hefner showed up at our run-through. He wanted to talk to Sonie so they went off to a corner table. Who was I to tell him he was interrupting our rehearsal? As Mr. Hefner left, he said he might come watch the act that night. Later, Sonie let me know that she and Hef were having problems. The spotlight man told me he had never lit a show with Mr. Hefner there. He was so nervous he didn't think he could do it.

Hugh Hefner *did* show up that night as promised and the light man panicked and couldn't do it. No one else knew the show, *so guess who wound up being the light man?* He showed me how to turn the follow spot on and off, tighten or widen it, slip in all the colored gels and how to dim out or black out. Running the lights that night was a good experience.

A short time later, Sonie invited Jack and me to a birthday party she was giving for herself. Because she and Mr. Hefner were having problems, she hadn't given him a wish list, although I knew she wanted a particular raincoat with a mink lining. I don't think Sonie ever asked for much, anyway. I never saw her wear expensive jewelry; she drove an inexpensive car and lived in a mediocre apartment in Westwood. In spite of their problems, Sonie felt she should let Hef know she was having the party so he could come if he wanted.

Sonie and a few friends spent all day preparing a buffet. It was the first party she had ever thrown and it was very nice. Not knowing how much alcohol to buy, she only had *one* bottle of champagne. It went pretty fast. We were about halfway through her buffet when the doorbell rang. She opened the door. There stood Hugh Hefner with a big present for her. It was the one thing she wanted – her raincoat with a mink lining. When Mr. Hefner learned she was out of champagne, he sent his chauffeur back to the mansion to bring a case back. In spite of this happy occasion, it wasn't long afterward that they broke up.

So did the act.

CHAPTER FIFTEEN

Fly Me To The Moon

NEIL ARMSTRONG

At a birthday party for Tony Orlando, one of the guests brought him a present, Neil Armstrong. He had just come back from outer space. He was asked to speak, which he did. I was told, and I don't know if it is true, that all the astronauts have been briefed on how to speak about their experiences. He was so charming and humble. Everyone wanted to shake his hand. When it was my turn, I said, "Do you have one more handshake in you?" He said, "Sure," and his hand came out to shake mine. For the first time I realized why fans are so thrilled to shake the hands of a movie star and say "I don't ever want to wash this hand!" After that encounter, I felt the same way.

BUZZ ALDRIN

When I casually mentioned to my son I was going to a cocktail party at Buzz Aldrin's, he got so excited, and asked me to get him an autographed picture. Mind you, he was not a baby now but a grown man. This was unusual for Chris, who had grown up with celebrities his whole life and never paid much attention. This was different. He had never asked me to do anything like this before, so I had to get that picture.

The party was so crowded, I could hardly get in the front door. I slowly worked my way around until I got in. Finally, I spotted 'him' surrounded by people.

"How will I ever get through to him and ask for 'the' picture," I thought. After quite a while, the party started to thin out. I waited my chance and finally saw a brief opening. I seized the moment, shook his hand and told him, "This is the first time my son had ever asked me to do anything like this before, so I can't disappoint him." Buzz indicated that if he was seen signing a picture, other people would start asking for one too. I must have looked so forlorn, he asked my son's name. I told him, "Chris." Then he said, "See the lady over there?" I nodded. "When you are ready to leave, ask her for the envelope." It was like a mystery movie. Sure enough, when I was leaving, she was at the door. I asked her if she had an envelope for me. She produced it out of thin air and I was gone with a treasure for my son.

Here I am, with astronaut Gordon Cooper.

GORDON COOPER

My next job was to stage a show at the Hollywood Bowl. It would have many ethnic dance groups performing. So many, there wasn't enough room backstage for them all. Groups were brought in one busload at a time. They would do their routine and would be bused out as another busload came in.

At a meeting in producer Bob Jani's office, we talked about having a major star do a dramatic, patriotic reading, while a children's choir sang. We discussed the best voices, like Gregory Peck, Charlton Heston, etc... We struck out with all of them. I kept reading the list of names on Jani's blackboard. One name jumped out at me, astronaut Gordon Cooper. After my experiences with Neil Armstrong and Buzz Aldrin, I thought he would be perfect. When all agreed, it became my job to make it happen. I gulped and made the call to his Beverly Hills office. I was able to get through to him. I told him of our Show. He asked if he could see the script and we made a date for the next day. I gave him the script and received another 'handshake.' He read his part and was happy with it. Whew!

I called the Choirmaster at the school and told him with whom the children would be singing. He asked if it would be at all possible if Gordon Cooper could rehearse at the school so the rest of the children would have the opportunity to meet him. After another call, we agreed that I would pick up Gordon and drive him there.

It was a good half hour away. While driving, I realized I had an astronaut all to myself. What could I ask him? The first question, of course, was "Did you ever see a flying saucer?" He said he had not but some of his buddies had. "They flew alongside the plane, then veered off and just disappeared." While driving home from rehearsal, he said he was hungry and asked if we could stop somewhere. We had a lovely lunch and talked some more. He asked about my work and seemed interested in my babbling.

I had to be at the bowl early the day of the show, so he drove himself. The show went off without a hitch. I hated to say good-by to my astronaut.

CHUCK YEAGER

Shortly after these experiences, Jack and I went to a friend's for dinner where I couldn't stop talking about my astronauts. They asked me if I had ever read Chuck Yeager's book, *Breaking the Sound Barrier*. I hadn't, so they loaned me their copy, which was fascinating reading.

Now back to work. A half time show at a college, I think in Wyoming, with pom-pom girls. We rehearsed in the gymnasium. The day of the game came and we were out on the football field. I looked up and saw written on a huge electric sign "Welcome Chuck Yeager." I couldn't believe it. I asked where I could find him and was told I could find him in the tower, watching the game with the mayor and some other dignitaries. He would come down in the elevator at halftime. During the first half of the game, I scurried back to my hotel and got the book. Thank goodness I had brought it to read on my trip. You can be sure I was right near the elevator before halftime. When the door opened, out they came. The group stopped about ten feet from where I was standing. As they were talking, Chuck just happened to glance my way. I held up the book, then the pen. He laughed and gestured for me to come over. He took the book and pen and signed it.

When I got back to LA, I invited my friends over for dinner and to return the book. My dilemma was, do I give them the signed book or buy them a new one? I gave them the book and told them to look inside. Now they started laughing and accused my husband of signing it. It took a lot of talking to convince them it was real. As much as I might have wanted to keep the book for myself, it was well worth the fun of giving it to them.

CHAPTER SEVENTEEN

Stages, Ballrooms, Arenas and Ice

RADIO CITY MUSIC HALL

The day after the 1970 Academy Awards show I received a call from Radio City Music Hall. The famous producer Leon Leonidoff had enjoyed the bicycle number ("Raindrops Keep Falling...") so much he wanted to know if I would choreograph it at Radio City. Would I? You bet!

Everyone knows Radio City has the Rockettes, the thirty-six dancers who do their signature kick line. But many people don't realize they have a ballet company too. I always thought if I ever staged anything at the Music Hall it would be for the Rockettes. But I had been asked to create the number with the ballet company.

After I settled into my hotel I jumped in a cab. The driver dropped me off in front of Radio City and it really took me back in time. I remembered the day so many years ago when I had auditioned to be a Rockette myself. I was supposed to come back when I had grown up. "I guess I *have* grown up," I thought to myself.

I held auditions for male dancers and got lucky because two of the original dancers from the Academy Awards telecast were in New York and wanted to be in the show. It was helpful to have them there because they knew the entire routine. Radio City got me the bicycles and the new dancers started learning the tricks.

The first time we rehearsed I was concerned about safety because the bicycles rushed on- and offstage. I roped off an area backstage to reduce the threat of injury. Before we started I called everybody out onstage. I stood in the middle of the theater at a lighted table and spoke into the microphone.

"These bicycles are dangerous," my voice boomed throughout the theater. "They will fly offstage, turn around and come back on." I went on a while longer about the importance of the riders taking every precaution. After rehearsal a couple dancers told me it was one of the best speeches they had ever heard.

"What speech?" I asked.

"About the dangers of the bicycles," they said.

I told them I didn't consider it a speech. I just wanted to be sure no one got hurt.

"But you didn't yell at us," they said. "You just talked normally."

While I was there I ran into Russell Markert, the dear man who originated the Rockettes and for whom I auditioned so many years ago. He was still the head choreographer, but would be retiring the following year. He had heard I might be asked to become a permanent fixture at Radio City Music Hall. I was doing pretty well in California and didn't want to go back to New York. I just wanted to do the shows periodically at "The Hall," as they referred to it.

"The Rockettes are asked to do many functions," he told me. "Someone might call and ask for twelve Rockettes, but

At Radio City Music Hall with Leon Leonidoff.

don't ever do that," he went on to advise me. "It takes all thirty-six dancers to create an impact." Then he told me something I thought was a bit pitiful. He said to be sure if I worked for Radio City to not let them break my heart. I guess his heart had been broken many times over the years.

ANN MILLER

The following year I created a couple of routines for Ann Miller for *Anything Goes* at the Muny-Opera in St. Louis. Ann told me she would call after opening night to let me know how it went. Opening night came and went and she didn't call so I called her. I found out she had been hit in the head by one of the hydraulic drapes and was hospitalized.

After that, Ann didn't dance for many months. She got dizzy. Finally, she called one day. "I'd like to get back to dancing," Ann said. "Will you come in and work with me?"

I worked with Ann quite a few times over the years, including helping her get ready for an appearance on *The Merv Griffin Show*. He had been so good to her that she wanted to do something *new*. She called me a few days later to tell me she wasn't doing the show. He wouldn't pay for the new orchestrations so she wasn't going to do it.

MARY MARTIN

Mary Martin starred in so many Broadway shows you could fill a book with the titles alone. She did *South Pacific, I Do, I Do,* and, of course, *Peter Pan.* In the early Eighties Mary hosted a PBS television program called *Over Easy.* The show was so successful she became the darling of San Francisco. Bill Brennan, a friend of mine from CBS, produced the show.

Janet Gaynor was the guest star one day. After the show, Mary, her manager and Janet were struck broadside while riding in a taxi. The accident was terrible, killing Mary's manager instantly and sending Mary and Janet to the hospital. Janet eventually died from injuries she had sustained, and Mary was told she might never walk again. Everyone was stunned.

Mary received therapy every day at a wonderful rehabilitation center. The doctors, nurses and therapists never gave up on her. Then — miracle of miracles — Mary got up on her feet. She started walking with the help of a walker. Eventually she graduated to a cane, and finally was able to walk on her own.

Mary was so grateful to the doctors, nurses and therapists she wanted to do something for them. The center needed many things they couldn't afford so Mary decided to put on a fundraiser. Bill Brennan called and asked if I was available to direct the show. I was glad to finally work with the wonderfully talented Mary Martin.

I flew to San Francisco for a meeting at Mary's lovely apartment. We talked all day about the songs she would sing and the celebrities who might participate. She got commitments from John Raitt, Lou Rawls, Van Johnson, Dolores Hope and, naturally, her own son, Larry Hagman, who played J.R. on *Dallas.* We wanted Robert Preston, who had starred with her in *I Do, I Do* to be the master of ceremonies. I said I'd call him. I got a notion that at some point in the show we could put Mary on her piano and have each star in the show sing something special to her. I'd see if I could get Sammy Cahn to write lyrics. The show conductor had been training a glee club of approximately fifty men. We decided to use the glee club, too.

Because Mary had so many costume changes, she said she'd feel more secure if her longtime wardrobe lady from New York could come and help her with her fast changes. The wardrobe lady, who was living in Palm Springs, agreed to come up especially for the show.

Before I left, Mary, who was forty-one when she originated the role of *Peter Pan* on Broadway, told me she had recently seen Sandy Duncan play the role on Broadway. She couldn't believe her eyes when Sandy was flown from the stage up to the top balcony and back down again. Mary had only been able to fly side to side. She always had it in her mind she wanted to do that. Now was her chance — at sixty-nine years old!

I went to see the Davies Symphony Hall. It was beautiful. It had a pit for the orchestra that was on a lift so it could rise up to stage level. There were four or five rows of seats like a mezzanine above the stage. Bill's idea for the set was a big staircase where Mary could make her entrance. The only problem was that it had to be built and would be very expensive.

After I returned to Los Angeles I kept thinking about that staircase. It seemed a shame to spend that much money on something we would only use for Mary's entrance. I came up with a cheaper alternative that could have just as much impact.

I thought the orchestra should be on stage and the glee club should be in the mezzanine. We would open with an overture of songs that were connected to Mary. As the glee club sang Mary's songs, Mary would slowly rise from the orchestra pit. The top of the balcony would see her first, building excitement and anticipation as she rose.

One of the first songs Mary was associated with was "My Heart Belongs to Daddy" from the Broadway show *Leave It to Me*. She performed it originally sitting atop a steamer trunk wearing a short fur jacket that showed off her legs. Her legs were still

Mary Martin and I listening to the music during rehearsal.

great, so I decided to recreate this moment as her entrance. I called Bill and explained my idea. He bought it and gave me the go ahead to develop the rest of the show.

I called Robert Preston. He couldn't have been sweeter. "I like lady directors," Bob told me. "I just worked with one, so we'll get along fine." I called Sammy Cahn and told him what I wanted. Sammy was so prolific it was hard for him to write just one chorus. Once he got started he wrote chorus after chorus. What a gift!

We didn't have a comedian, so I called Roy Gerber, an agent in Hollywood, and told him we wanted a clean act. He told me about an up-and-coming comic he thought would fit the bill. We asked, "Will he wear a tuxedo and work 'clean'?" He assured me this young man would be perfect. This young comic, who was just getting started, was Arsenio Hall.

We brought in Peter Foy, who had flown Mary in the original production of *Peter Pan* in 1954. "Flying by Foy" was the best in the business when it came to stage flying and would rig the theater ceiling. He would make Mary's wish come true. The harness Mary had worn in *Peter Pan* had been donated to the Smithsonian Institution, so we borrowed it back. Mary's figure had not changed at all over the years and it still fit!

A few days before the show, we began rehearsals. I didn't realize that when Mary did a Broadway show she didn't hold a hand mike. So, when she was singing with

John Raitt, she would forget to move her head with the microphone or she would start lowering her hand and didn't realize it. He was cute. He kept pushing her elbow up to remind her to keep the mike nailed to her mouth.

Larry Hagman did a wonderful rendition of "Deep in the Heart of Texas." (He and his mother are from Texas.) He went into a special material chorus of "Honey Bun" from *South Pacific*, singing about his mom. On cue, Mary came out in that great big sailor suit she had worn in that show and they did a duet that I staged.

I had not been forewarned that one day a week Larry does not talk. He never picked the same day. I had no way of knowing what day he wouldn't talk until that day. Wouldn't you know — it was the day of the rehearsal. He absorbed everything I told him and even sang songs. He just wouldn't talk. "Off-the-wall" is an expression that comes to mind.

In case you didn't know, Dolores Hope, Bob's wife, was a band singer when they met. Dolores was one of Mary's favorite singers. She thought she had a "clear, pure voice." So when Mary asked her, Dolores consented to perform a couple of songs. I must say, she was very sweet.

When Van Johnson walked into the rehearsal hall he spotted me immediately. "Well, Miss Franklin," he said, "What do you want me to do?" We had hugs and kisses. I hadn't seen him since we worked together at Billy Rose's Casa Manaña. I told him several of us dancers from Broadway had gone to see his first movie. We all applauded and carried on like crazy. We couldn't believe it when they dyed his gorgeous red hair black. Thank God they wised up and let him be himself.

The night of the show arrived and we were all excited. The orchestra was ready. The glee club was in the mezzanine. I went up into the light booth and slipped on my headset. I called to the stage manager and he said everyone was in place, including Mary, down in the orchestra pit on the trunk. The conductor was cued and he started the overture.

As the orchestra and glee club began performing Mary's numbers, the pit began to slowly rise. When the glee club started singing, "Cause it was Mary, Mary, Mary is a Grand Old Name," Mary began appearing to the audience in the balcony. They started applauding and yelling, which built tremendous excitement. Then the mezzanine saw her and then the loges. The excitement kept building. By the time Mary was in full view, the audience was on its feet, going wild. The orchestra started vamping "My Heart Belongs to Daddy." The orchestra had to vamp for quite a while before the audience had quieted down enough that Mary could start singing. When she finished, of course, the audience was back on its feet. What an opening!

I'm glad we trusted Roy, the Hollywood agent, and went with the unknown comic. Arsenio was perfect. Even so, I couldn't have imagined the heights he would attain.

Mary's and Larry's number went over terrifically, too. I found out later that when Larry was a boy he was in a show or two of Mary's and had been performing long before *I Dream of Jeannie* and *Dallas*.

Van's trademark was to wear red socks. His jacket was lined with red, too, which he showed to the audience. This got a good laugh.

Sammy Cahn came out and started his number with all the celebrities, minus the one we needed most: Mary Martin! My stomach flipped!

"*Where's Mary?*" I called through my headset from the lighting booth to the stage manager backstage. Everybody backstage raced to Mary's dressing room to find her. Meanwhile, Sammy Cahn, a.k.a. Mr. Talent, started an ad lib of funny little parodies. The stars around his piano were laughing at his jokes. I knew Sammy was doing bits from his one-man show. Mary still didn't appear so Sammy kept joking.

Now, about that wardrobe lady Mary brought up from Palm Springs. I wrote the order of the rundown of the show myself, including what costume or gown Mary was to wear in each number. I taped a copy to the mirror in her dressing room so she could easily read it.

I found out when Mary came offstage from her last number that the wardrobe lady put her into the Peter Pan costume and harness. Wrong! They realized the mistake when someone pounded on the door screaming she was late for the Sammy number. There was no time to take off the harness. They pulled off the costume and tried getting her into her gown which would not fit over the harness. Luckily, Mary had a full flowing dress she was to wear in the finale. The wardrobe lady put her into that. As soon as they got Mary to the wings, she walked on stage like nothing had happened. Van Johnson lifted her onto the piano.

"For God's sake," Van asked later, "what were you wearing?"

The number went off without a hitch and the audience was none the wiser, thanks to Sammy. Mary's next costume change was Peter Pan. The number started with a blackout. The audience heard pixie music and saw a laser light. It was a teeny spotlight going up and around the stage and out over the audience.

"Tink," Mary called out referring to the little fairy, Tinkerbell. "Tink, is that you?" The music sounded like Tinkerbell talking back to her. With that, a spotlight hit Mary. Mary was positioned on a platform on one side of the stage. She immediately took off and flew up to the balcony.

In all my years I never heard such a gasp from an audience. Here was Mary Martin, who everyone thought would never walk again, flying overhead. We prerecorded Mary's voice to "I'm Flying" because it wouldn't be spiffy for Peter Pan to carry a microphone. Mary started lip-syncing as she dipped into the pouch on her belt to sprinkle "pixie dust" over the audience. After several trips up to the balcony and back again she landed on stage.

For the finale, the stars lined up across stage and sang their final song. Colorful, helium-inflated balloons started coming up in front of them on the orchestra pit. Finally, the audience saw who was holding the balloons. It was the doctors and nurses from the trauma centers, dressed in uniform. Mary came downstage and thanked all of them.

"A wonderful time was had by all," as they say, especially me because I was given a healthy bonus for finding a way to cut out the expensive staircase. I never had that happen before.

SESAME STREET LIVE

Bob Shipstad, whose father was half of the Shipstad and Johnson's *Ice Follies* legacy, had asked me to direct and choreograph a *Sesame Street* traveling arena show called *Sesame Street Live*. I started by trying out music with Paul Walberg. All the numbers were fun to choreograph. The show audience was children and for children you can be as silly as you want. In fact, the sillier the better.

As I was also working with *The Playmates* at the same time, I was supposed to be in Japan for their entire four-day engagement, but on my second day I received a telegram asking if I could be in Canada in two days to record Jim Henson and Frank Oz for *Sesame Street Live.* They were in the middle of shooting a movie and it was the only day they could make these recordings. The show was in good shape so I knew it would be all right to leave, even though I hated to go. We were going to tour Japan the next day and I wanted to see the temples, but *c'est la guerre.* Dick took me to the travel office and helped me arrange my schedule and get my ticket for Toronto.

The next morning Dick put me on a bus for the airport. I was impressed with the white linen on the headrest. It was an enjoyable ride, but it was mainly on the freeway so I didn't see much of Japan.

My flight to Toronto was re-routed. Instead of connecting in Los Angeles I was flown through San Francisco. I thought I surely would miss that flight. As soon as we landed in San Francisco I got out of my seat and started racing. I got my luggage, went through Customs, took a bus ride to another terminal, checked in and made it to my gate which, of course, was the last terminal.

As I got onto my flight to Toronto, the stewardess closed the door behind me. I must have looked pale and thirsty. The stewardess didn't wait for me to take my seat. She asked if she could get anything.

"How about half a dozen Cokes?" I joked.

We landed in Toronto and I was shuttled to my hotel. I was supposed to get a call in the morning that someone would pick me up for rehearsal. The next morning came and I didn't get a phone call. I was getting nervous, and then I noticed a white piece of paper that had been placed under my door.

"Sorry for the inconvenience," it read, "but the water will be turned off from 8:00 a.m. until 10:00 a.m. on Saturday." I had a pretty good case of jetlag and I was certain it was Sunday so I wondered why they slipped an outdated note under my door. I called the front desk.

"What day is this?" I asked.

"Why, it's Saturday," the woman told me. I couldn't believe it. *I had gained a day!* I ordered breakfast from room service. Then I called a beauty parlor and made an appointment to have a facial, my hair done, a manicure and a pedicure. I was beginning to feel like a new woman. I had a leisurely dinner and went back to bed.

The next morning I got that call that I'd be picked up in an hour. Off we went to the recording studio. Jim and Frank were right on time. I was officially their director, but they didn't need much direction. I only had to occasionally get up and do a dance or show them how I staged a scene so they could match the physical energy in their voices. The pre-recorded music was played for them on earphones and they sang all the songs. It was quite an experience watching these two bearded men act like "Bert," "Ernie" and several other characters.

When the session was over I mentioned to Jim that my grandson, Matthew, would be thrilled to know I had worked with him. He asked me how old Matthew was and I told him and that he had a birthday coming up.

Jim told the engineer to put in a fresh tape. All of a sudden Jim and Frank, as "Bert and Ernie," started talking about Matthew's birthday party. They said they didn't get an invitation. They went on about how they didn't really want to go anyway. Then they decided Matthew was a good kid, and maybe they should go. This went on for a good three or four minutes. Sometimes Jim would throw in the voice of "Kermit the Frog." It was priceless. Needless to say, when I played it for Matthew he was totally awed!

From there, Paul Walberg and I flew to New York to record the other voices. It was interesting to match the people with the voices I had heard so often. The man who did "Cookie Monster" did several other voices. He had to do "Cookie Monster" last because it really ripped up his throat.

While in New York we were fortunate to see Henson's studios. It was several floors of an apartment building. They were making all the character costumes and heads for our show and it was faintly unnerving to see the smiling heads lined up on shelves.

I flew back to Los Angeles to find actors that were suited to these characters. They had to learn the songs and be able to manipulate the mouths by a wire that ran down one of the character's arms. It was fun to watch them sit around the piano and sing as their hands opened and closed in time with the words. Their hands had to move so fast to match the mouths — I don't know how they did it.

Sesame Street Live was to open in Minneapolis. Our stage was built in an arena and all our sets and props were made there. I gathered a wonderful group of local dancers and we rehearsed four weeks before opening. On opening night I had as much fun watching the children in the audience as I did watching the show. They screamed and clapped every time a new character was introduced.

Since I am so fond of tap, I made the character "Prairie Dawn" the lead dancer in an MGM-type number. I surrounded her with twelve monsters in top hats and tails. I had pre-recorded taps for all the dancers. "Prairie Dawn" wore a beautiful gown with feathers around the hem. After the show was over, I went into the lobby to overhear what the audience had to say. One lady said she didn't know how those monsters could tap so well with those "humongous" feet.

ICE

While we were in Minneapolis working on *Sesame Street Live*, Bob Shipstad asked me to direct, stage and design an ice show for Radio City Music Hall. The show would simply be called *Ice*.

"Why do you want me?" I asked Bob. "I'm not even an ice skater."

"I don't want this to be a typical ice show, Miriam," he told me. He wanted to blend skating with Broadway show music and classical music. He said this would be his most challenging ice show because it was a "pure vision of interpreting music while skating." He thought I was the perfect person to come up with this new and different look.

We spent many nights dreaming up ideas for the show, trying to keep to a reasonable budget. Bob and I went into New York and presented the idea to Radio City. It's hard to tell whether people like your ideas. You just go in there and give it your best. Evidently they were impressed because Bob got a call saying they wanted us to go ahead with the show.

Paul Walberg, who did the music for *Sesame Street Live*, was hired to do the music. He and I spent days and days and *days* listening to music and talking over ideas. The key to the success for this show was staging it for the theater, rather than an arena.

The stars were gold medal winners Peggy Fleming, Robin Cousins and Toller Cranston. We had three other pair skaters who skated in different styles: smooth, dancing and another style that includes overhead lifts. We also had a chorus of twenty-four skaters. I began designing the show, using the forte of each skater. I liked doing the show because skaters can get anywhere, fast.

I dreamed up a ballet for Peggy and Robin that would be in a ballroom scene where Toller was a thief who steals jewels from the leading lady. Paul and I found a

Toller Cranston, Robin Cousins, me and Sheila MacRae.

piece of dramatic music we thought was perfect. I had never heard the music before so I asked him where he got it.

"It's a score from a pornographic movie," he told me.

Bob sent Paul and me to Toller's home in Canada to describe Toller's ballet. Toller is an elegant man and said he only liked to skate to music that was symphonic. Anything else was beneath him. We played the music and he wanted to know where it came from. "It's from a movie," we told him. He said he didn't like movie music and wasn't sure he would skate to it.

We went back to Canada three times after this trip to find skaters. Each time we pushed Tollar to accept this piece of music. He finally came around. Toller and I became friends. It amused me when he asked for "dirt" about Hollywood. (I intended to get him a copy of *The National Enquirer*, but never got around to it.) Unless he reads this book, he'll never know he skated to music from a pornographic movie.

I thought it would be exciting to have a Slavic dance for the first-act finale. I envisioned ramps coming from the boxes on either side of the stage. I knew the male skaters in the show were so crazy they would do leaps and jumps that would create a dramatic effect. They had to use fake ice on the ramps but it was good enough to slide down.

I envisioned all of the skaters doing a sit-spin or camel-spin at the same time. These spins are usually reserved for the stars. I dreamed of twelve white grand pianos being pushed out on the ice by male skaters dressed in white tails. They would appear to play the piano. Of course, the pianos weren't real. The girls skated in and out of those pianos at one point. We had them all lined up and lowered the lids at the end of the number. In the finale, Peggy, Robin and Toller would walk out across the tops of the pianos.

I needed an assistant who could skate. Bob arranged for me to meet a young man he thought might work out. When we met I described what I felt the number should be. He kept interjecting his own creative thoughts. I could see I wouldn't get the show I wanted. Then Bob came up with Sara Kawahara who had worked with Peggy and many other great skaters. When we met, I described what one of the numbers should be. She became enthusiastic and I knew I had found my gal!*

Sara and I went to Canada, Chicago and Los Angeles to find the best skaters. Then we went into rehearsal at Lake Placid, New York. They have several ice rinks there, which was perfect because I could be working with the chorus in one rink and the pairs and solo performers in another.

I had another assistant named Cathy, also a wonderful skater. Cathy, Sara and I had our own chalet. There were two bedrooms upstairs and one down. We had a kitchen and a fireplace. Often, after rehearsals, we fixed dinner then sat in front of the fire and talked about the next day. Many times I would make up a dance step and show it to Sara. Then she would perform it on the ice. One morning we awoke to find that we were snowed in. They had to come dig us out so we could get out the front door! It was so cold we put on layers of sweaters under our coats. For days afterward we would rotate the order of sweaters so we weren't seen in the same one twice.

I arrived at the frozen rinks in my quilted down coat. It amazed me to see these girls in short costumes and bare arms. They told me skaters expend so much energy when they skate their bodies kept them warm. When I gave them a ten-minute break they would never sit. They would skate freestyle. At first it scared me to death to watch them because they would do tricks and jumps. But they never ran into each other.

One day I heard the Olympic ski jumpers were practicing. I asked Bob if we could take a long lunch and go see them. He was the best boss for whom anyone could ever work. He arranged a bus to take us up to the site. We stood at the bottom where they landed. A lift was running to take them back to the top but they took their skis off and walked up. I was told they didn't want their muscles to cool. It seemed like every minute a bell would ring and another skier would come down. I had seen all of this on television, but that is nothing compared with standing there watching them fly through the air above your head.

We rehearsed for about a month and then were supposed to take a bus to New York. When we were close to leaving, Bob said he didn't want to take the long bus ride back and asked Sara, Cathy and me how we felt about flying out on a chartered plane. We packed up and went to a small airport with a tiny waiting area. Someone asked if we minded waiting while they fixed something on the airplane.

*Sara Kawahara would go on to choreograph for Scott Hamilton and Michelle Kwan and win an Emmy for an Olympics opening ceremony.

"By all means, fix it!" I said.

The pilot's wife drove her car down to the end of the runway and turned on her headlights. I wondered what she was doing. Someone told me she was there so the pilot knew he had come to the end of the runway. I called my son, Chris, and told him what I was up to.

"Nobody's twisting your arm," he said, "so if you decide not to go, don't go. But if you do go, just sink down in your seat. Relax. Enjoy the adventure."

I decided to go.

I climbed up onto the wing of the freezing plane. I poked my head inside and saw six seats. When I saw this setup, I strongly considered not going. Then I thought about an all-day bus ride. I took my seat behind the pilot. Bob sat behind the co-pilot. Sara and Cathy sat behind us.

We had been joking before we got on board, but all of a sudden it became eerily quiet. The airplane engine was racing. The pilot started taxiing down the runway and just before we got to his wife in her car we lifted off. The sky was pitch-black; I had never seen such a dark sky. Every so often the pilot had to shine his flashlight onto the wings.

"Why are you doing that?" I shouted above the roar of the engine.

"I want to make sure ice isn't forming," he told me.

After climbing for about fifteen minutes the pilot yelled at us to look out the left window. The moon was just peaking out through those black clouds. I thought about what Chris had said. I sat back and tried to enjoy the adventure.

We began skimming across the tops of clouds that looked like ocean waves. I wondered why I was no longer nervous. It was sheer magic. Bob had brought a bottle of wine he intended to open once we leveled off, but he never mentioned it. We all just sat there staring out at the beauty on each side of us. When I saw runway lights off in the distance, I felt sorry it was all coming to an end.

We awoke early the next morning and went to Radio City Music Hall. We couldn't wait to see the ice and the set pieces they had constructed. They took out a few rows of seats so they could enlarge the stage. It was amazing to see how they made the ice. The back elevator held the whole orchestra. On some numbers it would come up and be the backdrop. It was the most beautiful setting for a show.

The rest of the skaters arrived by bus that night and we started rehearsing the following day. The show came together beautifully. Usually ice shows have an announcer for each act making it sound like a sports event. I wanted this to be more like a Broadway show so I had no announcements. The audience could read the program.

We opened to terrific reviews. *The New York Times* remarked that "under the direction of Miriam Nelson, 'Ice' maintains a throbbing pace all through its 90 minutes …'Ice' is a champagne show."

Isn't it ironic that I got the best review of my career from *The New York Times*, no less, for something I had never done before!

After the show had been running a few days, Jack flew to New York to see it. I must say, he was impressed. He stayed a few days and we had fun in the city. The morning we were leaving for Los Angeles it started snowing. Halfway to the airport we could barely see out the windows and our driver had to keep stopping to clean them. It took us three hours to get to the airport. By the time we arrived we learned that all planes had been grounded. We had the driver wait while we went into the airport to find a hotel so we would be near in case we could take off the next day. We called around in the city. Everything was booked. We kept calling until we finally found a hotel.

"One of the worst blizzards known to New York," the papers declared the following morning. New York became a small town. Everyone was out on the streets building snowmen and throwing snowballs. There was absolutely no transportation. We walked all the way up to Central Park and had lunch at The Tavern on the Green. Central Park looked like a winter wonderland. After three days, we were able to fly home.

Bob called and asked if I wanted to fly with him to New York for the close of the show. I told him I did and I'd like to bring my son. Chris was a grown man by now, in his mid-thirties, and I hadn't been in New York with him since he was four, when Gene was in "Lend an Ear." I looked forward to showing Chris the city and my new show *Ice*. We went to the World Trade Center, the Battery, museums and saw several Broadway shows. We had the best time together.

I wanted to take Chris to dinner at The River Café. It was under the Brooklyn Bridge and I had heard a lot about it. It was hugely popular and it was difficult to get a reservation. I heard that one of the girls in *Ice* dated a man who knew the owner. I asked for her help. She said she was no longer seeing him, but if I used his name, it might carry some weight. I called, dropped his name, and indeed, we got a reservation.

Chris and I got out of our taxi in front of the restaurant on Water Street, in Brooklyn. I don't know *who* this man whose name I was "dropping" was, but I had a feeling there was a Mafia connection. We were ushered through the waiting crowd like royalty and seated at a table by the window so we could watch the boats go up and down the river. A very attentive captain hovered over us. We were both impressed. They wanted to give us a drink on the house. Neither of us drank much but we both got the giggles. Chris told me things he had done as a boy that I had never known. It was a very special evening for me.

DOROTHY "DIVA" KIRSTEN

My phone rang one afternoon. "This is Dorothy Kirsten," a classically rolling, high-pitched voice said from the other end. "I'd like to speak to Miriam Nelson." Dorothy was one of the most celebrated opera singers of the time, even more heralded than Beverly Sills. "What would an opera diva want with me?" I thought. I opened my mouth to ask, "*The* Dorothy Kirsten?" but she continued talking.

"Buz Kohan suggested I call," she went on. (Buz is a fine comedy writer who wrote special material for SHARE shows and the Julie Andrews special.) "He thought you might be the right person to produce my gala." She wanted to raise money for Alzheimer's Disease. We met for lunch the following day.

Dorothy told me her husband, Dr. John D. French, a former brain surgeon at UCLA, was in an advanced stage of Alzheimer's. She was keeping him at home, although it was difficult, because he would get up in the middle of the night and wander. She had been to several facilities that cared for people with memory loss but didn't like any of them. She decided, with the help of an architect, that she would design a place herself. She knew it would take a lot of money to build and this was the reason for the gala.

On a recent flight across the country, she had been seated next to Nelson Riddle. Before the flight was over she had talked him into conducting the show. She also got Julie Andrews and many other stars. *Gratis.* Dorothy was persuasive. Before lunch was over she got me, too. I'm glad, because this was the beginning of a wonderful eight-year association.

Dorothy had played Vegas, done her own TV series and appeared in several movies. Even so, she didn't know many of the current, popular stars. Unless they sang opera or had concert quality voices she felt they couldn't sing. Dorothy was kind of square that way. I teased her about it. I'd call her "Dorothy Diva" and we would laugh.

The night of the gala, me with Dorothy and Julie.

Sometimes she'd call and leave a message on my tape: "Hello, Miriam," she'd say in that distinctive voice. "This is your diva, Dorothy."

Dorothy wanted her gala to have the utmost class. Truthfully, she isn't the only person who likes a show with taste. We complemented each other perfectly. If there was a female singer in the show, she wanted her in a formal to the floor. No miniskirts. The men were dressed in black tie, of course.

We wanted to feature Helen Hayes in one of the shows. Dorothy and Helen had found out not too many years before that they were cousins. They traced their lineage to a famous opera singer.

Helen often stayed with a friend in Beverly Hills and invited Dorothy and me to lunch. It was a wonderful afternoon with lots of "girl talk." We talked about Helen's love of gardening, Dorothy's love of painting and my interest in beading. We also went over the script with Helen.

The next day was the show. We planned to rehearse it prior to the actual performance. I drove to the Century Plaza Hotel through a pouring rain. Helen was coming to rehearsal to get the feel of the place. She was quite petite, so I had a step unit for her to get on the podium. The person who was to bring Helen to the hotel was having car trouble. I called Jack to ask if he'd pick her up.

"I'm having coffee and reading the Sunday paper," he told me, and I knew that meant he didn't want to do it. Then he said, "Am I crazy?! You're talking about the First Lady of the American Theater. I should be thrilled to pick her up!" Jack could always tell a joke. Helen told me he had her laughing the entire way to the hotel.

The rehearsal went off great. A room had been taken for Helen at the hotel so she could rest before the show. One of Dorothy's volunteers was in charge of bringing Helen down to the ballroom at the proper time.

The show started with a terrific overture from Johnny Green, our conductor. I sat next to the soundman and wore a headset connecting me to the light booth and backstage. The show was going as planned. As Helen's entrance was drawing near, I got a frantic call from the stage manager. "Helen's not backstage yet," she said. I quickly called Helen's room but she wasn't there. I had the stage manager tell Johnny Green not to start her play-on. Johnny smartly told the audience that Dorothy requested he play one of his own compositions. He sat down at the piano and played "Body and Soul." As he was playing the sound man's wife ran up to me. "There's a little lady sitting on a couch outside the ballroom," she said. "Maybe it's her." I charged out there. Sure enough, there sat Helen. I took her hand and raced her through the ballroom to backstage. We signaled Johnny and he struck up her entrance music. She was on! I could have killed that volunteer worker. Imagine, *losing Helen Hayes!*

Over the years, I've had so many good times with Dorothy. She liked to cook and I spent many dinners at Dorothy's home with her and her good friend, companion, seamstress and an all-around *everything*, Vicky. Sometimes Dorothy would call and say, "I'm in the mood for Mexican food." We'd meet at Tampico Tilly's in Santa Monica, where we'd enjoy the restaurant's trademark giant margaritas. One night I drove us both there.

"That margarita was so good," Dorothy said as I was driving us home, "I could have had two."

Top: Another year, Dorothy talked Bob Hope into performing at her gala. Here I am giving last minute advice to Bob. Bottom: Another year, Peter Matz, Me, Robert Merrill, Carol Lawrence, and Art Linkletter.

"Dorothy," I told her. "*You did.*"

On a beautiful day in August 1985, I went to the dedication for the opening of the John D. French Alzheimer's Foundation. Governor George Deukmejian made a speech and we toured the facility, which was truly amazing. By now, Dorothy could no longer keep her husband home. One night he had turned on all the gas jets then went back to bed. He was the first resident at the new facility and was treated royally. Dorothy lived to see her dream come true.

MERCI, AMERICA

Marcia Israel, one of the first female entrepreneurs in America, was helping with many charity events in Los Angeles and had been contacted by the French government to present a big gala at the Beverly Hilton Hotel to celebrate the 50th anniversary of D-Day. It was to be called *Merci, America* and Anne Jeffreys had recommended me to Marcia to produce the show.

To give this a French motif, I went to Grosh, a theatrical rental house, which specializes in theatrical curtains and backdrops. I chose a backdrop with little French shops and the Eiffel Tower in the background. I then went to a prop house and rented streetlamps for the lobby and both sides of the stage. I also rented a flower cart that was filled with flowers and placed on one side of the stage.

The Beverly Hilton has a large reception area for cocktails, separated from the dining room and stage by a curtain. The curtains were drawn so the guests couldn't see into the dining room until we were ready for them.

We had one of France's most popular singers, a friend of Gregory Peck and his wife, Veronique. Mr. Peck agreed to introduce her. The orchestra was seated at one side of the stage. During rehearsal the singer asked if the piano could be a little closer to her so I had it moved. My theory has always been, if you can do something to make a star happy, then do it! A happy star behaves better and does a better show.

I had a run-through with the last act, which was a large French children's choir who sang "Le Marseilles."

At the time, Mr. Peck was having back trouble. We arranged for him and his wife to enter through a side door so he wouldn't have to mingle at the cocktail party. I was still on stage rehearsing when I noticed he was sitting ringside. I hadn't had time to change into my formal yet. I finished with the choir and got them offstage.

"Is the music ready?" I called.

"Yes."

"Is somebody there to pull the curtain so the people can come in for dinner?"

"Yes."

Mr. Peck surprised me by asking, "Who's going to light all these candles?"

I looked out at all the tables; each had a lovely silver candelabrum with white candles, but they were not lit. I jumped off the stage and ran up to the maitre'd and told him we couldn't open the curtains until the candles had been lit. He had his waiters hopping!

I had asked my son Chris to cut together the energetic and familiar sections of *An American in Paris* as I wanted that music to be playing as the guests entered the dining room. They opened the curtain on the dining area and stage. I cued the music. It looked like something right out of Paris. Then I raced backstage like a bunny to change before anyone saw me. The show went off without a hitch, thanks to Mr. Peck.

Viva La France!

CHAPTER EIGHTEEN

Recent Past, Wonderful Present and Glorious Future

Everything is changing every minute of every day, whether we are aware of it or not. Periodically, major events happen that remind us nothing lasts forever.

My husband, Jack, began having trouble with his heart in the late Eighties. He also had problems with his liver although he didn't drink. He didn't complain about his health, but I knew he was having trouble because he started waking up in the middle of the night.

I started nagging him to please see a doctor. I tried everything I could think of to get him to go. He kept telling me he'd make an appointment, but day after day he didn't. He always had an excuse. To this day it mystifies me why he wouldn't go in and find out what was wrong. I've heard other women tell that the men in their life refused medical attention. What is it? Is it that the male ego makes them unwilling to ask for help? What kind of fear causes this denial?

In the middle of one night in March of 1988, I heard a thud outside the bedroom. I awoke and raced into the hallway and found Jack lying unconscious on the floor. When I witness a medical crisis my mind goes blank and I can't think clearly. I can't even watch hospital shows on television. All the drama surrounding medical crises just sends me to pieces. The sight of Jack lying on the floor was beyond my comprehension and what happened afterward is kind of a blur. I do know I was nearly hysterical, trying to get Jack to respond. When I couldn't get a response, I immediately raced to the phone and called the ambulance. I'm sure it wasn't long before the paramedics arrived, but it felt like forever.

Several paramedics raced into the apartment and went to Jack's aid immediately. They pulled him in to the living room and began working on him. It was as though I was watching a television show. I stood there blankly, unable to accept this was real, as they transferred him to a gurney. One of the fellows asked me if I wanted him to call somebody. He was very kind. It must have been obvious I was in shock. As I've written, I have been blessed by the most amazing group of wonderful friends throughout my entire life. There are hundreds of names I could have come up with, but only one

I invited my son, Chris, my great grand daughter, Emma, me of course and Emma's dad, my grandson, Christian, to a SHARE Show rehearsal.

came to mind: my son, Chris. I called Chris and told him what happened.

I got in the ambulance and rode with the crew to St. Joseph's Hospital in Santa Monica. Jack remained unconscious. On the way my mind began to clear. I prayed that Jack wouldn't die. The ambulance pulled into the hospital and they wheeled Jack into the emergency room. I was ushered into the waiting room. Chris arrived soon after us. A short while later the doctor came in. He told us Jack wouldn't last long. He didn't. He died at two o'clock the following morning. I didn't want to go home alone to that empty apartment, so I stayed with Chris and his wife, Jenna.

I don't remember if it was Chris or me, but one of us called Missy. I didn't see her until a few days later, at the funeral. Missy and I had been estranged for several years. As she grew into a young woman, she began drinking excessively and taking drugs. I felt she was manipulating her father into giving her money. I thought Jack was "enabling" her; that's the term everyone was using at the time. Jack and I had many disagreements over Missy and how to handle her — really, it was the only thing that we ever disagreed about in our marriage.

I don't cut people out of my life easily. I only did it one other time when I learned Gene was having an affair. As tragic as it is, there are times when it is in a person's best interest to avoid contact with others, even if they are related by blood or by marriage.

We held a memorial service for Jack out at the cemetery, where my mother was buried. Gene came to the service and sat next to me. I asked each one of our grandsons to talk. I helped Josh put together something. "We called him 'Papa Jack,'" he said as

Carol Arthur, me, Claiborn Cary, and Tyne Daly in "Queen of the Stardust Ballroom." Carol is the wife of Dom DeLuise and Claiborn is Cloris Leachman's sister and a wonderful singer.

he gave several examples of times that Jack had been a good grandfather to him.

"He was the one that played ball with us and took us to games."

I couldn't help but wonder what Gene thought about that. Gene remarried twice and had two other children. He really hadn't spent much time with Chris or his grandsons. I think Gene missed out on so much and I wonder if he regretted it.

After the service I went back to Chris and Jenna's. I stayed with them for about a week. The loss hit me so I hard I did a lot of running around. I don't even know where I went, but I remember I'd get in my car and go places. Meanwhile, my wonderful friends began to surround me with love and support.

I've written how Sheila MacRae was there for me when I divorced Gene and she was there when Jack died. Never underestimate the importance of friends in your life! That's one big lesson I've learned. Sheila invited me to go with her to Shirley Jones's house in Big Bear. We sat there in the Jacuzzi on the back deck, looking up at the mountain and talked and talked. We talked about life in general, but mostly we talked about Jack. I felt such a mixture of emotions over his death. I couldn't reconcile why in the world he had refused to seek medical attention. It left me frustrated and feeling angry at him, but there was no way to vent it. He was gone. I was left to deal with it.

I'd seen enough loss and grief in my life to know that the best antidote for me is to work. The following week I went to a SHARE meeting and focused on the needy children that the girls and I helped. The other thing that helped me get through difficult times was dancing. Looking back over my life, I think I've danced away most of my troubles.

Marge Champion called me from the Berkshires in Massachusetts and invited me to stay with her. "By the way," she said, "bring your tap shoes. We're doing a show."

Marge had seen the play, *Stepping Out*, in London and always wanted to do it. At her suggestion, the Stockbridge Playhouse got the rights to do it. Marge directed and I choreographed. Sheila played one of the roles. I had my good friends around me when I needed them most. They are the sisters I never had. I also appeared in Marge's 1992 Long Beach Civic Light Opera production of *Queen of the Stardust Ballroom*.

Every summer I spent about a week with Marge at her home in Massachusetts.

AL HIRSCHFELD

One weekend while I was there, her houseguests were Al Hirschfeld, the noted caricaturist, and his wife, Louise. Marge and Louise were very protective of Al and told me he liked to read the paper in the morning and be quiet, so I was not to disturb him. Well, the next day I woke up early, dressed, walked into the living room

Me with Al Hirschfeld. What a talent!

and sure enough, there sat Al quietly reading the morning paper. I don't know why but the devil got into me and I said, "Al, have you seen my shoes? I think somebody stole my shoes." He went right along with my silliness and said, "I think there is a thief in this house, my shoes are missing, too!"

We had a lot of fun. Marge and Louise won't ever know about it unless they read it here.

RELIGIOUS SCIENCE OF THE MIND

When I got back to Los Angeles, a longtime friend, Howard Kreiger, called and asked if I wanted to go to a Religious Science of the Mind service with him. I discovered Religious Science of the Mind back in the 1950s after my divorce from Gene, but when I married Jack I stopped going. Jack had been raised as a Protestant in the Midwest, but he certainly didn't mind if I went to Religious Science services. I just got busy and didn't go.

I knew how much the church had sustained me before and it seemed right for me to be going back. I went with Howard and have been attending services regularly ever since. I can honestly say after every single service I attended (and it's been over fifteen years now) I have walked away feeling as though I've learned something that I could use to improve my life and myself.

After Jack passed away, I tried to keep up with our properties in Palm Springs, but it was just too much. I sold them and felt relief from the burden of looking after them. I only had our apartment in Santa Monica to be concerned about. I was free to explore a new passion: traveling.

CRUISING

"How would you like to lecture on a cruise ship?" Marge asked when she called from New York in the early Nineties. I knew Marge and other movie stars who had done these cruises, but not being a star myself, I was amazed that she was asking *me*.

"What do you mean by 'lecture'?" I asked.

"You talk about the stars you worked with," she told me, "and if you have film clips, show them." She told me I only had to do a one-hour talk and, in exchange, I got to cruise for free. I sure liked the idea of a free cruise, but was unsure about being a lecturer. I told Marge I had a bit of a fear of public speaking. Marge told me I'd be fine. She said she was going to give my number to the woman who booked the lecturers. That was the end of that.

Sure enough, a few days later I got the call inviting me to lecture on the Royal Viking Sun on a three-week cruise to Brazil. All expenses would be paid, including air fare, and I could even bring a friend. I called Marge.

"You got me the gig," I said, "so do you want to go?"

The hardest part about doing the show was putting it together. If I had my book back then, I could have read excerpts. But all I had were my scrapbooks and memories. I initially wrote down the names of the biggest stars (Judy Garland, Bette

Davis, Ingrid Bergman, Carol Channing, Ethel Merman, George Burns and Dean Martin were at the top of the list) and I remembered the stories that you've been reading about. The talk was only to be for one hour, but I found I could have gone on for several.

Unfortunately, I have no clips of my Broadway shows. I don't even know if they exist. I owned some of the movies and television shows I had done and rented others. I went to the best editor in the business — my son, Chris — and asked him to put all my film clips together. He put ten seconds between each of the clips so the operator would know when to turn it off and on. During those breaks I talked about the upcoming clip.

I wrote out a general script and began to rehearse it. My friend, Diane Davisson, helped me by typing it into the computer. I could gauge how funny the stories were by her reaction.

I flew to New York where I met Marge, then we flew on to Madrid. We spent a couple of days in that beautiful city before we went on to Portugal to board the cruise ship. I never thought I'd make a good sailor because I sometimes get queasy traveling. I packed all the proper seasick medication, but never had to take any of it.

A nice crowd assembled for the lecture. As I mentioned, I didn't have it word-for-word, because I didn't want to sound rehearsed. I wanted to sound natural. As I started telling my stories, the oddest thing happened. I started to relax. I felt like everyone was in my living room and I was telling them my stories. The experience changed me. I realized I could talk naturally in public.

After I finished I discovered I enjoyed mingling with the guests.

Lecturing on the cruise, where people seemed to enjoy my stories.

They told me some stars didn't want to mingle but preferred to remain distant. Not me. I loved getting acquainted with everyone.

The comments I had were complimentary. I was told that most of the celebrities usually filled a lot of their lecture time showing movies. I ran short clips of myself and the stars I had taught. They said they liked the variety.

I also discovered I loved cruising. The cruise ship was really luxurious in a sort of old-world way. We had a room next to the captain's room, with our own balcony. We even had our own valet. Occasionally we'd eat out on our balcony.

Once, when Marge and I were out on the poop deck, Jacques Cousteau's son, Jean-Michel, was there talking about his father's trips. Another time there was a sighting of whales.

Seeing some of the sights in Rome.

A couple of years later I got to cruise with another good friend, Anne Jeffreys. She was lecturing on a Crystal Cruise ship on the Mediterranean and invited me as her guest and told me to bring my film clips. We flew to Rome to see the sights before leaving for our cruise. I know Rome wasn't built in a day, but we felt we covered it in about that time. We saw the Coliseum, the Sistine Chapel and many other famous places. We also discovered pistachio ice cream.

We began our cruise and had fun stopping at the various ports, although I had the hardest time remembering their names. I almost missed the ship at Malta (I remember the name of that place by associating it with "Chocolate Malta") because I found a ring I couldn't live without and Anne and I were signing all our traveler's checks to pay for it. After we paid, I took the ring and we ran all the way to the ship. We boarded, they pulled up the gangplank and pulled away. We found out later two ladies did miss the ship.

I wound up doing my little show on that cruise. It was fun.

Top: Anne Jeffreys and me on our "Roman Holiday." Bottom: On other travels with my dear friend Anne Jeffreys and our hats!

They have such fabulous food on these ships. But if Annie and I did gain a pound it wasn't from the food on the ship. It was from pistachio ice cream cones we ate in every port.

THE NORTHRIDGE QUAKE

Annie and I cruised the same year that I had the biggest scare of my entire life. I was awakened in the middle of the night on January 17, 1994, by the sound of a rumble. It grew louder by the second and my bed began vibrating. I thought a 747 was going to hit the building. What happened next was like something out of an Irwin Allen movie.

The walls of the bedroom started bouncing side to side and up and down. Pictures fell off the wall. Perfume bottles scuttled across the top of my dresser. Cracks started forming down the walls. I couldn't believe my eyes. I sprang from bed and pressed my arms against the walls. In my shock I thought I could hold up the walls. I didn't know it at the time, but I was experiencing one of the worst earthquakes to hit the area in the century. It would be named the Northridge Earthquake and anyone who is old enough to remember it can tell you vivid stories about its destruction. It triggered two earthquakes out in the ocean, down below my 17th-story apartment.

I don't know how long the shaking lasted, but it felt like an eternity. And then there were smaller aftershocks. I didn't dare move, for fear the entire building would come crashing down upon me.

After the quake was over, Chris, who lived in Burbank, started calling. He couldn't get through to me so he got in his car and drove down. I heard him calling through the door.

"Mom, are you there?" I found the strength to get up off the floor and head for the door. "Are you all right?" he called through the door. I told him I was and I saw the kitchen for the first time. The contents of the refrigerator and broken glass and food were everywhere. The folding door on the pantry had fallen off and several cans were in front of the door. I had to clear the area before I could open the door. I was petrified as I thought the building was going to fall down around us.

Chris and I walked down the stairwell, got into his car and drove away. I told him that when I heard his voice at my door, all of the labor pains I endured when he was born were worth it. The following day we came back to my apartment because I wanted to see the damage with a clear head and, hopefully, get a few personal belongings. All the windows down Wilshire Boulevard were "red tagged" — meaning you couldn't go back in.

We were allowed to go back into my apartment, in spite of the extensive damage. Of course, the elevators were down so we used the stairs. We began cleaning up the apartment and putting the furniture back in place. The answering machine was lit and I realized I had received a call. I wasn't allowed to take furniture, but I did grab some personal effects and a few clothes. Afterward, friends jokingly referred to me as "One-Dress Miriam." SHARE members gave me clothes to wear.

I stayed with Chris and Jenna for a couple of weeks. We had no idea how long it would take to repair the apartment. I really didn't want to move out of there and be on my own, but I couldn't stay with Chris and Jenna until they finished my apartment. I began hunting for a new apartment. I wanted room for my piano and wall space for my buffet (both pieces survived the quake).

I found a two-bedroom, two-bath apartment in West Los Angeles and made plans to move in. I got movers who went in and moved everything out of my Santa Monica apartment. I was offered "right of first refusal" when the apartment was remodeled. It took four years for them to repair the building. I did go look at it when it was ready to be leased. They took away half of my living room so they could add another apartment. The remodeled apartment wouldn't have had enough room for all my belongings. Besides, I didn't think I would have been able to sleep there so I stayed where I was. To this day the sound of a teacup hitting a saucer can send my stomach in knots.

Me with Eddie Albert, Jody and Joni Berry.

EDDIE ALBERT

Later that year (1994), Nanette Fabray told me Eddie Albert was thinking about putting together a one-man show. She arranged a dinner for the two of us to get together to talk business, but Nan had an ulterior motive. Eddie was now a widower and Nan thought that he and I would be compatible and we all sort of knew that was the real reason for the dinner.

Eddie and I did enjoy each other's company. Afterwards, we got together frequently. He told lots of funny stories and I always have had a soft spot for a man with a sense of humor. We'd frequently have dinner at his house. Eddie was an environmentalist and he often brought me produce from his garden. We talked a lot. I got the sense that his wife, Margo, had ruled the roost. I think he was a bit lonely and looking for a woman to guide his life. He talked about his failing memory. He worried he might be getting Alzheimer's.

"I guess it's too late to think about marriage," he kind of threw out on the phone one night.

"Yes, it is," I said.

He never called me again.

GOWER CHAMPION

I had other things on my mind. Ever since my cruises I wanted to get out and see places I'd never been. I wanted to go, go, go! In January of 1996, Marge called again to say she was putting together a group — nine of us — to go on a cruise ship. The ship was going around the world, but we would take it only as far as Australia. The theme for the show would be the music from shows Gower Champion had done.

Gower had died in 1980. I remember talking to him a few days before *42nd Street* opened. I called him to ask if he wanted to take an ad in our SHARE book. Of course he said "Yes." We talked about his show.

"I'm sure you're going to like it," he told me. "I think it's some of my best work." He sounded so good and happy. He said he was coming to Los Angeles as soon as the show opened. He wanted to see his doctor for a routine checkup. I knew he had a blood disease and had to have transfusions periodically. He was going to take a place at the beach to rest. But it never happened. Marge called a couple of days after we talked.

"Gower died," she told me.

I was in shock.

According to the September 8, 1980 issue of *Newsweek*: "It is sad that just before his death at 59 Champion may have done his best work."

Marge and I boarded the ship in San Francisco. We had five days to plot out the show. She had already suggested that I perform "Tap Your Troubles Away" from *Mack and Mabel*, a show Gower had directed. I was able to get an early start on my solo. The rest of the cast was picked up in Hawaii. We rehearsed every day. Everyone did a solo and we also sang together.

The act started with special material Peter Howard and I wrote to "Lullaby of Broadway" from *42nd Street*, which was Gower's last show. As I rehearsed, I learned I had something new to contend with: tapping on a swaying floor. The only time I could get into the showroom was 8:00 in the morning. I went every morning for forty-five minutes. It's a funny feeling to dance on a floor that rolls from side to side. Sometimes I'd start a step in one spot and wind up in another, without intending to be there. You can get used to anything, I guess, because after awhile it didn't bother me. I could "go with the roll."

I really appreciated the casts of the other shows being performed on the ship. One show had dancers with an adagio couple. Every time he had her up over his head and the ship was rolling, I could feel for them. One night he let out a "Whoa!" but he never dropped her.

Each of us did an individual show. Peter Howard, who conducted many Broadway shows, put together a wonderful evening of singing and piano playing. Max Showalter, whom I'd known for over forty years, was also wonderful. People recognized him from all the movies he'd been in. He talked to everyone and became the darling of the ship.

I gave my lecture one afternoon. Another day I taught a tap class. I had a pretty good turnout, which surprised me. Even Marge brought her tap shoes so she could take my class. They were able to learn several easy tap steps. Donald Saddler, who has choreographed many New York shows, did a lovely ballroom number with Marge.

On shipboard with Max Showalter, me, Donald Sadler and Marge Champion.

We rehearsed putting our show together every day. We performed it two days before we docked in Cairns. The captain came back after the show carrying two bottles of champagne. During the trip he invited us up on the bridge for cocktails and then for a lovely dinner in his quarters.

"This is a five-star ship," he told us. "You've all just added one more."

When we reached Australia our "leg" of the journey had ended. Marge and I decided to tour Australia and New Zealand before flying home. We rented a car and went sightseeing.

It was such a long trip back home. We flew to Hawaii and stayed overnight to break up the trip. The next afternoon Marge flew on to New York and I flew to Los Angeles.

Several days after we got home Marge called from New York. "Did you hear about our ship?" she asked. The ship got off course and broke off some significant bits of coral. The ship had to be evacuated. Our Captain was put in jail in Egypt. It cost the coast guard a few million dollars to get him out. I'm sorry to say he was fired.

GENE NELSON

When I got back to Los Angeles, Chris told me that his father Gene was ill and in a coma. Chris, his wife Jenna and I went to the Motion Picture Home where we visited Gene along with Diane Davisson, a friend and former student of Gene's. We were all there when he died on September 16, 1996. Chris asked me to organize a memorial service. I had a catering service provide a lunch. I think Gene would have been pleased.

THE GREENHOUSE

Marge and I recently worked together, along with Debbie Reynolds and our mutual friend, Anne Jeffreys. We had been invited to an exclusive spa called The Greenhouse, in Texas. This place usually goes for $1,000 per day. We stayed there for a week and got to take advantage of all the amenities. We were served breakfast in bed. We got massages, had facials, took aerobics classes and swam. The four of us showed clips of our movies and talked to the guests at The Greenhouse. Each of us spoke on a different night. It was a blast.

At the Greenhouse we were treated like Queens. Marge Champion, me, Debbie Reynolds, and Anne Jeffreys.

MARGE CHAMPION

Marge has an apartment in New York and a lovely house in Stockbridge, Massachusetts. Her son, Greg, lives here in Los Angeles with his wife, daughter and son. Marge comes out to visit them and I go back East once a year to visit her.

Top: At a photo shoot with the ladies of MGM: Jane Powell, me, Marge Champion, June Allyson, Ann Miller and Cyd Charisse, on the back lot. Bottom: Helping the director with my dancer's trick.

Another time, Marge called to say she was coming to California to be part of a publicity layout for *Vanity Fair* magazine. It was called "The Ladies of MGM." Even though I was not an MGM Lady, she said I knew every one, so why not come and hang out with them and have lunch. I did, and it was great fun. The ladies were June Allyson, Cyd Charisse, Ann Miller, Jane Powell, and, of course, Marge.

The director/photographer wanted the girls to be arm in arm walking toward the camera. Well, they lined up and when he yelled action, they started out not quite together and all on different feet. After a few unsuccessful attempts Marge said, "Our friend Miriam is a choreographer — why don't you let her start us." He agreed. I went up to the girls and said, "Start on your left foot." I walked out of the shot and yelled: "And 5, 6, 7, 8!" They all started on the same foot and were together. The director wanted to know how I did it. I said, "It's a dancer's trick."

I guess I could write an entire book about the good and bad times Marge and I shared. The marriages, divorces, births and deaths (including her second husband, Boris Segal, and her son, Blake, who was killed in an automobile accident). She was recently interviewed on the radio show *Fresh Air*, and she told Terry Gross, the interviewer, how important friends have been to her throughout her life, even more important than husbands. I couldn't agree with her more.

PROFESSIONAL DANCERS SOCIETY

In the mid-Eighties, I began participating in another wonderful charitable Show Business foundation called "Professional Dancers Society" (PDS). Composed of ex-dancers, choreographers and people who simply love dance, each year it honors people who contributed to the history of Hollywood dance with an annual Gypsy Award Luncheon. Many of the people I have had the pleasure to work with (Ann Miller, Bob Hope, Sammy Davis, Jr., Milton Berle, Donald O'Connor, Angela Lansbury and Debbie Reynolds) and some of my dearest "Gal Pals" (June Allyson, Marge Champion and Nanette Fabray) have been honored. They also hold a "Fall Ball" and over the years have given scholarships to young dancers and held picnics and other functions to bring dancers together. Now associated with The Actor's Fund, PDS has donated a substantial amount of money to support living quarters for retired dancers and actors. A wonderful lady I first met in SHARE, Joni Berry, is currently the Chairman of the Board and the legendary — and inimitable — Mitzi Gaynor is our very own Madame President.

JOHN TRAVOLTA

Whenever we hold meetings to discuss who we are going to honor with a "Gypsy Award" for our big annual fundraiser, John Travolta's name continues to come up. John's place in Hollywood Dance History for *Saturday Night Fever*, *Grease*, *Hairspray* and nearly every other film he has starred in, is well-deserved. When I got a call to work on a movie he was starring in (*Michael*), I hoped that I might have an opportunity to finally "confirm" him as the next Honoree. The film had been completely shot but "they" were not happy with the last scene and came up with another

Top: At this PDS show, special material was performed in my honor by Billy Barnes, Tad Tadlock, Earl Holliman, Stan Mazin, Rusty Frank and Peter Flahiff. Bottom: My master class for Traditions in Tap developed quite a fan club.

ending. It would now end with Travolta dancing down the street. My first day on the job I was figuring it out. The second day I met him! We worked out the dance routine and all the time I was trying to find a perfect way to approach him about the PDS Gypsy Award. I don't know why I was so nervous, but I was. What if he said "no"? During one of the breaks, we were just making small talk when he asked me what kind of dancing I liked best. Of course, I said I was a tapper. To my surprise, he jumped up from his chair and did a tap step. So I did one... then he did

another and I did one. He was so good, sort of like Gene Kelly in style. After a few tap exchanges, I asked him where he studied. He said "...at Fred Kelly's Studio." Fred was Gene Kelly's brother. Well, if that didn't break the ice? I now felt comfortable enough to tell him all about PDS' fundraiser and how we have always wanted to honor him. He asked the date of our next event. When I told him he said he would check his schedule and get back to me. Well, he found he was to be shooting on another movie but "maybe another time" he would be available. I was finished with *Michael* but, to all our delight, a lovely check came to PDS from John for two thousand dollars. Of course, now more than ever, we want to honor him.

Here with long time girl friend, Nanette Fabray.

Religious Science teaches that we continuously are creating our lives. I wake up each morning, at the age of (*gulp*) eighty-eight, and plan my day. For me, it is gratifying to be told I am inspiring younger generations. I treasure comments from younger people who tell me I give them hope. Even people in their sixties, seventies and eighties tell me they admire the fact that I don't let myself get old and that I enjoy my life.

I still choreograph, produce shows, travel and dance, although I can't jump as high as I used to or twirl around as fast.

I feel especially blessed to be able to spend time with the light of my life, my great-granddaughter, Emma, who was born to Jill and Christian on August 26, 1999. The things that come out of that darling little mind! My next writing project will be about her sayings. I already have a title: "A Little Book about a Little Girl."

I have been asked to teach "Tap" master classes in Estonia, Finland and Sweden and recently returned from Estonia where I performed in a tap dance show. It is so exciting to see how Europe has embraced tap dancing and is producing some of the best "Tappers" in the world.

The Professional Dancers honored me on my 80th birthday.

I am still active in both SHARE (we presented our 50th Anniversary Show in 2007!) and PDS, producing their shows.

I cannot tell you how I appreciate the recognition I am receiving in this new millennium — which I honestly never thought I would live to see! When we're fulfilled and busy with a full-time career creating shows, and dance and entertainment, it really does not go through our minds that we need Awards and Honors. But gosh, they are nice!

My tap performance in James Gray's 2008 "Fruitcake Follies."

It all began when I was the Honoree at PDS' "Fall Ball" in 1999 and continued with a SHARE "Member of the Year" Award and a Lifetime Achievement Award from "Rhapsody in Taps" in 2003. In May of 2004, I was the Honoree on "National Tap Day" in 2004. In November, 2007, "Tradition in Tap" recognized my "Contributions to Tap" and I had a wonderful time teaching a workshop in New York with my "Best New Friend," author, producer and dance instructor Rusty Frank. Rusty also has invited me to appear in several of her instructional DVDs and in November, 2008, I went to Munich, Germany to perform and teach with Rusty. I was also interviewed for a Turner Classic Movies Archival project.

Since life is not about "just taking bows," I am fortunate to be able to continue working. It introduces me to young dancers and creative people who enrich my life with their "new" ideas and energy. I recently choreographed my sixth show at the beautiful Civic Light Opera in Downey, California, *A Funny Thing Happened on the Way to the Forum.* Recently, a dear friend, James Gray, who produces shows, sings, acts and is a sometime prop man for television, said to me, "You put a one-woman show together, I'll get it booked." I'm already busy working out the dance routines, selecting music and writing lyrics. I believe a key to staying young is to always look forward to the next adventure. Someone recently asked me if I would ever retire.

"Not as long as the phone keeps ringing," I said.

I love my work. I'm so grateful I've had the opportunity to work with and get to know so many wonderful and talented people. My life dancing with the stars, I can't imagine doing anything else.

Oh! Excuse me; I have a phone call…

I think I hear the phone ringing...

INDEX

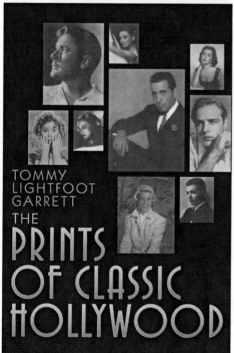
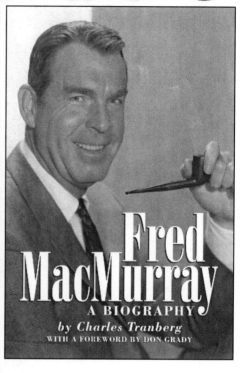

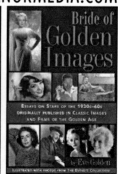

Printed in the United States
150771LV00002B/3/P

9 781593 933333